Forecasting Government Budgets

Forecasting Government Budgets

Methods and Applications

Aman Khan and Kenneth A. Kriz

LEXINGTON BOOKS
Lanham • Boulder • New York • London

Published by Lexington Books
An imprint of The Rowman & Littlefield Publishing Group, Inc.
4501 Forbes Boulevard, Suite 200, Lanham, Maryland 20706
www.rowman.com

86-90 Paul Street, London EC2A 4NE

Figure 7.1. Permission to reprint granted by Mackinac Center for Public Policy

Figure 7.9. Published 2014 by the American Meteorological Society.

British Library Cataloguing in Publication Information Available

Library of Congress Cataloging-in-Publication Data

Names: Khan, Aman, author. | Kriz, Kenneth A., author.
Title: Forecasting government budgets : methods and applications /
    Aman Khan and Kenneth A. Kriz.
Description: Lanham : Lexington Books, [2023] | Includes bibliographical
    references. | Summary: "Written in a simple and easy to understand manner,
    Forecasting Government Budgets presents some of the frequently used methods,
    simple as well as advanced, in budget forecasting. Although written primarily for
    graduate students in public administration and management, students from other
    disciplines will also find it useful"—Provided by publisher.
Identifiers: LCCN 2022040505 (print) | LCCN 2022040506 (ebook) |
    ISBN 9781793613103 (cloth ; alk. paper) | ISBN 9781793613127 (paper ; alk. paper) |
    ISBN 9781793613110 (ebook)
Subjects: LCSH: Budget—United States—Forecasting. | Finance, Public—United
    States—Forecasting.
Classification: LCC HJ2053.A6 K63 2023 (print) | LCC HJ2053.A6 (ebook) |
    DDC 336.73—dc23/eng/20220909
LC record available at https://lccn.loc.gov/2022040505
LC ebook record available at https://lccn.loc.gov/2022040506

In Loving Memory of Our Parents

Contents

Preface

Budgeting is about future—future revenues and future expenditures. For a government to be able to function effectively, in particular, to be able to carry out its activities in a planned and organized manner, it has to have a sound knowledge of future revenues and expenditures. Forecasting provides that knowledge by producing estimates of revenues and expenditures based on past and current information to indicate whether the government will have sufficient resources to effectively carry out these activities. Without good and reliable forecasts, a government will not only find it difficult to plan its activities, but will also find it difficult to cope with the increasingly demanding and complex environment in which it operates.

Budget forecasting is not a recent development, although it has received more attention in recent years. Early history of forecasting indicates that an act of Congress in the 1800s required the Secretary of Treasury to submit revenue estimates to Congress, along with plans and analyses of specific levels of expenditure. There is no concrete evidence that confirms that the department seriously followed this requirement. However, the 1974 Congressional Budget and Impoundment Control Act requires that the budget include a multiyear forecast as part of government's regular budget preparation and submissions process. Two other factors have also contributed to this trend: The development of a wide range of forecasting methods over the years and the easy availability of microcomputers with enormous computational and data storage capacity that was not available some years ago. The latter, in particular, has made it possible to take advantage of many of these methods that were previously difficult to use without high-speed, mainframe computers.

As important as forecasting is, it is equally important to keep in mind that a forecast is not an end rather it is an input into the decision process. It is a prediction of what will happen or is likely to happen in the future, based on an analysis of the past and current activities of an organization. Put simply, forecasts are not the actual values that one would observe at some future points in time, but rather they are estimates of the actual values that will occur in the future. The probability that the forecasts will be successful depends, to a large measure, on the process that can identify the forecasting activities and their sequence so that important elements of the process are not left out. Although one will seldom find forecasts that are perfect, decisions will have to be made with the best possible information available. The real challenge in forecasting is not whether forecasts are good and reliable, although that is the desirable objective, rather how to continue to develop and use the existing methods to produce better forecasts.

Interestingly, forecasting is just as important, if not more, at the subnational level, where all 50 states and many local governments prepare multiyear revenue and expenditure forecasts as part of their regular budgetary activities. This is particularly important for these governments, as state and local governments are required by law to balance their budget, especially the operating budget, which means that the projected revenues of a government must balance the projected expenditures for it to be able to run its everyday operations without incurring a deficit or budget shortfall. This does not mean that the government will not have budget deficits; in all likelihood, it will. But without good and reliable forecasts, it will be difficult to determine the measures that will be necessary to balance the budget or ensure conformity between revenues and expenditures. Also, important to keep in mind that, unlike the federal government, the state and local governments do not have the same latitude to raise revenues easily to meet the growing expenditure needs because of political, economic, and other constraints. Forecasting can help these governments to get a good sense of what future budgetary situation would look like so they can better prepare to deal with the future revenue and expenditure needs.

From a methodological point of view, what makes forecasting interesting, as well as challenging, since the central focus of the current text is on forecasting methods, is the wide array of methods that are available to a forecaster, and the number has been consistently increasing over time. Selecting the best method for forecasting is a challenging task, even for a seasoned forecaster, because the methods vary in complexity. While there may be an inherent tendency toward complex methods because of their analytical sophistication and the level of forecasting details they can produce, methods such as simple arithmetic average or simple trend line can be just as useful for forecasting problems that are not complex. Besides they are easy to deal with where in-house expertise, especially at the local level, is not always available. This text provides a broad array of methods, starting with those that are simple and analytically least demanding and then gradually moving to methods that are more advanced.

Finally, given the sheer number of forecasting methods, it is impossible to cover every single of these methods in a few chapters or even in a single book. The present text is an attempt to cover those with a long and established history, including some that are emerging, providing a useful guide that one would find helpful when preparing a government budget.

Acknowledgments

No job is the product of a single individual. It is often the result of family members, friends, and coworkers. A book is no exception. We owe our family members immensely, in particular, our spouses and children, without whose love and affection this book would have never been completed. Our deepest thanks and appreciation to each of them. We also want to extend our thanks to the members of the editorial board, in particular, to Carter Moran, Acquisitions Assistant, for nicely preparing the materials for production, Sara Noakes, Associate Acquisitions Editor, for carefully seeing it through its completion, to Monica Sukumar, Production Manager, and Taylor Breeding, Assistant Production Editor, as well as other members of the production team for doing an outstanding job of putting it all together. And, finally, a very special thanks to Julie Hirsch, Senior Vice President of Publishing, Rowman & Littlefield Publishers Group, without whose unfailing support throughout the entire process, this book would have never been possible.

Introduction

Forecasting is an essential part of the government budget process, but it is also literally one of the most difficult tasks to perform appropriately. And even if everything is done correctly, with the tools and techniques that are necessary to do the forecasts, the world, as the saying goes, can intervene and render forecasts inaccurate. For instance, a forecast that is carefully prepared using appropriate methods and the forecast results appear to be fairly accurate and statistically sound in light of the past, and current behavior of the data can be rendered ineffective if there are sudden changes in the economic and financial decisions of a government. The changes in policy decisions, after the forecasts have been prepared, are common in government and are often necessary in view of changing economic and noneconomic conditions, but they can pose serious challenges to a forecaster,[1] but, fortunately, most forecasters are aware of this.

Despite these and other shortcomings, forecasts serve a valuable purpose: They are essential for planning, management, and decision-making. This leads us to a story concerning the Nobel Prize winning economist Kenneth Arrow. Early in his life, he served on a team of weather forecasters for the Air Force during World War II. Known as somewhat of a freethinker (and extremely skilled with statistics), Arrow and his team of forecasters studied the forecasts that they were providing to the upper level of decision makers. Then Arrow wrote a carefully worded memo to the decision-makers with the results of their assessment—that the forecasts were so inaccurate as to be worthless. They asked to be relieved of the responsibility for making the forecasts. The response from the generals: "We understand that the forecasts are inaccurate. But we need them for planning purposes" (Bernstein, 1998, p. 203).

We begin our discussion of forecasting government budgets, which is the focus of this text, with a dictionary definition of forecasting, followed a

discussion of the role forecasting plays in public budgeting, and of the forecasting process, a brief survey of forecasting, and concludes with an overview
of forecasting methods used in the text.

WHAT IS FORECASTING?

Before getting into the details of forecasting, it will be helpful to set expectations by providing a working definition of forecasting. While it may seem
truly academic, a working definition and the lessons it contains can be a good
starting point. For instance, the Merriam-Webster online dictionary defines
forecasting as:

> a: To calculate or predict (some future event or condition) usually as a result of
> study and analysis of available pertinent data.
> *The company is forecasting reduced profits.* Especially: to predict (weather
> conditions) on the basis of correlated meteorological (see METEOROLOGY
> sense 1) observations
> *They're forecasting rain for this weekend.*
>
> b: To indicate as likely to occur
> *Optimists are forecasting an immediate upswing in business.*

The combination of these definitions actually provides a good working
definition of forecasting. Forecasting involves calculating or predicting a
future event or condition, utilizing available data, and especially using correlated observations to indicate what is most likely to occur. We would add
one other element to this definition, that forecasts directly consider the risk of
a forecast being inaccurate and communicate this uncertainty to users of the
forecast. Therefore, the essential elements of a forecast are:

1. A prediction of a future event or condition
2. The use of available data, especially correlated observations
3. An indication of what is most likely to happen, and
4. An explicit delineation of the risk of the predicted event or condition not
   occurring.

The first element seems straightforward, a prediction of a future event or
condition, but immediately we can run into difficulties with definitions. As
we will see shortly, most parts of the budget, both on the revenue or expenditure side, come from some base of activity and the rate at which it is taxed
(for tax revenues), charged (for fees or fines), or is brought by a citizen to the

government for a benefit (for expenditures). So, if we are forecasting into the future, at some level, we cannot know what changes the government might make in either the base (e.g., exempting certain income for taxes or adding a class of persons eligible for a benefit for expenditures) or the rate (changing the absolute rate or the rate structure for taxes, fees, or charges, or the benefit level for expenditures). Consequently, most forecasters pursue forecasts assuming current policies will continue. One notable exception concerns a policy that potentially affects revenues or expenditures and is scheduled to "sunset" at some point in the future (e.g., many provisions of the Tax Cuts and Jobs Act of 2017 were scheduled to sunset in 2025). As a sunset date approaches, forecasters face a dilemma. No matter what course they take (assume the policy will sunset or assume it will not), they are potentially creating biased forecasts. The only recommendation for this situation is to present both scenarios to decision-makers and let them judge which is more likely to reflect the future.

As for the second element, using all available data, this should be fairly straightforward. One twist does arise when considering the "correlated observations" clause. If the data have a long memory process, where many lags of the data are correlated, the question comes as to how many lags of data should be included in the model. Lags are past observations of a variable. There are some measures which will be discussed in Chapters 4–6 that can help us make the decision, but the basic idea is that we should include all lags of a variable that increase the predictive power of the model without unnecessarily complicating it.

As for the third and fourth elements, forecasters should include two important things in forecasts, point estimates (forecasts) and confidence (or credible) intervals. Point forecasts are the forecasters' best estimates of what will happen in the future. Although we will discuss a much more precise definition of these items in Chapter 3, at this point, we introduce them by analogy. Most of us are aware of political polls (and the news is replete with these estimates, especially during election times). The results of political polls are typically reported with a point estimate of support and a "margin of error" (so in a recent poll, one candidate received 48 percent support, with a margin of error of 3.1 percent). This latter figure reflects the amount of sampling error in a survey, in other words, in repeated samples, this is the amount that our estimate is expected to vary by. So, the estimate of the true support is 48 percent plus or minus ($\pm$) 3.1 percent. Therefore, we can expect the results of an election, if it were held today, to be anywhere from 44.9 percent to 51.1 percent. While government budget forecasters do not generally concern themselves with political polls, the idea is the same, we will produce measures of what we think best represents the level of revenues, expenditures, and other figures (the point estimate) and a range of potential outcomes (confidence intervals, equivalent to the margin of error for polling data).

Contrast with Projections

One of the issues with understanding real forecasting comes because many things that are not really forecasts are offered as if they were. Consider this graph from the Office of Management and Budget in 2015 (Figure 0.1). This shows two different projections of budget outcomes, one from 2010 and then the current projection. It should be obvious that this is not a forecast, as it does not contain two of the essential elements identified above. While it does make a prediction about a future condition (US federal debt as a percentage of GDP), it obviously does not consider all data. While the actual data to the left of 2010 and 2015 contains obvious variation, the "forecasts" are very smooth (one should be able to note that they use the word "projections" in the chart, but these values, in fact, come from the US federal budget and what the OMB states are associated revenue forecasts). There is an indication of what is most likely to happen, but no accounting for the risk or uncertainty of reality not matching the forecast. Looking at this chart, one would be tempted to assume that there was little uncertainty associated with these projections, something which is probably intended. It is also ironic that the projections from 2010 were fairly inaccurate, yet the 2015 projection is offered without a sense of uncertainty.

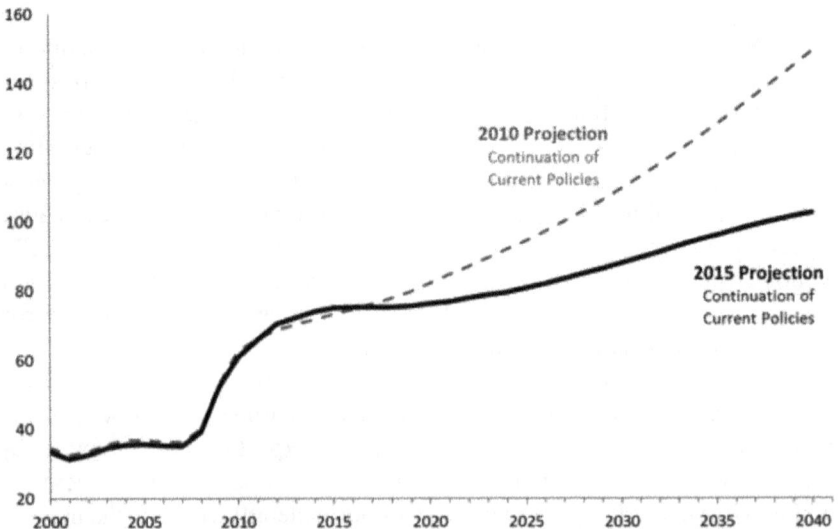

Figure 0.1 "Forecasts" from the US Office of Management and Budget. "2010 projections" are based on the FY 2011 Budget baseline; "2015 projections" are based on the FY 2015 Budget baseline. *Source*: United States Office of Management and Budget, https://obamawhitehouse.archives.gov/blog/2015/03/11/long-term-budget-outlook

THE ROLE OF FORECASTING IN PUBLIC BUDGETING

Forecasting is an integral part of the public budgeting process. The reason this is the case comes down to something called revenue constraints. When we think about what a government is asked to do, it boils down to providing essential public goods and services in order to increase social welfare. Social welfare is the aggregate satisfaction of society. What governments face is a "constrained maximization" problem; they would like to enact many programs to enhance (maximize) social welfare but cannot enact them all because of constraints. These constraints are what the combination of economic condition, revenue and expenditure bases, and political acceptance yield in terms of resources—revenues. Economic condition provides a constraint for revenues and expenditures through limiting the amount of resources available to governments to carry out desired expenditures and through creating demand for public expenditures themselves.

Revenue and expenditure bases provide constraints in terms of how much revenue can be raised or how much expenditure is required. All revenues and expenditures of government are based on a simple formula: Revenue (expenditure) = base*rate. For tax revenues, the base may be some flow of economic activity (e.g., sales for the sales tax), a flow based on other variables (income for the income tax, where income is based on economic activity), or the stock of some asset (property value for the property tax). For charges, fees, or fines, the base is the activity on which the charge is collected (transaction for charges or fees, crimes, or violations for fines). For expenditures, the base is how many people or businesses require payment (e.g., for Medicaid expenditures, the number of enrollees or transactions).

Finally, political acceptance provides a constraint for what can be done to change bases through law (e.g., exempting certain income from an income tax base) as well as a constraint for how much rates can be changed. Many local government officials are fearful of raising property tax rates, even in the face of financial difficulties. They fear a strong political backlash and diminished prospects for reelection.

In the face of these constraints, budget forecasting provides estimates of the base for revenues and expenditures, and sometimes total revenue or expenditure, in cases where rates are legally or effectively frozen at the same level. Not surprisingly, budget forecasts most often happen early in the budget process. Most often accompanied by economic forecasts, they provide upper limits for revenues and expenditures. In many state governments, a formal forecast is required prior to our incidental to the start of the budget process. In Illinois, for example, 20 ILCS 3005/7.3 requires the Governor's Office of Management and Budget (GOMB) to "annually submit an Economic and Fiscal Policy Report to the General Assembly outlining the long-term economic and fiscal policy objectives of the state, along with the economic and fiscal policy intentions for the upcoming fiscal year and the subsequent four fiscal years.

The report also includes a review of the current fiscal year's enacted budget compared with the current outlook for the fiscal year, along with fiscal and policy options that GOMB recommends for consideration by the General Assembly and the Governor to remedy any budgetary shortfalls in the current year or the five following fiscal years" (Sturm, 2019). This requirement must be met before the budget process can begin. Effectively this requires a full economic and fiscal forecast. In some states, an updated set of forecasts are required prior to budget passage. In Illinois, although not required, this update has become standard. In Texas, the process requires that the state Comptroller certifies the forecasts to ensure that the government will have enough revenue for the next two years (since the state has a biennial budget) before the Governor can sign it into law.

Figure 0.2 shows the budget process for education finance in the state of Michigan (Olson and LaFaive, 2007). It starts with preliminary forecasts before cost estimates of educating students are even considered. It provides a sense of the base revenues that will be available to fund education programs. Although not seen directly in the graphic, during January (at the same time as Step 3 of the graphic), a "Consensus Revenue Estimating Conference" is held. This updates and solidifies revenue forecasts that will go into the budget requests. The idea here is that without the ability to fund programs, even the most cost-efficient and effective public programs cannot be sustained. They truly form the base for expectations of revenue availability.

FORECASTING PROCESS

The forecasting process starts with collecting data necessary to develop an understanding of the forces affecting the most likely outcome in the form of revenue, expenditure, or base. Depending on the resources available to the forecaster, this data can be from public or private sources. One issue which immediately must be addressed during this process is the frequency or periodicity of the data. One can often get data at high frequencies, such as months (for things like unemployment rates, government program case counts, or revenue receipts) or even weeks (unemployment claims). Recently, many other high-frequency data sources have been developed (e.g., the Opportunity Insights website at https://tracktherecovery.org/ for example). There is no firm guidance for the appropriate frequency of the data other than to note that government budgets are usually done on an annual basis. So, higher

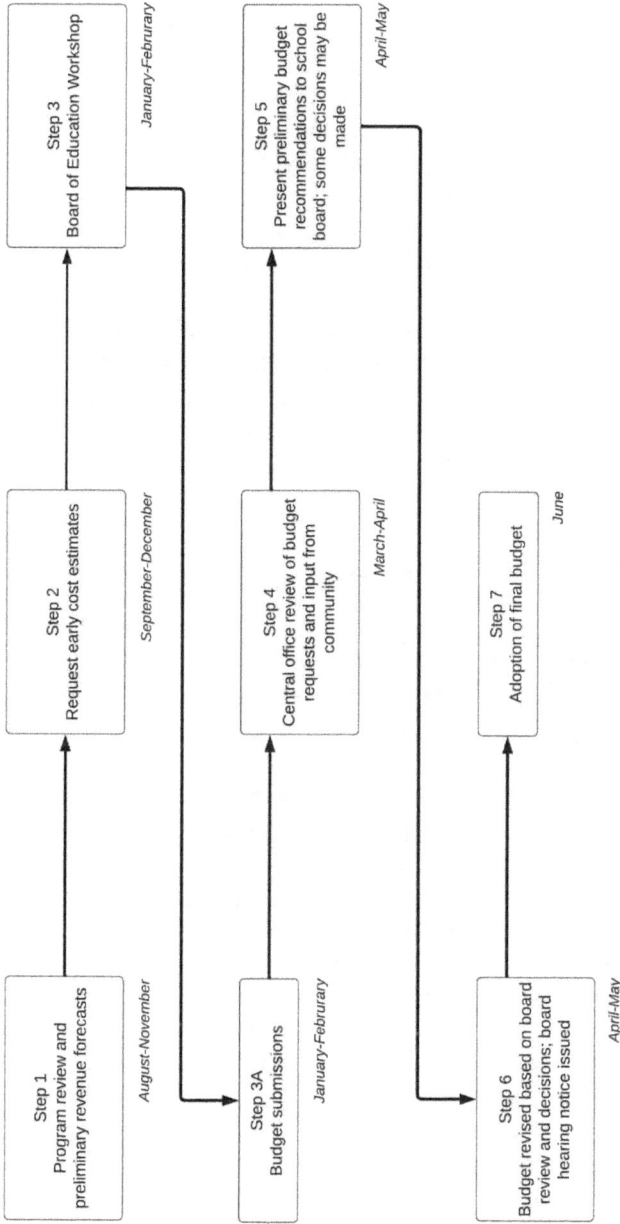

Figure 0.2 Budget Process Flow Chart, State of Michigan School Funding. *Source*: Olson and LaFaive, 2007, Graph 26. Permission to reprint granted by IEEE Proceedings.

frequency data will have to be converted into an annual basis, either during the model estimation process or after, for presentation to decision-makers.

Once we have gathered the relevant data,[2] then we have to decide how to save them for analysis. There are many choices for formats and many choices of software that can be used. The main point here is to pick a format to save the data which offers flexibility in terms of which analysis platforms can be used. More importantly, select a format the forecaster is comfortable with.

The next step is to analyze the data. The rest of the book details many techniques for analyzing data. For now, we will just summarize these techniques into two broad categories, graphical analysis and statistical analysis. Regardless of the technique used, the basic approach is to try to develop an understanding of the data. One of the things that forecasters often refer to is the data generating process that lies behind the data. These are the underlying forces and trends that shape how data move through time. Figure 0.3 shows an example of a graphical analysis technique. When referring to this particular data (shown by the black line), the first obvious force in the data is an evident upward trend. While we will have a more formal definition of this in later chapters, it is not difficult to see, even without training in statistical analysis that there is a trend in this data. And trends are one of the major components of a data generating process. Another major component is the cycle of the data. A careful look at the figure shows how the data follows a broad trend, but then it oscillates around that trend (we have added a dashed line through the data in red to show the trend). The data oscillating around that trend provides evidence that there is a cyclical process at work. In future chapters, we will talk about all of the parts and demonstrate how to use statistical techniques to reveal them.

Ultimately, what one will be producing is a statistical model of the data generating process. The next step is to test that statistical model. We apply the statistical model to the data and assess how well it "fits." At this point, we must make a distinction between forecasting and statistical inference. There is a difference in intent between models of statistical inference and forecasting models. The goal of statistical inference is to discover relationships between variables in a sample that rise to the level where we can make an inference between that sample and the overall population. So, we might test the relationship between poverty and crime rates using data from several cities in an attempt to develop good public policy to fight crime. We would then assess how likely the effects we see in the sample are to be seen in the larger population. In forecasting, the focus is less on generalized results in the population. Rather, the main concern is for the predictive ability of a model in the particular contacts that are being analyzed. In Chapters 1 and 3, we will be discussing how we assess the goodness of fit of forecasting models.

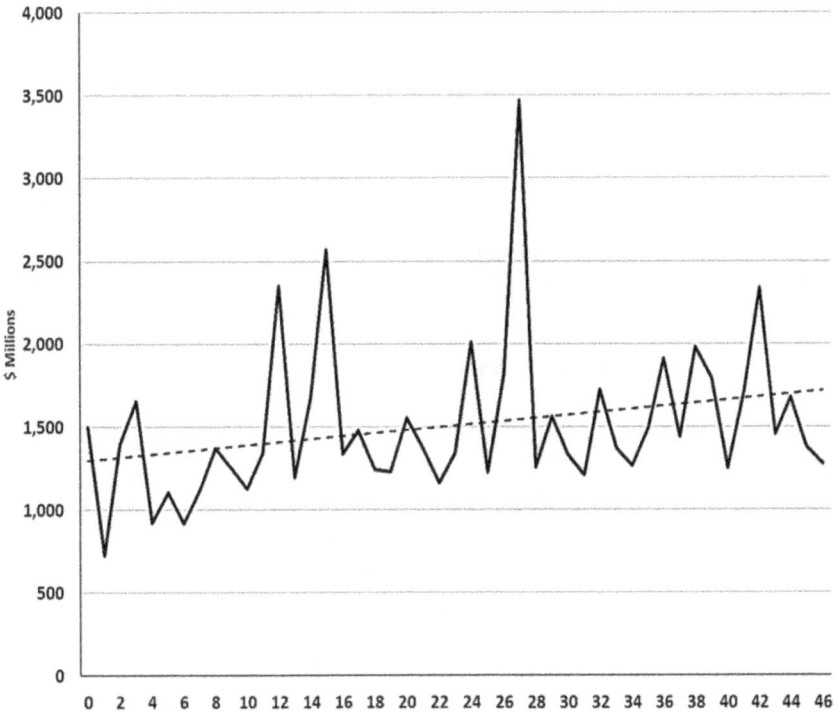

Figure 0.3   Individual Income Tax Receipts (solid line) with Fitted Trend (dashed line), State of Illinois.

Once we have developed and tested a good forecasting model, the final step is to make the forecasts and document them. This produces another set of choices for forecasters. The first choice regards the time period over which the forecast will be issued. Many governments only have a forecast for the next fiscal year plus one or two fiscal years into the future. However, some governments have more recently been interested in medium-term forecasting (3–5 years) in order to develop financial plans and sustainability analyses. Another choice involves frequency of the forecasts; traditionally, budget forecasts are done on an annual basis. However, tracking estimates may be produced on a quarterly or even monthly basis. The sole advice here is to work with the appropriate officials in order to develop the desired length of the forecast as well as the frequency. As for documentation of the forecasts, typically, a combination of graphical, text-based, and tabular presentations would be useful. The one requirement must be to present an estimate of the uncertainty or estimated error involved in the forecast. Earlier, we stated that one of the key elements of a true forecast is documentation of the uncertainty. Without it, we are producing projections and not forecasts.

Figure 0.4 shows a graphical representation of the data forecast of the Illinois individual income tax receipt data, as of April 2020, with the estimate in blue as well as the 95% confidence interval for the estimate in the gray shaded area. As one can see, the confidence interval is very wide for this particular forecast, driven by limited data availability (there are less than 5 years of monthly observations that go into the forecast) and by volatility (especially later in the period as COVID-19 and the associated delay of the individual income tax deadline reduced collections dramatically). This is a fact that decision makers need to consider when assessing revenue forecasts.

A BRIEF SURVEY OF FORECASTING

Forecasting has a long history. Considering the primary focus of this text is on forecasting, with an emphasis on forecasting methods, we thought that it would be useful to briefly look at the development of some of these methods, including those that have not been discussed here, to get a sense of how they developed, their development tracks, and their use. Over time, the methods have proliferated both in number and complexity. It would be impossible

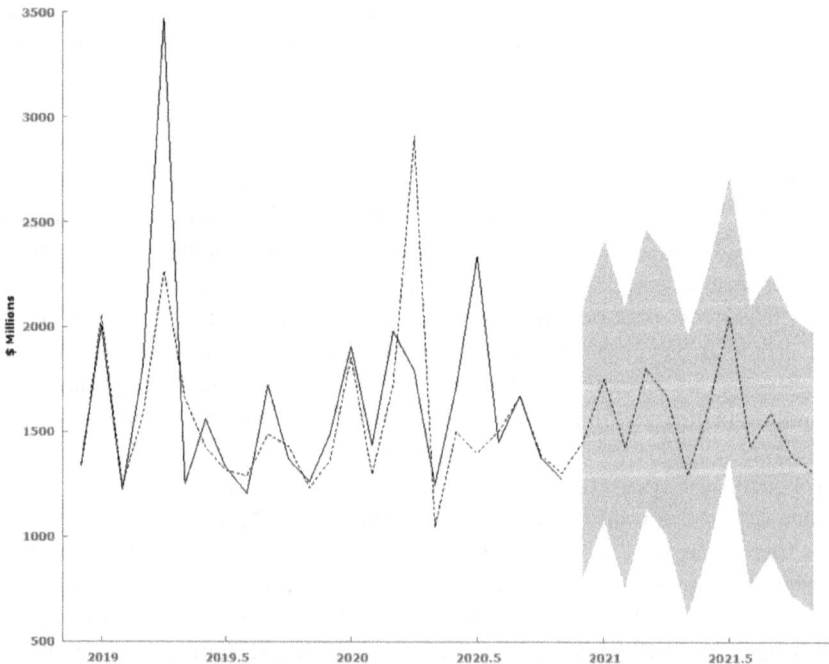

Figure 0.4 Actual (solid line) and Forecast (dashed line) Individual Income Tax Receipts, State of Illinois.

to capture the richness of these methods in a few pages. We will, therefore, focus on those that have been extensively used in areas such as economics, business, policy analysis, and public budgeting.

The literature on forecasting has developed over several years into two broad tracks, one that emphasizes the development of methodologies and techniques for forecasting, and the other that examines forecast accuracy, biases, and forces that affect the accuracy of forecasts. The first track is older, starting in the nineteenth and early twentieth centuries, with the first works examining phenomena using statistical methods. However, it was in the 1940s and 1950s when forecasting was first starting to gain traction as a discipline and area of inquiry, though forecasting as an enterprise extends back to prehistoric times. The ancient Babylonians, for instance, were known to forecast the future based on the "distribution of maggots in a rotten sheep's liver" (Hyndman and Athanasopoulos, 2018), and the story of the Oracle of Delphi is one of the classic tales in ancient history. However, until the advent of computerized records in the 1930s and 1940s, data were not generally available to conduct systematic forecasts. In light of the emphasis in the book on forecasting methods, we will discuss it in two steps: First, the development of forecasting methods and techniques, followed by a quick discussion on forecast accuracy and bias.

Methods and Techniques of Forecasting

Many early works set the stage for the forecasting revolution. A good example is Schuster's (1906) investigation into the periodicity of sunspots, using the concept of periodogram, which forms the basis for time series models to this day. A study by Yule (1927) refined the analysis of sunspot data, further establishing the knowledge of serial correlated processes and providing the basis for the development of autoregressive (AR) models. Two subsequent studies by Macauley (1931) and Slutzky (1937) focused on the use of moving average (MA) processes, a term that frequently appears alongside AR models. Macauley, in particular, used them as ways to smooth time series data on interest rates and security prices, and Slutzky used data from a lottery in France to develop the notion that MA processes underlie much of what was until then thought to be random sequences.

The earliest systematic forecasts followed two main strands, qualitative and naïve quantitative. The classic example of qualitative forecasting was Delphi, developed in the 1940s and 1950s at the RAND Corporation to aid in the Cold War effort to understand strategic military planning issues (Dalkey and Helmer, 1962). Around the same time, Holt (1957) and Winters (1960) were extending the earlier work of Macauley and Slutzky to develop the concept of exponentially weighted MAs.

Interestingly, as the development of naïve forecasting models such as MAs and exponentially weighted MAs was taking place, large complex macro-econometric models were also being developed. Researchers such as Klein and Goldberger, working with the Cowles Commission for Research in Economics and the work of Jan Tinbergen, the Dutch economist who received the first Nobel Memorial Prize in economics, developed structural macroeconomic models consisting of dozens of equations describing the way the economy worked (Adelman and Adelman, 1959). These models were then "shocked" with impulses to estimate what would happen in the economy given a certain change in the current period. Although the models have been heavily criticized for their reliance on aggregated historical data, implying fixed preferences and behaviors (Lucas, 1976), they remain a bulwark of macroeconomic forecasting. The Federal Reserve Bank uses a version of the model developed by Klein and Goldberger for its monetary policy analysis, as do many commercial forecasters such as S&P Global, formerly IHS Markit, IHS Global Insight, and the Wharton Econometric Forecasting Associates formed by Klein.

The 1970s saw another major development in forecasting methodology. George Box and Gwilym Jenkins formalized the work that had occurred over a decade by combining autoregressive and MA models cited earlier into a unified framework for identifying, estimating, and checking models of univariate time series observations. Their book, *Time Series Analysis: Forecasting and Control* (1970), is one of the seminal texts in time series analysis. The autoregressive integrated moving average (ARIMA) methodology they pioneered allowed forecasters significant flexibility in developing models to deal with correlated and nonstationary (trending) data. Although the methodology has evolved over time, their general approach to forecasting has been and continues to be the foundation for scores of studies, from economics to business, to policy analysis.

Over the next two decades, there was an explosion of interest in advanced forecasting methodologies. Vector autoregressions (Geweke, 1978, 1982; Litterman, 1979; Sims, 1980, and others) were introduced into the modeler's toolkit, allowing for feedback relationships among forecasted variables in an ARIMA framework. Vector error-correction models (Engle and Granger, 1987; Johansen, 1988; Johansen and Juselius, 1990) were introduced to address the problem of cointegration among variables (shared trends in the data that cause problems of inference and estimation). Dynamic factor models (Jöreskog and Goldberger, 1975; Geweke and Singleton, 1981) were developed to more measure latent variables from many different indicators in time series models. These models are fundamentally "nonstructural" in that they do not contain a set of equations that described the workings of the economy, in contrast to the structural models describe above that were developed in the 1950s and 1960s.

The 1970s through 1990s also saw the development of structural models, such as computable general equilibrium (Batchelor and Bowe, 1974), econometric input-output models (Conway, 1979), and most notably, dynamic stochastic general equilibrium (DSGE) models. These models were built and estimated for a wide range of forecasting and policy analysis problems (Kydland and Prescott, 1982). This later round of structural models held the promise of providing forecasts based on "microfoundations" of behavior. However, their record of accomplishment in terms of forecasting has been less impressive than first purported.

Most recently, "Big Data" methodologies such as support vector machines (Lee and Billings, 2002), neural networks (Zhang, Patuwo, and Hu, 1998), and machine learning processes such as bagging (Breiman, 1996) have been developed. Using methods that underlie artificial intelligence, these models propose to rethink the forecasting process by automating it and emphasizing nonlinear relationships in contrast to the mostly linear methods that have come before. As with the newer structural models, their forecasting record is mixed in real-world applications.

Forecast Accuracy and Bias

Studies of forecast accuracy and bias date back to the late 1960s and 1970s. Some of the earliest works involved macroeconomic variables and corporate earnings forecasts. The results turned out to be fairly pessimistic in terms of the accuracy and bias of forecasts. For instance, Zarnowitz (1967) examined errors in forecasts of Gross National Product (GNP, the precursor measure to Gross Domestic Product, GDP) and industrial production for the period 1951–1963. He used forecasts from four different sources-private-sector forecasts, forecasts by groups of business economists, forecasters from various industries, governments and academic economists, and a poll including a large number of forecasts. The study found that the average error in GNP forecasts was about 2.0 percent, but that figure would make a difference between a good and bad business year. The study also found that the errors in forecasting were about half of the errors that would have occurred from a naïve model where the prediction was the previous year's GNP. For industrial production, the average errors of annual forecasts were in the range of 4-5 index points, compared to a year-to-year variation of 8-10 points. In addition, the study found substantial bias in the longer-term forecast records for both GNP and industrial production, although the level of bias was less for industrial production.

Similarly, using data from five different investment firms on the earnings per share of 185 corporations in 1962 and 1963, Cragg and Malkiel (1968) found that the predictions of security analysts in the investment firms performed only slightly better than the historical earnings growth of the corporation in predicting future corporate earnings. Further, the existing market price-to-earnings ratio did not perform better than either the past growth rates or analysts' forecasts. Most of the earlier studies of forecast accuracy held some humbling results for those who believed in the ability of forecasting to clarify future outcomes.

Makridakis (1986) summarizes the results of the early studies into six lessons:

1. There is no one methodology that has been shown to be clearly superior to other methodologies.
2. Judgmental (qualitative) forecasts are not more accurate than quantitative forecasts, with the exception of certain applications. Human forecasters tend to be optimistic and underestimate future uncertainty.
3. Forecasts using econometric methods are not necessarily more accurate than those that used time series extrapolation methods.
4. Large, complex, or statistically sophisticated methods do not necessarily produce more accurate forecasts than smaller, relatively simpler methods.
5. Adaptive methods are not more accurate than nonadaptive ones.
6. Methods that give equal weight to all data are less accurate than models that weigh the most recent data more heavily.

Interestingly, early studies on budget forecasting in the public sector came to some of the same conclusions as those observed by Makridakis and others, cited earlier. A good example is a study by Bretschneider and Schroeder (1985). Using data from Kansas City, MO, for five-year revenue forecasts, the authors found that simple exponential smoothing models could perform just as well as econometric forecasting models, depending on the revenue source. Much also depends on the desired budget level and risk-aversion level of budget setters, as to which forecasting methodology one would prefer. In a follow-up study on the use of commercial, economic forecasts for Kansas City revenue forecasting, the authors found that the variance of forecasts is minimized by either using simple extrapolation techniques on explanatory variables of GNP and the Consumer Price Index (CPI) or through simple time series forecasting methods on revenues (Bretschneider and Schroeder, 1988). The commercial forecasts from major forecasting firms added little value to the forecasting process

Over the next two decades, there were numerous studies of forecast accuracy and bias in the public sector, especially with regard to the federal budget. The general pattern of results observed by two leading federal organizations (OMB and GAO) showed little bias and generally produced accurate forecasts of the economy and major receipt categories, while forecasts of budget out-lays showed evidence of bias. To cite an example, Blackley and DeBoer (1992) examined the OMB forecasts during the 1976-1988 period and found little evidence of forecast bias in economic variables and receipt categories except for corporate profits and the corporate income tax. However, they found no evidence of significant forecasting bias in total outlays, as well as several categories of outlays.

More recently, many studies have suggested the presence of over-forecast-ing bias. For instance, Krause and Corder (2007) found substantial evidence of overly optimistic macroeconomic forecasts from OMB over the period 1979-2003. However, they found less optimistic forecasts came from the Social Security Administration (SSA) during that period. The results further suggested that the difference between the forecasts can be attributed to the SSA being more stable over time than OMB, which is subject to greater level of political appointments.

For state and local governments, however, a different pattern emerged. The results of numerous studies suggested that subnational governments consis-tently underestimate revenues. Feenberg et al. (1989) analyzed the rationality of own-source revenues and grant receipts from New Jersey, Maryland, and Massachusetts. They found that all states under forecast own-source rev-enues, but New Jersey and Massachusetts showed rationality in grant receipt forecasting. They also found that long-term own-source revenue forecasts showed less bias, but not enough to make them satisfy tests of rationality. A study by Gentry (1989) confirmed downward bias in several categories of revenues in the New Jersey data but found that forecasts of several categories exhibited rationality.

There were a few studies during the initial period of research into fore-cast bias had slightly different answers to the question of accuracy and bias. Cassidy, Kamlet, and Nagin (1989), for instance, found a much smaller level of under forecasting revenues, much of which they attributed to economic uncertainty during the period under study. They also find no evidence for an institutional bias toward under forecasting driven by the desire to create fiscal surpluses, a theory that had been advanced in earlier works. Bretschneider and Gorr (1992) found evidence for the overestimation of sales tax revenue in states and suggested that state forecasting agencies faced different institu-tional and political incentives to either over-or-under forecast depending on the economic and budgetary situation they faced.

However, later studies such as those by Rodgers and Joyce (1996) and Voorhees (2006) found significant evidence confirming the underestimation bias for revenues by state governments, attributing much of it to incentives faced by forecasters. Voorhees especially talked about the "asymmetric loss function" faced by forecasters and politicians, namely that under forecasts of revenues result in the ability to make upward adjustments in expenditure plans, resulting in little loss to governments, while over forecasts lead to the need to make politically unpalatable decisions to cut budgets or increase taxes during the middle of the fiscal year. Recently, Williams (2012) undertook an extensive study of five different forecasts of revenues for New York City. He found that property tax revenue is over forecast, while "all other taxes" and federal grants are under forecast. He explained that there are technical reasons for the property tax and grants results and suggested that more research is needed on the reasons for forecast bias results. Importantly, he found little support that forecasters with different incentives have different biases, finding that only one forecaster produced forecasts that were significantly different from the others in terms of bias. This tends to argue against the notion of institutional factors being responsible for forecast bias.

AN OVERVIEW OF METHODS USED

As it should be obvious by now, forecasting methods available to a forecaster are far too many to cover in a single book. For the ones we will discuss in this text, we can divide them into roughly two types: Naïve and informed. Those using naïve forecasting models consider very little information when making a forecast. Naïve trend forecasting is an example. We may note when analyzing some data that over time a certain variable has trended upward at a fairly constant rate, say 2 percent. We can simply apply this information to forecast out into the future a 2 percent growth rate. This by itself would not be a forecast but a projection. However, we could come closer to a forecast if we include estimates at a 1.5 percent growth rate and a 2.5 percent growth rate to create a measure of uncertainty. This type of forecast is more accurately called a scenario analysis and suffers from similar problems as a projection. Another type of naïve forecasting, one that is more qualitative in nature, would be to consult numerous experts about what they think the growth rate or a particular value of a variable in the future would be.

The majority of what is covered in this text are informed models that belong to the realm of quantitative forecasting. Quantitative forecasting models are the most frequently used in professional forecasting. They range from very simple forecasting models that are close to being naïve in nature to more sophisticated quantitative models involving frameworks such as artificial intelligence. The former only considers a few facts when they are being developed. An example of this is a smoothing model discussed in Chapters 1 and 2. In this type of model only information on past trends and cycles is used to develop a forecast. Moving to more informed models such as univariate ARIMA models use the information on correlations of a variable over time. We will discuss this type of model in Chapters 4 and 5.

More sophisticated quantitative models involve forecasts of many variables and their relationships. Two examples of this type of model are time series regression models and vector autoregressive models. We will discuss time series regression models further in Chapter 3 and vector autoregression in Chapter 6, but the basic logic is to investigate the relationships between the variables we wish to forecast and some other variable that represents an important determinant of the value of that variable. For example, we might be interested in the relationship between economic activity represented by GDP and income tax revenues. We start by analyzing historical data to see how these two variables are related over time. Perhaps we will find that there is a relationship where if we know the value of GDP, we can predict with greater accuracy the values of income tax revenues in a given year. Then we can develop forecasts of GDP using quantitative or qualitative methods and use those in turn to forecast income tax revenues.

Vector autoregressions and their cohort vector error corrections, on the other hand, represent one of the more sophisticated forecasting models that would fall into this category. At their core, however, these models are just an extension of time series regression analysis. The extension is that we consider both contemporaneous values of variables and lagged values. For our example of GDP and income tax revenues, we would therefore investigate not only the contemporaneous relationship between the variables but the relationship between income tax revenues and the lags of GDP. At the same time, we analyze the relationship between GDP and the lags of income tax revenues. In this way, we can produce forecasts of both variables, which will be based on their own values and the values of the other variable.

Another category of more sophisticated quantitative models that have been receiving considerable attention in recent years are models designed to deal with specific circumstances. We discuss in this text three such models—ensemble forecasting, state-space forecasting models, and neural network. Ensemble forecasting is used when the results of traditional forecasting are problematic. Ensemble forecasts are developed by incorporating information from many individual forecasts into a combined one. State-spaced forecasting model combines information from many different variables where each reflects a certain portion of a concept underlying a variable. Finally, neural network models use human thought processes to capture and process information in ways that traditional models cannot hope to achieve. All three models are discussed in chapter 7 before we conclude the text with some additional remarks on forecasting.

SUMMARY

This chapter provided an overview of budget forecasting. It started by defining forecasting and contrasting it with projections. Projections are relatively uninformative in that they do not capture the risk of a forward-looking estimate. Forecasts explicitly capture risk of error in the estimates. It then described the forecasting process. Developing a good forecast requires many steps and is an iterative process. The chapter discussed the notion of forecasting as a way to discover the "data generating process" of the variable being forecast and introduce the notion of goodness of fit as a goal of forecasting. Finally, it concluded with a brief introduction to the development of forecasting methods, how they evolved over time and their relevance to the materials discussed throughout this book.

NOTES

1. These decisions are quite common in government. A case in point is a recent forecasting study by Kenneth Kriz for a major U.S. City. One of the things that most affected the study, in particular the revenue forecasts for the city, was a tax credit offered by the state government to businesses in the area. The forecast included the usage of that tax credit using historical data, obtaining a "fit" of the model to the data which was acceptable. Then, merely one month into the new fiscal year, the largest employer in the city decided to take a credit that was three times larger than the total tax credits offered in the previous 10 years. As a result, the forecasted revenues, including the estimated uncertainty, were rendered useless, in spite of the fact that the study was well received by the Council when initially presented. The lesson: forecasts that seem good, properly done, and reliable, can easily fall apart in the real world. One way to deal with problems such as this, especially for the forecaster, is to map out a cone of uncertainty, discussed briefly in the concluding chapter, to allow the decision makers the opportunity to exercise strategic judgment.

2. Gathering relevant data involves a multi-stage process, such as removing any unwanted observations from the data set, fixing structural errors, filtering unwanted outliers that can skew the forecasts, dealing with missing observations, and so forth, commonly known as data cleaning. The point is to make sure that the data gathered are clean, consistent, and reliable. One way to ensure this, in particular, that they are reliable is to use published sources with a long history and established record. Most government published data, especially at the federal level, as well as those for state and local governments would fall into this category.

Part I

BASIC TIME SERIES MODELS

Chapter 1

Basic Time Series Models I

A time series is a sequence of equally spaced observations of a variable defined in continuous time. Time series models use past or historical observations to predict the future values of a forecast variable. The primary purpose of these models is to discover the pattern that underlies these observations and to extrapolate them into the future to produce desired forecasts. Since the forecasts based on time series models rely entirely on historical data, it is quite natural for these forecasts to contain some elements of past and current conditions. This is likely to be true in the short run than in the long run, which means that time series models will produce reasonably accurate forecasts in the short-term but not necessarily in the long-term. Similarly, for the same reason, these models are less likely to predict accurately when significant changes occur in an economy such as turning points (Gilchrist, 1976).

There is a wide range of time series models, from analytically simple to models that are complex, data-intensive, and machine driven, and the number of choices has been increasing over time (Diebold, 1998; Makridakis et al., 1998). This chapter discusses some of the commonly used time series models that are simple and relatively easy to use. They are naïve model, percentage average, simple moving average, double moving average, weighted moving average, exponential moving average, and simple trend line. The chapter concludes with a brief discussion on measures of forecast accuracy.

NAÏVE MODEL

The easiest way to forecast a government budget (revenue, as well as expenditure) is to assume that next year's budget will be exactly the same as the current year, which means that there will be no change in demand or the cost of providing government services and, consequently, no change in the level of revenue that will be needed to provide them, other than for inflation. This is known as naïve forecasting. Since a naïve forecast assumes the current conditions to be the same as last year, it often serves as the initial decision tool to make the appropriate changes in a budget.

We can use a simple expression to describe it, as shown below:

$$\hat{Y}_{t+1} = Y_t \qquad\qquad (1.1)$$

where Y is a revenue or expenditure variable, Y_t is the current value of Y, and $\hat{Y}_{t+1}$ is the value of Y at time $t+1$.

PERCENTAGE AVERAGE METHOD

Simplest among the time series models is the percentage average method. Its simplicity lies in the fact that it uses measures such as simple arithmetic average to do the forecast. The model is based on the assumption that the future values of a forecast variable tend toward the average of its past occurrences. In other words, the average of the past values of a variable can provide a good basis for its future values. The procedure for using the method is quite simple: Simply take the differences between any two adjacent observations in a series, calculate their average, and use that as a basis for forecasting the future values, say, for next year, $t+1$, as shown below:

$$\hat{Y}_{t+1} = Y_t + \left(Y_t\right)\left(\text{Average Change}\right)$$

$$= Y_t + \left(Y_t\right)\left(\sum_{i=1}^{n} \left(Y_{t-(t-i)} / Y_{t-i}\right)\right) / (n-1) \qquad (1.2)$$

where $\hat{Y}_{t+1}$ is the predicted value of the forecast variable Y at time $t+1$, Y_t is the current value of the forecast variable Y, Y_{t-i} are past values of the forecast variable Y (for i = 1, 2, ……., n), and n is the number of observations in a series.[1] Since the average change is a constant, c, Equation 1.2 can be written as $\hat{Y}_{t+1} = Y_t + cY_t$, which in essence becomes the same as the equation described under naïve forecast, except that the constant term is derived by taking the average of the past changes or some other predetermined measures. For example, suppose that a local government wants to forecast its property tax revenue (PTR) for next year, $t+1$. Let us say that we have the revenue data for the government for the last 15 years. Table 1.1 shows the data and their percentage changes.

Thus, to forecast the revenue for next year, $t+1$, all one needs to do is apply the extended expression for Equation 1.2 to the data, as shown below:

$$\hat{Y}_{t+1} = Y_t + (Y_t)\left(\sum_{i=1}^{n}\left(Y_{t-(t-i)} / Y_{t-i}\right)\right) / (n-1)$$

$$= (164.840) + (164.840)\left[(0.00686 + 0.00874 + \ldots\ldots + 0.00688) / (15-1)\right]$$

$$= (164.840) + \left[(164.840)(0.00517)\right]$$

$$= 164.830 + 0.85217$$

$$= 165.68217$$

or 165.68217 x \$1,000,000 = \$165,682,170, which is the amount of revenue the government will collect next year, $t+1$.

We can repeat the above process to produce forecasts for any number of years in the future. For instance, for year 2, $t+2$, the forecast value for $t+1$ will serve as the constant, instead of Y_t, so that $\hat{Y}_{t+2} = \hat{Y}_{t+1} + \left(\hat{Y}_{t+1}\right)\left[(\ldots\ldots\ldots) / (n-1)\right]$, and so forth. However, it is worth noting that when past forecasts are used to forecast future values of a variable, the errors in past forecasts automatically become part of the error in any future forecasts. A second problem with the

Table 1.1 Property Tax Revenue: Percentage Change

Time (T)	(Year-Period)	PTR, Y ($Million)	Change (Δ)	Percentage Change
t-14	1	164.840	-	-
t-13	2	165.970	0.00686	0.686
t-12	3	167.420	0.00874	0.874
t-11	4	166.290	-0.00675	-0.676
t-10	5	168.370	0.01251	1.251
t-9	6	169.250	0.00523	0.523
t-8	7	171.470	0.01312	1.312
t-7	8	170.870	-0.00350	-0.350
t-6	9	171.960	0.00638	0.638
t-5	10	172.680	0.00419	0.419
t-4	11	173.930	0.00724	0.724
t-3	12	173.050	-0.00046	-1.046
t-2	13	174.560	0.00408	0.408
t-1	14	175.920	0.00779	0.779
t	15	177.130	0.00688	0.688
t+1	16	-	-	-

Σ = 0.07231 6.230

$\bar{Y}$ = 0.00517 0.445

model, which is common to arithmetic averages, is that if a series contains extreme values (outliers), it will skew the average, which, in turn, will distort the forecasts. The problem can be easily corrected by discarding the outliers and replacing them with interpolated values or increasing the length of the series to even out some of the skewness in the data.

SIMPLE MOVING AVERAGE

Simple moving average (SMA), also called single moving average, is the simplest and most widely used among the family of time series models, especially where short-term forecasts are concerned. Like the percentage average method, it relies on arithmetic average, but instead of using a single average, the model uses a series of averages, called moving averages, which are obtained by taking the average of the most recent observations in a series. The procedure is quite simple: As new observations become available, a new average is calculated by dropping the oldest observation from the average and including the newest one. The newest average is then used to forecast the value for the next time period. Thus, the number of observations in the average always remains constant.

However, the method requires that the number of time periods included in the average is specified in advance, such as three, six, nine, etc. There is no prescribed method for determining the number of periods in a moving average. The general pattern of the data should guide the decision as to the number of periods one should include in the model. Moving averages can be used for any time series but are typically used for monthly data of a short time span because they can help smooth out the data by constantly updating the averages. Thus, a series containing three months of data is called a three-month moving average, six months of data is called a six-month moving average, and so forth.

The following presents the mathematical expression for the method:

$$\hat{Y}_{t+1} = \sum_{i=1}^{n} \frac{Y_{t-n+i}}{n}$$

$$= \frac{Y_t + Y_{t-1} + \ldots\ldots + Y_{t-n+1}}{n} \tag{1.3}$$

where $\hat{Y}_{t+1}$ is the forecast value of Y at time $t+1$, Y is the actual observation, Y_{t-n+i} is the past observations of Y (for $i = 1, 2, \ldots, n$), and n is the number of observations.

To give an example, suppose that a local government wants to forecast its monthly revenue from parking meters. Parking meter revenue can be fairly significant, especially for large governments. Let us say that the government has the data for the last 11 months, from January through November.

The objective of the government is to forecast the revenue for the month of December using a three-month moving average. Table 1.2 shows the monthly inflow of data for the government.

To obtain the revenue for December, $t+1$, we simply plug in the data for the three most recent months in the expression in Equation 1.4 and calculate the average, as shown below:

$$\hat{Y}_{(December)} = \frac{Y_{Nov} + Y_{Oct} + Y_{Sep}}{3}$$

$$= \frac{250 + 200 + 175}{3}$$

$$= 208.33$$

The result produces a revenue of $208,330 (208.33 x $1000) for the month of December.

We can repeat the process to forecast the revenue for January, $t+2$, in a similar fashion, so that

$$\hat{Y}_{(January)} = \frac{Y_{Dec} + Y_{Nov} + Y_{Oct}}{3}$$

$$= \frac{208 + 250 + 200}{3}$$

$$= 219.333$$

Table 1.2   Parking Meter Revenue: Simple (Single) Moving Average

Month	Time (T)	Actual Revenue, Y_t ($1000)	Revenue Forecast (Three-Month MA) ($1000)
January	t-10	250.00	-
February	t-9	200.00	-
March	t-8	225.00	-
April	t-7	275.00	225.00
May	t-6	300.00	233.33
June	t-5	250.00	266.67
July	t-4	225.00	275.00
August	t-3	200.00	258.33
September	t-2	175.00	225.00
October	t-1	200.00	200.00
November	t	250.00	191.67
December	t+1	-	208.33*
January	t+2	-	219.33*

*Forecasts.

or 219.333 x $1000 = $219,333 and continue to do so for any number of months into the future.

A quick glance at the results would indicate that the revenue forecast for December is much lower than the actual revenue for November, which is the most recent month. On the other hand, the revenue for January shows an increase of about $12,000 over December, but still much lower than the revenue for the previous January. The fluctuation in revenue from parking meters can be due to a variety of factors such as the months for which the data are collected, special events such as sports and musical festivals, weather conditions, and so forth.

Fluctuations in revenues are quite common in government, as they are in the private sector. For instance, governments tend to collect more revenue during certain times of the year, such as property taxes when they become due, sales tax during the holidays when consumer spending goes up, utility revenue, say, from water during the summer months when the consumption is usually high, and revenue from electricity during the winter months when the consumption is high. The forecasts for the Parking Meter revenue, by and large, appear consistent with this underlying pattern, although there may be other factors.

An important concern with moving averages, in general, is how to find the initial value when no previous forecasts are available. The rule of thumb is to substitute the first observation of the series (March, in the current example) for the first forecast. Another alternative is to take the average of three or four most recent observations and use that average as the forecast for the initial value. Although they are considered *ad hoc* measures, they tend to be quite effective when no information is available on previous forecasts.

DOUBLE MOVING AVERAGE

Simple moving averages have an inherent weakness in that the forecasts tend to lag behind the actual values, especially when the actual values show a consistent increase or decrease. To illustrate, let us say that we have a new set of revenue data for our parking meter example that show a slow but consistent increase in revenue for the first eight months, from January through August (Table 1.3). However, looking at the forecasts produced by the simple moving average (Column 4), they appear to lag behind the actual revenues consistently for the most part, except for a couple of months. Although some lags are not unlikely, depending on the rate of increase or decrease in the data over time, consistent lags can underestimate the values that can easily get reflected in the forecasts. The double moving average (DMA) can considerably overcome the problem.

Table 1.3 Parking Meter Revenue: Double Moving Average

Month	Time (T)	Actual Revenue, Y_t ($1000)	Three-Month Forecast, Y' ($1000)	3 x 3 Forecast, Y'' ($1000)	a	b	Forecast (a+b)
January	t-10	250.00	-	-	-	-	-
February	t-9	251.00	-	-	-	-	-
March	t-8	253.00	251.33	-	-	-	-
April	t-7	255.00	253.00	-	-	-	-
May	t-6	258.00	255.33	253.22	257.44	2.11	-
June	t-5	262.00	258.33	255.55	261.11	2.78	259.55
July	t-4	267.00	262.33	258.66	266.00	3.67	263.89
August	t-3	270.00	266.33	262.33	270.33	4.00	269.67
September	t-2	268.00	268.33	265.66	271.00	2.67	274.33
October	t-1	267.00	268.33	267.66	269.00	0.67	273.67
November	t	268.00	267.67	268.11	267.23	-0.44	269.67
December	t+1	-	-	-	-	-	266.79*
January	t+2	-	-	-	-	-	-

*Forecast.

The term DMA is somewhat of a misnomer in that it does not double the moving average, as the name implies. It is essentially the moving average of the moving average. The following shows the expression for the DMA for a three-month moving average, N = 3:

$$Y_t' = \frac{Y_t + Y_{t-1} + Y_{t-2}}{N = 3} \tag{1.4}$$

$$Y_t'' = \frac{Y_t' + Y_{t-1}' + Y_{t-2}'}{N = 3} \tag{1.5}$$

where Y_t is the actual revenue for a given month t, Y_t' is the simple (single) moving average forecast, Y_t'' is the double moving average forecast, and N is the number of months used in forecasting, which will be three in our case.

Now, applying the expressions in Equations 1.4-1.5 to the data, we get the following forecasts for March, t-8, and May, t-6:

$$Y_t' = \frac{Y_t + Y_{t-1} + Y_{t-2}}{N = 3}$$

$$= \frac{253 + 251 + 250}{3}$$

or \$251,330 for March, and

$$Y_t'' = \frac{Y_t' + Y_{t-1}' + Y_{t-2}'}{N = 3}$$

$$= \frac{255.33 + 253.00 + 251.33}{3}$$

or \$253,220 for May.

It should be worth noting that while both SMA and DMA follow the same computational procedures, the forecast for the double moving average is slightly different in that its values are aligned adjacent to the most recent period used to calculate the single moving average. This explains why the first forecast for DMA was the Month of May (Column 5). Also, in a DMA, the initial forecasts produced by the single and the double moving averages are not the final forecasts, rather they provide values for two new terms, a and b, similar to the intercept and slope coefficients in a regression model, which are then used to produce the forecasts.

The following expression shows how to use the two terms, a and b, to produce the DMA forecast:

$$Y''_{t+1} = a_t + b_t \qquad (1.6)$$

where a and b are given by the expressions

$$a_t = 2Y'_t - Y''_t \qquad (1.7)$$

$$b_t = \left(\frac{2}{N-1}\right)(Y'_t - Y''_t) \qquad (1.8)$$

Equations 1.7 and 1.8 need a little elaboration. Since the MAs often lag behind the actual values, Equation 1.7 makes an adjustment for the most recent forecast to avoid the problem. It does so by adding to the single moving average, Y'_t, the difference between the single and the double moving average, $Y'_t - Y''_t$, so that $a_t = Y'_t + (Y'_t - Y''_t) = 2Y'_t - Y''_t$. To further improve the forecast, Equation 1.8 also makes an adjustment in b_t, based on the difference between the single and the double moving average, $Y'_t - Y''_t$, with an allowance for the number of periods, N, used in the moving average.

Thus, to forecast the revenue for the month of December, $t+1$, first, we find (estimate) the values of a and b for the month of November and then plug the estimated values into the expression in Equation 1.6 to obtain the revenue for the month of December, as shown below:

$$a_{(November)} = 2Y'_t - Y''_t$$

$$= 2(267.67) - 268.11$$

$$= 267.23$$

$$b_{(November)} = \left(\frac{2}{N-1}\right)(Y'_t - Y''_t)$$

$$= \left(\frac{2}{3-1}\right)(267.67 - 268.11)$$

$$= -0.44$$

$$Y''_{(December)} = a_{(November)} + b_{(November)}$$

$$= 267.23 - 0.44$$

$$= 266.79$$

which turns out to be \$266,790 and repeat the process for the month of January or any number of months in the future. Table 1.3 also shows the estimated values for a and b and the final forecasts for the DMA.

One final point about DMA is that while it addresses the lag problem of the single moving average, it also requires more data than a single moving average. The rule of thumb is that if SMA uses three periods of data, the DMA will need six periods of data, and if SMA uses six periods of data, the DMA will need 12 periods of data, and so forth; hence, the term double.

WEIGHTED MOVING AVERAGE

Moving averages, single or double, have an inherent weakness in that they assign equal weight to all the observations in a series, including the most recent observations. Common sense tells us that most recent observations usually contain more information about what is likely to happen in the future than the earlier observations, meaning that the most recent observations should be given relatively higher weights than the earlier observations. Weighted moving average corrects the problem by assigning differential weights to the observations in a series.

Equation 1.9 shows the expression for a weighted moving average.

$$\hat{Y}_{t+1} = \frac{\sum_{i=1}^{n} (w_i)(Y_{t-n+i})}{\sum_{t=1}^{n} w_t}$$

$$= \frac{w_1 Y_t + w_2 Y_{t-1} + \ldots\ldots\ldots\ldots + w_n Y_{t-n+1}}{\sum w_i} \qquad (1.9)$$

where w_i represents the ith weight corresponding to the observations of the forecast variable, Y, and the rest of the terms are the same as before. Since recent observations contain more information, the weights decline with increasing time in that the most recent observation will have the highest weight, the second most recent observation will have the second highest, and so forth.

To give an example, let us look at the monthly Parking Meter revenue data again (Table 1.2). Assume that the government decides to assign a weight of 3 to the most recent month (November), a weight of 2 to the second most

recent month (October), and a weight of 1 to the third most recent month
(September). The inflow for the month of December, $t+1$, will thus be

$$\hat{Y}_{(December)} = \frac{w_1 Y_{Nov} + w_2 Y_{Oct} + w_3 Y_{Sept}}{\sum_{i=1}^{3} w_i}$$

$$= \frac{3(250) + 2(200) + 1(175)}{3 + 2 + 1}$$

$$= \frac{750 + 400 + 175}{6}$$

$$= 220.83$$

or 220.83 x \$1000 = \$220,830. The result appears to be much higher than the
earnings obtained with the SMA for the same month; the difference can be
attributed in part to the weights assigned to the data.

It should be worth noting that the weights we assigned to the problem were
somewhat arbitrary, although they maintained the order structure of time.
There are two fundamental ways to assign weights to a series: informal, as
we did in the present example, and formal, using a formal (mathematical)
structure, which requires a logical basis for determining the weights. A good
example of the latter would be normalized weights, where the sum of the
weights is equal to 1. Normalization produces a relative measure of time.
Applied to the current problem, this would be $w_1 = 0.5$ (3/6) for November,
$w_2 = 0.333$ (2/6) for October, and $w_3 = 0.167(1/6)$ for September, indicating that November (the most recent month) is three times as important as
September (the least recent month), which is half as important as the month
of October (the second most recent month).

The unweighted case then emerges as a special case, where $w_i = 1/n$ (for all
i). The result of the forecast with normalized weights is shown below:

$$\hat{Y}_{(December)} = \frac{w_1 Y_{Nov} + w_2 Y_{Oct} + w_3 Y_{Sep}}{\sum_{i=1}^{3} w_i}$$

$$= \frac{0.5(250) + 0.333(200) + 0.167(175)}{0.5 + 0.333 + 0.167}$$

$$= (125.00 + 66.60 + 29.23) / 1$$

$$= 220.83$$

or 220.83 X $1000 = $220,830 which incidentally came out to be the same as the nonnormalized weight. (If we reversed the weights, the result would be different).

Finally, it should also be worth noting that caution is exercised when the weights are assigned, regardless of the model used. If too high a weight is assigned to the most recent observation, the weighted average may overreact to an irregular movement. On the other hand, if there are no significant differences in the weights, the result would not be any different from a simple arithmetic average. The number of time periods included in a series may also have an effect on the forecast. In any case, experience and a clear understanding of the observations and their pattern should be a useful guide to suggest how many time periods would be appropriate.

EXPONENTIAL MOVING AVERAGE

Both simple and weighted moving averages have an important requirement that all prior observations past the nth period must be available, which may be a problem if the series initially does not contain sufficient observations. Exponential moving average, also known as single exponential smoothing (since it uses a single parameter), corrects the problem by using only two observations or data points to forecast—the most recent observation and the most recent forecast. As such, it is considered the most parsimonious among all the moving average methods, especially where there are data limitations.

While there are some differences, there is also a similarity between the exponential moving average and the weighted moving average in that they both assign differential weights to the observations. In the case of the exponential moving average, they are called smoothing constants or "alpha" weights, or simply α. The weights, which range between 0 and 1 ($0 < \alpha < 1$), are not selected in any ordered fashion, rather they are selected in such a way that their values reflect the degree to which past observations are taken into account. For instance, if α has a high value, say, close to 1, it gives greater weight to the most recent forecast meaning that large changes can result from new observations. On the other hand, if α has a low value, say, close to 0, it gives greater weight to the old forecast meaning that only small changes can result from new observations. It should be worth noting that there is no correct procedure for selecting α—much depends on the judgment of the forecaster.

The computation of the method is somewhat more involved than either the simple or weighted moving average, as can be seen from the following expression:

$$\text{Exponential Moving Average}, \hat{Y}_{t+1} = \alpha Y_t + (1-\alpha)\hat{Y}_t \qquad (1.10)$$

where Y_{t+1} is the exponential moving average, Y_t is the most recent value for variable Y, α is the weight assigned to the most recent value (smoothing constant), $(1-\alpha)$ is the complementary weight, and $\hat{Y}_t$ is the most recent forecast for Y.

Since the method relies on two data points, it is necessary to have a reasonably good forecast for the most recent month. However, the forecast may not always be available to a forecaster, in which case the forecaster may use the average of the series or the forecast based on the initial value of α. Since we already have the forecast for the month of November (Table 1.2), based on the three-month moving average, we can easily plug in the value to obtain the forecast for the month of December. That is,

$$\hat{Y}_{(December)} = \alpha Y_t + (1-\alpha)\hat{Y}_t$$

$$= (0.9)(250) + (0.1)(191.67)$$

$$= 225.0 + 19.167$$

$$= 244.167$$

or 244.167 x \$1000 = \$244,167. Note that 250 (\$250,000) is the most recent revenue, Y_t, and 191.67 (\$191,670) is the most recent forecast, $\hat{Y}_t$, based on the SMA. Interestingly, we could have also used 197.80, corresponding to $\alpha = 0.9$, which is the weight we assigned to the most recent value, Y_t (Table 1.4). The result would be slightly different, but close, as shown below:

$$\hat{Y}_{(December)} = \alpha Y_t + (1-\alpha)\hat{Y}_t$$

$$= (0.9)(250) + (0.1)(197.80)$$

$$= 225.0 + 19.78$$

$$= 244.780$$

or \$244,780. It should be worth noting that when faced with two recent forecasts that are close, it is up to the judgment of the forecaster which one to use. The rule of thumb is to use the one obtained with the α value, since it is the basis for the forecast in an exponential moving average, rather than the one obtained with a single moving average.

Table 1.4 shows three exponential moving averages, based on three α values, selected at random: 0.1, 0.5, and 0.9. Since, in reality, there can be many such values of α, there will be many such forecasts, which raises the

Table 1.4   Parking Meter Revenue: Exponentially-Smoothed Values for Different α's

| | | | Exponentially | Smoothed | Values |
Month	Time (T)	PMR, Y_t ($1000)	α = 0.1 (Estimated)	α = 0.5 (Estimated)	α = 0.9 (Estimated)
January	t-10	250.00	-	-	-
February	t-9	200.00	250.00	250.00	250.00
March	t-8	225.00	245.00	225.00	205.00
April	t-7	275.00	243.00	225.00	223.00
May	t-6	300.00	246.20	250.00	269.80
June	t-5	250.00	251.60	275.00	297.00
July	t-4	225.00	251.40	262.50	254.70
August	t-3	200.00	248.80	243.70	228.00
September	t-2	175.00	243.90	221.80	208.00
October	t-1	200.00	237.00	198.40	177.90
November	t	250.00	233.30	199.20	197.80
December	t+1	-	235.00*	224.60*	245.80*
		MSE	1629.40	1620.70	1469.34

$$MSE = \frac{\Sigma(Observed - Estimated)^2}{n}\left[for\ n=10, \alpha=0.9\right]$$

$$=[(200-250)^2 + (225-205)^2 + (275-223)^2 + (300-269.8)^2 + (250-297)^2 + (225-254.7)^2$$

$$+(200-228)^2 + (175-208)^2 + (200-177.9)^2 + (250-197.8)^2]/10$$

$$=\left[2,500 + 400 + 2,704 + 912.04 + 2,209 + 882.09 + 784 + 1,089 + 488.41 + 2,724.84\right]/10$$

$$= 14,693.38/10$$

$$= 1,469.338$$

*Forecasts.

question: How does one obtain the α value that will produce the best possible forecast? As noted earlier, there is no hard and fast rule for determining this value, but the convention is to use a trial-and-error approach until one finds the α value that will produce the minimum forecast error. The errors can be calculated using methods such as mean-squared error (MSE) or any other methods (discussed later in the chapter). According to the table, the α value that will produce the least amount of error is 0.9.

The exponential smoothing discussed here is appropriate for a time series that moves randomly around a constant average, called stationary. Stationary means it has no trend or seasonal pattern. However, there are variations of exponential smoothing that can effectively deal with both trends and seasonal patterns in a data series. In fact, a whole family of smoothing techniques has been developed over the years that can deal with varying conditions in a series (Gardner, 2006, 1985), some of which are discussed in the next chapter.

TREND LINE

One of the most popular time series models among budget practitioners is the trend line, partly because it is analytically simple and partly because of its statistical appeal. A trend is a continuous movement in a time series. Trend line provides a visual presentation of the movement in a certain direction—upward or downward. For certain types of revenues, as well as expenditures, it is possible to obtain a fairly accurate forecast with a simple trend line than with SMA or exponential smoothing, especially if the forecast variables are affected by long-term trends in underlying economic and demographic variables. For instance, cities and states with growing populations and economic activities will have an upward trend in their property tax base and sales tax collections. In contrast, if the same cities and states have consistently declining economic activities, they will show a downward trend in their tax base and revenue collections. Trend line projections are quite useful in both cases.

Basic Structure

Trend lines are generally expressed in terms of degrees. A first-degree trend is a straight line, the second degree is a curve, where the highest exponent of the independent variable, T, in our case, is 2 (quadratic), the third degree is a curve where the highest exponent of the independent variable is 3 (cubic), and so forth (Figure 1.1). The number of degrees indicates the number of times the curve shifts directions. The first-degree does not change direction, the second-degree changes once, the third degree twice, and so forth. Although higher degree polynomials can be used in forecasting, in most instances, the first and second degrees and maybe the third degree are what one would need.

Conceptually, a trend line is a special case of regression models (discussed at length in Chapter 3) with one major difference: It is expressed as a function of time, whereas, for a regression model, it could be any variable of interest, single or multiple. The following presents a simple expression for a first-degree trend line:

$$Y_t = a + bT \tag{1.11}$$

where Y is the dependent or forecast variable, T is the independent variable representing time, and a and b are the intercept and the slope coefficient, respectively.

The expression in Equation 1.11 assumes a linear or straight-line relationship (degree one), meaning that for any value of T, Y will change by a constant amount equal to the value of the slope, b. The slope indicates the

Forecast Variable (Y)   Forecast Variable (Y)

0   Time (T)   0   Time (T)

(a) First Degree-Linear   (b) Second Degree-Quadratic
(Y= a+bT)   (Y=a+bT+cT²)

Forecast Variable (Y)   Forecast Variable (Y)

0   Time (Y)   0   Time (T)

(c) Second Degree-Quadratic   (d) Third Degree-Cubic
(Y=a+bT+cT²)   (Y=a+bT+cT²+dT³)

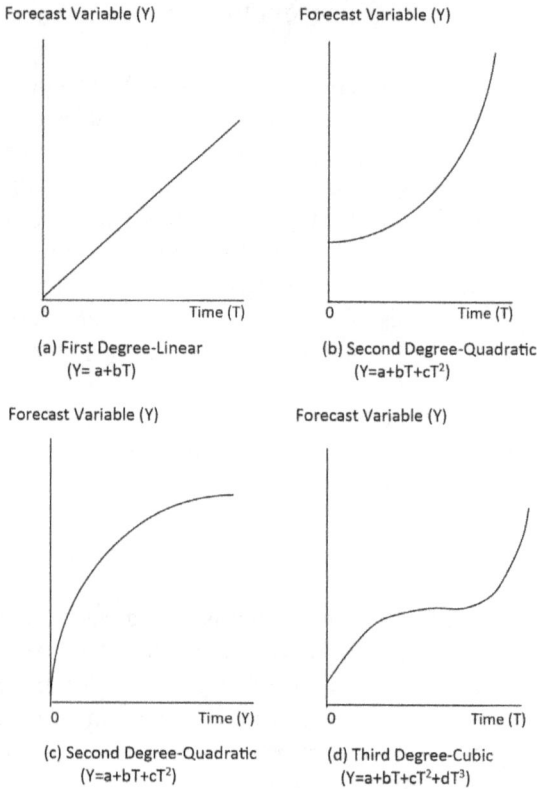

Figure 1.1   Polynomials – first, second, and third degree.

amount by which the forecast variable Y will change for one unit change in the independent variable and can be obtained by the expression

$$\hat{b} = \frac{\Sigma(Y - \bar{Y})(T - \bar{T})}{\Sigma(T - \bar{T})^2} \tag{1.12}$$

where $\bar{Y}$, $\bar{T}$ are respectively the arithmetic means of Y and T, and $\hat{b}$ is the estimated value of b. The intercept, a, on the other hand, measures the value Y will assume in the absence of the independent variable T and is obtained by the expression

$$\hat{a} = \bar{Y} - \hat{b}\bar{T} \tag{1.13}$$

where â is the estimated value of α, and the rest of the terms are the same as before.

The Model Parameters

In general, the slope of the model in Equation 1.13 can be positive or negative, although the convention is to express the relationship in the positive term, $Y = a + bT$. A positive slope ($b > 0$) indicates a positive relationship between the dependent variable Y and the independent variable T, meaning that Y will change in the same direction as the direction of change in T; that is, if T goes up, so will Y, and vice versa. A negative slope ($b < 0$), on the other hand, indicates an inverse relationship between Y and T, meaning that as T goes up, Y will go down and vice versa. The slope, however, is seldom 0 because if it is zero it will mean the absence or total redundancy of the explanatory variable. From a forecasting perspective, when $b > 0$, it means the values of the forecast variable, Y, will increase over time (since our independent variable is time), and when $b < 0$, it means the values will decrease over time. On the other hand, if $b = 0$, it means the values of Y will remain the same.

Similarly, the intercept term can be positive, negative, or zero. When it is 0, it means that Y will have a value 0 when $T = 0$. In other words, there is no intercept. When the intercept is negative, it means that Y has a negative value when $T = 0$, in which case the forecaster has to decide if it is the right model to use. And when it is positive, which is usually the case in most studies, it means that Y has a positive value when $T = 0$. The model is solved by the *ordinary least squares method* (OLS), which allows for a unique solution to the model.[1]

Tests of Significance of the Estimated Parameters and the Model

Once the model has been estimated, it is important to ensure that the observed estimates are statistically significant. Two sets of tests are typically used for this purpose: One, the tests of significance of the estimated parameters, and two, the test of significance of the estimated model, especially where multiple independent variables are involved. For the tests of significance of the estimated parameters, the convention is to use *t*-tests, corresponding to the number of parameters in the model.[2] Thus, if there are *n* parameters in a model, there will be *n* such tests. To test for the significance of the model, the convention is to use an *F*-test,[3] which tells us if the estimated model is a good fit, called the test of goodness-of-fit. The procedure is essentially the same as that used for the *t*-tests. The test is necessary to ensure that the model, $Y = a + bT$, as a whole is significant. On the other hand, it is not necessary when it includes a single independent variable, as in the current example. In fact, the tests of significance of the estimated parameters should be sufficient to guarantee the statistical soundness of the estimated model (see Chapter 3 for details).

Model Application

To illustrate the method, let us use the data for property tax revenue (PTR) we used earlier, for the percentage average method. As before, our objective is to forecast the revenue from property tax for the government. We do this in two steps: first, estimate the model and then use the estimated parameters to do the forecasts.

The results of the estimated model are presented below:

$$\hat{PTR_t} = 164.2330 + 0.8418T$$

$$(489.9466) \quad (22.8326)$$

$$\text{MAPE}=0.2305 \quad R^2=0.9757 \quad F=521.3266 \quad DW=2.2977$$

The model appears to be quite good, as evidenced by low mean absolute percentage error (MAPE), high t ratios (values, in parentheses), high R^2 (coefficient of determination), high F value (goodness of fit of the model), and a fairly good DW statistic.[4] In general, the higher the t value, R^2, and the F value, the better the estimated model. Both t values turned out to be quite high and statistically significant at less than 1 percent level of α, with $p < 0.001$, which can be easily checked against the critical t value (found in any standard statistics textbook). The R^2 also came out to be quite high at 97.57 percent.

The model, as a whole, also appears to be quite good, as given by the high F value, significant at less than 1 percent level of α, with $p < 0.001$, which, as before, can be checked against the critical value of F (found in any standard statistics textbook). The DW statistic also came out to be reasonably good, indicating no visible autocorrelation, a common problem with time series data. In general, if the estimated coefficients are significant, the chances are high that the model will also be significant, and vice versa.

Diagnostic Checks

Generally speaking, time series with trends are more common for economic than noneconomic data because economic data tend to reflect underlying patterns much better than noneconomic data. Consequently, forecasters often find it useful to fit some sort of trend model when dealing with revenue or expenditure forecasts. In most instances, the trend is obvious and detailed testing is not necessary but in the event that one has some doubt, it is important to use applicable measures to see if there is a trend in the data before running the model.

The simplest way to detect a trend in a series is to plot the data on a two-dimensional plane (with forecast variable on the vertical axis and time on the horizontal axis) to see if there is a discernible trend. As long as the data do not take a turn upward or downward or move in a wave-like fashion, it is an indication that there is a trend in the data. Alternatively, we can use formal statistical tests that can tell us if there is a trend in the series, in particular the direction of the trend—if it is positive or negative. Two types of tests are generally used for this purpose: nonparametric and parametric. Nonparametric tests do not make any assumption about the distribution of the population from which the sample observations have been drawn, such as normal, approximately normal, binomial, rectangular, and so forth; as such, they are often called distribution-free methods. Parametric tests, on the other hand, assume that the sample observations have come from a normal or any of the other forms of population distribution.

Nonparametric Tests

A good example of nonparametric tests applied to a trend line is Spearman's ρ (rho),[5] also known as Daniels' Test. It is essentially a nonparametric version of Pearson's Product Moment Correlation similar to Spearman's rank correlation coefficient, based on paired observations, and is given by the expression

$$\rho = 1 - \frac{6\sum_{i=1}^{n} d_i^2}{n\left(n^2 - 1\right)} \tag{1.14}$$

where ρ is the Spearman's rank correlation coefficient which ranges between ± 1 ($-1 \leq \rho \leq +1$), d_i is the ith rank deviation ($i = 1,2,\ldots\ldots,n$). The deviation, d, is obtained by taking the difference between the rank orders for time and the values of the forecast variable. In general, if ρ is positive, the trend is upward, and if it is negative, the trend is downward.

We can easily apply the procedure to our property tax revenue (PTR) problem to see if the data depict any trend. As can be seen in Table 1.5, the result produces a perfect relationship between PTR and time, given by $\rho = 1 - [(6\Sigma d^2)/n(n^2-1)] = 1 - [(6\Sigma d^2)/(n^3-n)] = 1 - [(6)(6)/(15^3-15)] = 1 - [(36)/(3360)] = 1 - 0.0107 = 0.9893$, indicating a strong upward trend in the series.

Table 1.5   Property Tax Revenue: Estimated Values, Time, and Rank Order

Time (T)	(Period)	PTR, Y_t ($Million)	PTR, $\hat{Y}_t$ ($Million)	Rank Order Y	Rank Order T	d	d²
t-14	1	164.840	165.075	1	1	0	0
t-13	2	165.970	165.197	2	2	0	0
t-12	3	167.420	166.758	4	3	1	1
t-11	4	166.290	167.600	3	4	-1	1
t-10	5	168.370	168.442	5	5	0	0
t-9	6	169.250	169.284	6	6	0	0
t-8	7	171.470	170.126	8	7	1	1
t-7	8	170.870	170.967	7	8	-1	1
t-6	9	171.960	172.191	9	9	0	0
t-5	10	172.680	172.651	10	10	0	0
t-4	11	173.930	173.493	12	11	1	1
t-3	12	173.050	174.335	11	12	-1	1
t-2	13	174.560	175.176	13	13	0	0
t-1	14	175.920	176.018	14	14	0	0
t	15	177.130	176.860	15	15	0	0
t+1	16	-	177.702*	-	-	-	-
t+2	17	-	178.544*	-	-	-	-
t+3	18	-	179.385*	-	-	-	-

$\Sigma d = 0 \; \Sigma d^2 = 6$

*Forecasts.

Parametric Tests

Like the nonparametric tests, there is a range of parametric tests that one can also use for this purpose. The most frequently used among these is the *t*-test.[6] It is based on the well-known Pearson's Product Moment Correlation coefficient, r, and is given by the expression

$$t = \frac{r\sqrt{n-2}}{\sqrt{1-r^2}} \tag{1.15}$$

where t is the test statistic, t, r is the Pearson's Product Moment Correlation coefficient, given by the expression

$$r = \frac{\Sigma(T - \bar{T})\Sigma(Y - \bar{Y})}{\sqrt{\Sigma(T - \bar{T})^2}\sqrt{\Sigma(Y - \bar{Y})^2}} \tag{1.16}$$

The test is carried out in three simple steps: First, obtain the value of r, which we know to be 0.9878 ($\sqrt{R^2} = \sqrt{0.9757} = 0.9878$); as such, it is not necessary for us to go through the computational process for r. Next, find the t value using the expression in Equation 1.16, and then follow the standard procedure for *t*-tests. Since we know r, we can plug it into the expression in Equation 1.15 to obtain t; that is, t = $r\sqrt{(n-2)} / \sqrt{(1-r^2)} = 0.9757\sqrt{(15-2)} / \sqrt{1-0.9757} = 3.5179 / 0.1559 = 22.5651$; which is close to our observed *t* value. Finally, conduct the test by setting the null and alternative hypotheses, as H_0: $\rho = 0$ and H_A: $\rho \neq 0$.

In general, if the hypothesis is rejected for a positive t at an acceptable level of significance, called α, the trend is upward. On the other hand, if it is rejected for a negative t, the trend is downward. When it cannot be rejected, there is no observable trend in the data. Given that our observed t for the slope coefficient was reasonably high (22.8326), we can safely assume it to be statistically significant at any acceptable level of α (which can be easily checked against any standard t table). As for the direction of the trend, also given that the observed t was high and significant, we can suggest a strong upward trend in the series.

Theoretically, both diagnostic checks are not necessary for the same series once we can make a safe assumption about the distribution of the population from which the data in the series were drawn. If not, it does not hurt to conduct both tests. If the results point in the same direction, it will reinforce the soundness of the fitted model. Interestingly, both our nonparametric and parametric tests show a strong upward trend in the revenue data in our example, indicating that revenue will increase with time.

Forecasts

Once the tests of the estimated model indicate that it is statistically sound, we can proceed with the forecasts for the next year or next several years. To do so, as before, all we need to do is plug in the value of T, which for next year will be 16 (15+1), where 15 is the current year, t, multiply it by the estimated slope coefficient, and add it to the constant, so that

$$P\hat{T}R_{t+1} = 164.2330 + 0.8418T$$

$$= 164.2330 + 0.8418(16)$$

$$= 164.2330 + 13.4688$$

$$= 177.7018$$

or 177.7018 x $1,000,000 = $177,701,800. The result shows a marginal increase in revenue from the previous year.

To forecast the revenue for *t*+2, as before, we plug in the new value of T, which will be 17 (15+2), multiply it by the slope coefficient and add it to the constant, so that

$$\hat{PTR}_{t+2} = 164.2330 + 0.8418T$$

$$= 164.2330 + 0.8418(17)$$

$$= 164.2330 + 14.3106$$

$$= 178.5436$$

or 178.5436 x $1,000,000 = $178,543,600, and repeat the process to produce forecasts for any number of years into the future.

We do the same to forecast the revenue for *t*+3, that is, plug in the value of T, which will be 18 (15+3), multiply it by the slope coefficient and add it to the constant, so that

$$\hat{PTR}_{t+3} = 164.2330 + 0.8418T$$

$$= 164.2330 + 0.8418(18)$$

$$= 164.2330 + 15.1524$$

$$= 179.3854$$

or 179.3854 x $1,000,000 = $179,385,400 and repeat the process to produce forecasts for any number of years into the future but would not be necessary in the current example because we had a small series to start with. Table 1.5 shows the forecasts.

It should be worth noting that since the model uses a linear trend, the revenue will increase by a constant amount, but it is unrealistic to assume that growth will take place at the same rate for all future years. This may explain why this type of model is useful for short-term rather than long-term forecasts. To avoid the problem, the data must be updated continuously as new information becomes available and repeat the forecast. Ideally, all forecasts should be updated on a regular basis, regardless of the method used to capture the most recent changes in the data.

Another point worth noting is that the process we used to forecast the future values of our revenue variable could also be used to estimate its past values. It is called backcasting, or ex post forecasts (for past values), as opposed to ex ante forecasts (for future values) of the forecast variable. The backcasts allow us to see how good our estimates are in light of our estimates of the past values. Obviously, the closer the estimates of past values are to the actual values, the greater the fit and the better the estimates.

A cursory glance at the table of the estimated values (Table 1.5, Column 4) would show that they are fairly close to the actual observations, indicating a reasonably good-fitting model. This is also reflected in figure 1.2. Note that the dashed line in figure 1.2 represents the actual data, while the solid line represents the fitted line. The shaded area represents 95% confidence intervals constructed around the forecasts (Table 1.6).

Confidence Intervals

The forecasts produced so far are what one would call "point forecasts." As noted previously, they are expected values, not the actual values, but they allow us to set up intervals about them called "interval forecasts" to indicate with a certain degree of confidence where the actual values are expected to lie. This is important, especially from a decision-making point of view, since

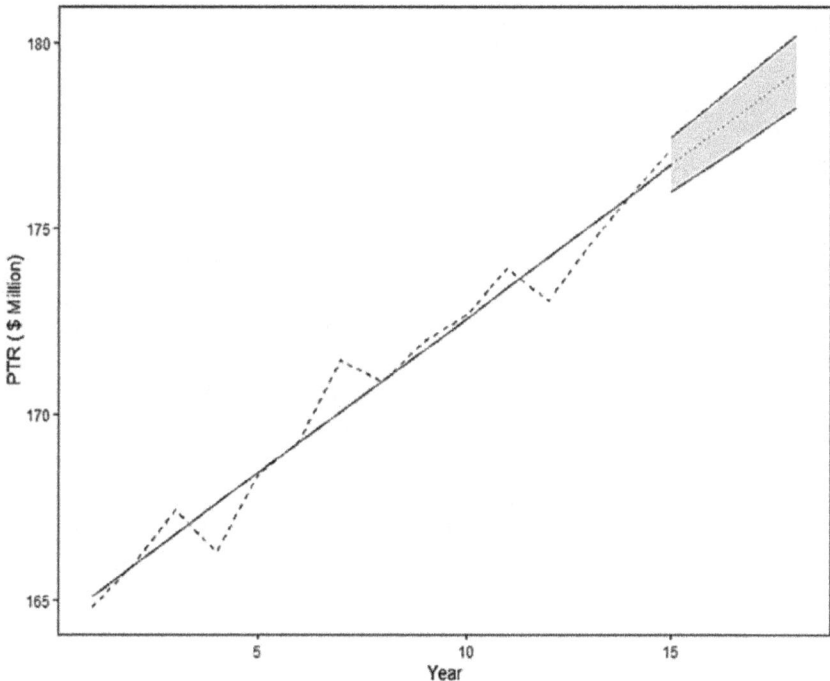

Figure 1.2 Observed and Fitted Line for PTR with 95% Confidence Bands.

Table 1.6   Revenue Forecasts for Property Tax with Confidence Intervals

Time (Period-Year)	Point Forecast ($Million)	95% CI Lower Bound	95% CI Upper Bound
t+1 (Yr. 16)	177.7018	176.3693	179.0343
t+2 (Yr. 17)	178.5436	177.2111	179.8761
t+3 (Yr. 18)	179.3854	178.0529	180.7179

it gives the decision makers a range of options when making budgetary decisions rather than restricting them to a single value.

The confidence intervals for PTR for next year, $t+1$, are calculated in the following way:

$$C[Y_{t+1} - (t_{\alpha/2})(SE_y) < Y_{t+1} < Y_{t+2} + (t_{\alpha/2})(SE_y)] = (1-\alpha)$$

$$C[177.7018 - (2.160)(0.6169) < Y_{t+1} < 177.7018 + (2.160)(0.6169)] = (1-0.05)$$

$$C[177.7018 - 1.3325 < Y_{t+1} < 177.7018 + 1.3325] = 0.95$$

$$C[176.3693 < Y_{t+1} < 179.0343] = 0.95$$

where C is the notation for confidence intervals, $\hat{Y}_{t+1}$ is the estimated value of Y at time $t+1$, $t_{\alpha/2}$ is the t value for a two-tailed distribution corresponding to $(1-\alpha)$, α is the probability of error (i.e., the probability that the observed estimate could have occurred by chance), $SE_{\hat{y}}$ is the standard error of estimate,[7] and $(1-\alpha)$ is the confidence level.

According to the interval estimates above, there is a 95 percent chance (i.e., we are 95% confident) that the actual revenue the government will collect from property tax next year will be between $176.34 million and $179.03 million, and the year after next will be between $177.21 and $179.88, and so forth. Table 1.6 shows the 95 percent confidence intervals for the revenue forecasts.

It is important to note that the selection of the confidence level is the discretion of the forecaster. For instance, we could have used a different confidence level, such as 90 or 99 percent, but 95 percent is considered fairly standard. In general, the higher the confidence level, the greater is the likelihood that the estimates will be reliable, as long as the model conditions hold.

Conditions Affecting Trend

In spite of its apparent simplicity and ease of use as a forecasting model, there are situations where it may be difficult to fit a trend line to a series, in particular when a major turning point occurs that can bring about a permanent change in the series. This is usually the case when there is a major change in a government policy that substantially shifts the direction of movement in the data. The trend line may also be difficult to fit to a series if there are random changes that cannot be easily explained. For instance, a sudden increase in government expenditure for a single period or two because of an unforeseen event that could not have been predicted would be a good example.

Also, there is a common perception about trend line that it can only be applied to situations where a series exhibits a linear trend, but, in reality, it can be applied to any situations where data may show a second- or third-degree trend. The rule of thumb is to plot the data first and then determine whether other forms of trend, such as a curvilinear or exponential trend, would best fit the data.

DECOMPOSING A TIME SERIES

An important consideration in time series models is the need to analyze the pattern that underlies the data so that the method most suitable or best approximates the pattern can be selected for forecasting. Decomposition serves an important purpose in this regard since it is primarily used to discover the underlying pattern in a time series. Four types of data patterns are commonly recognized in a time series: trend (T), seasonal (S), cyclical (C), and irregular (I). A trend pattern exists when there is a longer term (secular) increase or decrease in the data. Sales data, gross national product (GNP), and many other businesses and economic indicators follow a trend pattern in the movement over time. A seasonal pattern exists when a series is influenced by seasonal factors such as the quarter or month of the year or the day of the week. A cyclical pattern exists when the data are influenced by longer term economic fluctuations such as those associated with a business cycle. Finally, any movement in the data that cannot be explained by any of these patterns is explained by the irregular component.

Most data series include some combinations of the four patterns expressed either as a multiplicative ($Y_t = T \times S \times C \times I$) or an additive ($Y_t = T + S + C + I$) model. The multiplicative model assumes that, while the components are tied to different factors, they are also related to one another. The additive model assumes that while each component is independent of the other, they do not influence the values of the others. In other words, the high seasonal value will not influence the value of the trend or cyclical components. Regardless, the actual estimation of these patterns is an involved process. Forecasting models such as exponential smoothing are usually capable of distinguishing between these patterns, but they do not try to identify and estimate these individual components.

A number of methods have been developed over the years that try to identify, as well as estimate these components, the most widely recognized among them are the Census X-11, Census X-12, and Census X-13. Census X -11, which uses a multiplicative model, was originally developed by the National Bureau of Economic Research (NBER)—a private, nonprofit research organization. It consists of four phases, each of which is used to adjust the series in such a way as to facilitate the isolation and estimation of the four components (S, C, T, and I), which, in turn, are used to forecast business cycles and other macroeconomic goals.[7] Like Census X-11, Census X-12 uses a multiplicative model (S x C x T x I) because most economic time series data contain seasonal variations that increase with the level of the series. It uses an iterative process that runs through a series of steps until the components are successfully isolated.

Most of these steps involve the use of a weighted moving average to the data, but, as is common with moving average, it results in loss of data at the beginning and the end of the series because of averaging. To overcome the problem, it uses a seasonal ARIMA process (discussed in Chapter 4) that extends the original series in both directions with forecasts which makes it possible to adjust the observations using the full weighted moving averages. Census X-13, which is an enhanced version of Census X-11, includes a self-explanatory, versatile user interface and a variety of new diagnostics to detect and remedy any inadequacy in the seasonal and calendar effect adjustments, the details of which, including the ARIMA version, can be obtained from the US Census Bureau (US Bureau of Census, 2017).

MEASURING FORECAST ACCURACY

Forecasts are not actual values; they are estimates of what the actual values will be in the future. The difference between actual values and those estimated is the forecast error. The objective of any forecasting is to produce forecasts with as little forecast error as possible. For the government, in particular, this can have a significant effect on how the budget decisions are made. A positive forecast error, by and large, indicates that the model has underestimated the actual values and a negative forecast error indicates the opposite. Both over- and underestimation can have an effect on the government's decision whether to continue to provide existing services, undertake new initiatives, raise taxes, or cut expenditures. While forecasting models play an important role in this, the quality of data, familiarity with the forecasting problem, and the skill of the forecaster are also important in producing good and reliable forecasts.

The effectiveness of how best a forecasting model has been used is determined by the error it produces. Obviously, the lower the error, the more accurate the forecast is. The simplest way to measure the accuracy of a forecast is to plot the actual values against the forecasted values to see the level of error in a forecast, but, unfortunately, the plots do not give a precise measure of accuracy other than providing a visual impression of performance. A more effective way to deal with the problem is to use measures that would provide a precise picture of accuracy that is simple and also easy to interpret. There is a wide range of such measures that can be used for this purpose. Most of these measures are based on simple statistical concepts such as mean, $\bar{X} = \sum_{i=1}^{n} X_i / n$, variance, $s^2 = \left[\sum_{i=1}^{n} (X_i - \bar{X})^2\right] / n - 1$,

standard deviation, $s = \sqrt{\left[\sum_{i=1}^{n} (X_i - \bar{X})^2\right] / n - 1}$, and covariance,

$Cov_{XY} = [\sum_{i=1}^{n} (X_i - \bar{X})(Y_i - \bar{Y})] / (s_X s_Y)$, where X and Y are the variables

of interest, and n is the number of observations.

This section discusses four such measures that are frequently used in calculating forecast errors: MSE, mean absolute deviation (MAD), mean percentage error (MPE), and MAPE.

Mean-Squared Error

The simplest of the measures used in determining forecast errors is the mean-squared error (MSE). It is obtained by taking the average of the squared differences between the observed (actual) and the estimated (forecast) values and is given by the expression:

$$MSE = \frac{\sum_{i=1}^{n} (0_i - E_i)^2}{n} \tag{1.17}$$

where O_i is the ith observed value, E_i is the ith estimated value (for i = 1, 2, ..., n), and n is the number of observations in a series

To give an example, suppose that we have the following annual data (actual) for a revenue variable Y, observed at the end of each fiscal year, and their corresponding forecasts: $Y_{t-5} = \$100$, $\hat{Y}_{t-5} = \$105$; $Y_{t-4} = \$125$, $\hat{Y}_{t-4} = \$122$; $Y_{t-3} = \$160$, $\hat{Y}_{t-3} = \$158$; $Y_{t-2} = \$175$, $\hat{Y}_{t-2} = \$177$; and $Y_{t-1} = \$200$, $\hat{Y}_{t-1} = \$203$. The MSE for the forecasts, therefore, will be 10.2, obtained in the following way:

$$\text{MSE} = \left[(100-105)^2 + (125-122)^2 + (160-158)^2 + (175-177)^2 + (200-203)^2\right]/5$$

$$= (25+9+4+4+9)/5$$

$$= 51/5$$

$$= 10.2$$

In general, the higher the MSE, the greater will be the forecast error.

Since it is based on the squared differences of the original series, the MSE produces results that are much larger than the actual differences. One way to avoid the problem is to take the square root of the MSE to produce a statistic called root mean-squared error (RMSE). The new statistic, which has the same attributes as the MSE, is given by the expression $\sqrt{MSE} = RMSE$.

$$RMSE = \sqrt{\frac{\sum_{i=1}^{n}(0_i - E_i)^2}{n}} \tag{1.18}$$

Thus, for the current problem, the RMSE will be $\sqrt{MSE} = \sqrt{10.2} = 3.19$, which is much lower than the MSE, as expected. The advantage of using RMSE is that it is expressed in the same unit as the original values of the series, which makes it easy to interpret the results.

Mean Absolute Deviation

Although easy to use, MSE has an inherent problem in that it penalizes a forecasting model much more for large errors than a model for small errors. MAD corrects the problem by averaging the magnitude of the forecast errors in absolute terms, as given by the following expression

$$MAD = \frac{\sum_{i=1}^{n}|0_i - E_i|}{n} \tag{1.19}$$

where O_i is the *i*th observed value, E_i is the *i*th estimated value (for i = 1,2,......,n), and *n* is the number of observations in a series.

Since, in most error calculations, the positive and negative differences cancel themselves out, producing a 0 error, presenting the differences in absolute terms would correct the problem considerably. Put differently, when we have two models in which the positive errors exactly cancel out the negative errors in one and small absolute errors in the other, chances are that we would prefer the second one. Both would have the same average error, but the second model would produce a small MAD.

As can be seen from the following result, when applied to the same data, MAD produces a value of 3, which is much lower than MSE:

$$\text{MAD} = \left(|100 - 105| + |125 - 122| + |160 - 158| + |175 - 177| + |200 - 203| \right) / 5$$

$$= (5 + 3 + 2 + 2 + 3) / 5$$

$$= 15 / 5$$

$$= 3$$

Interestingly, like RMSE, the MAD is measured in the same units as the original series, which may partly explain the lower value. Another advantage of using MAD is that it is more robust than MSE since it does not get easily affected by extreme values.

Mean Percentage Error

On occasion, it may be necessary to determine if the forecasting method is biased in that it consistently produces high or low values. Mean Percentage Error (MPE) is an appropriate measure in this case. If the method is biased, the MPE will produce a value of zero; if it is consistently overestimating, the MPE will produce a large negative value, and if it is consistently underestimating, the MPE will produce a large positive value. It is obtained by dividing the forecast errors by the actual observations, then taking an average of their percentage errors, and is given by the expression

$$MPE = \frac{\sum_{i=1}^{n} (PE_i)}{n} = \frac{\sum_{i=1}^{n} \frac{(O_i - E_i)}{O_i}}{n} \times 100 \quad (1.20)$$

Using the same data as before, we obtain the following value for MPE:

$$MPE = [((100 - 105) / 100) + ((125 - 122) / 125) + ((160 - 158) / 160)$$

$$+ ((175 - 177) / 175) + ((200 - 203) / 200) / 5] \times 100$$

$$= \left[(-0.05 + 0.024 + 0.0125 + 0.0114 - 0.015) / 5 \right] \times 100$$

$$= -\left[0.0171 / 5 \right] \times 100$$

$$= -0.00342 \times 100$$

$$= -0.342$$

The result produces a negative value of less than one percent, indicating that the forecasts are not necessarily biased or underestimated but have a slight tendency to overestimate.

Mean Absolute Percentage Error

A fourth commonly used measure, which contains elements of both MSE and MAD, is the MAPE. This measure is particularly useful when the size of the forecast variable is important in determining the accuracy of the forecast. MAPE provides an indication of how large the forecast errors are in comparison to the actual values of the series. It is obtained by averaging the magnitude of absolute percentage errors and is given by the expression

$$MAPE = \frac{\sum_{i=1}^{n}|PE_i|}{n} = \frac{\sum_{i=1}^{n}\left|\frac{(0_i - E_i)}{0_i}\right|}{n} \times 100 \qquad (1.21)$$

where PE_i is the ith percentage error (for i = 1, 2, ..., n), and n is the number of observations in a series.

As before, we can use the same data for MAPE we used for the previous three measures. The result will produce an error of 2.26 percent, which is lower than both MAD and MSE, as can be seen from the following calculations:

$$MAPE = [|((100-105)/100| + |((125-122)/125| + |((160-158)/160|$$

$$+ |((175-177)/175| + |((200-203)/200|)/5] \times 100$$

$$= \left[|0.05 + 0.024 + 00.0125 + 0.0114 + 0.015|/5\right] \times 100$$

$$= \left[0.1129/5\right] \times 100$$

$$= 0.0226 \times 100$$

$$= 2.26$$

Of the four, MAPE is considered a better measure because it contains elements of both MSE and MAD. The measure is particularly useful when the size of the forecast variable is important in determining the accuracy of the forecast and, more importantly, when comparing forecast accuracy across multiple time series (Hyndman and Koehler, 2006).

Other Measures

In addition to the above four, there is a host of other measures that are also used to measure forecast accuracy, such as Theil's inequality coefficient, Hannan-Quinn information criterion (HQC), Schwartz information criterion (SIC), Akaike information criterion (AIC), and a variation of AIC, called final prediction error (FPE), among others. To provide a brief narrative of each criterion, Theil's inequality coefficient, also known as Theil's U, has been extensively used in economic studies to measure how well the forecast values compare against the observed values. HQC is essentially a measure of goodness-of-fit of a model and often used for model selection rather than determining forecast accuracy. Likewise, SIC, also known as Schwartz-Bayesian Criterion, is used for model selection, especially when a finite set of models are compared. AIC, which has been extensively used in forecasting studies such as ARIMA, measures the amount of information loss by a model. Lastly, the FPE, which is defined as the one-step-ahead prediction error variance, when the LS estimates of autoregressive coefficients are used for determining the order of an autoregressive (AR) model.

SUMMARY

Forecasting lies at the heart of budgeting in government. Without good and reliable forecasts, it would be difficult for any government to plan and effectively carry out its operations. This chapter has introduced several basic time series models used in budget forecasting. They are conceptually simple, have low data requirements, and are relatively easy to use. Included in the discussion were the naïve model, percentage average method, single moving average, double moving average, weighted moving average, exponential moving average, and simple trend line. The chapter concluded with a brief discussion of measures frequently used to determine forecast accuracy.

NOTES

1. The least squares method is a mathematical procedure for fitting a line to a set of observations (Y and T, in our case) such that the sum of the squared deviations between the observed and estimated values of Y, $\sum(Y - Y)^2$, (i.e., the error variance, $\Sigma e2$) is minimized. That is,

$$\text{Minimize} \sum \hat{e}2 \ = \sum (Y - \hat{Y})^2 \qquad [1]$$

where ê is the difference between the observed and estimated value of Y; that is, $\hat{e} = Y - \hat{Y}$, and $\hat{Y}$ is the equation of the regression (fitted) line, $\hat{Y} = \hat{\alpha} + \hat{\beta}T$, so that $\hat{e} = Y - \hat{\alpha} - \hat{\beta}T$, substituting for $\hat{Y}$. Since $\hat{Y} = \hat{\alpha} + \hat{\beta}T$, Equation 1 can be rewritten as

$$\text{Minimize} \sum \hat{e}^2 = \sum(Y - \hat{a} - \hat{b}T)^2 \qquad [2]$$

Equation 2 is, what one would ca. ll, a minimization function, which can be easily solved using simple differential calculus, and with some algebraic manipulations, to produce the equations (not shown here) for the estimated intercept and slope, and , that will satisfy the minimum variance requirement in Equations 1 and 2. (For a detailed discussion of the method, see any standard econometrics textbook).

2. To conduct a *t*-test, we must first find the *t* values, corresponding to the estimated parameters $t_{\hat{a}} = \hat{a} / S_{\hat{a}}$ r the intercept and $t_{\hat{b}} = \hat{b} / S_{\hat{b}}$. r the slope, where the. subscripts are, respectively, the standard errors of a and b. Next, use the standard test procedure to see if the observed *t* is greater than the critical value of *t* (found in any statistics textbook, under the *t* table) for a given level of *p* (called the *p*-value, i.e., the probability of error) to determine that it did not occur by chance. If it is greater than the critical value of t, the estimated parameters are considered statistically significant at that level of *p*, and vice versa.

3. Like the *t* test, to conduct an *F*-test, one must first obtain the *F*-value, given by the expression for the trend line, $F = \left[\hat{b}^2 \sum_{i=1}^{n} (T - \bar{T})^2 \right] / \left[\left(\sum_{i=1}^{n} e^2 \right) / (n-k) \right]$ where $e^2 = (Y - \hat{Y})^2$ where *n* is . the number o. f observations in a series, and k is the number of parameters in the model, which will be 2 in the current example. Once the F-value is obtained, this is followed by the standard test procedure to see if the observed F is greater than the critical value of F (found in any statistics textbook, under the F table) for a given level of *p*. If it is greater than the critical value of F, the model is considered statistically significant and a good fit.

4. The tests conducted here are fairly standard, as they are based on conventional test statistics. However, there are tests related to model assumptions that are frequently used to determine if the assumptions have been violated to further ensure the statistical soundness of the model. Four assumptions are commonly associated with these tests: (1) normality (the error terms are normally distributed with 0 mean, $\mu=0$, and constant variance, σ^2), (2) homoskedasticity (the variance of the error term is the same for all values of the explanatory variables), (3) no serial or autocorrelation (the error terms of one period are not related to the error terms of the preceding period, and (4) no multicollinearity (the explanatory variables are not perfectly correlated with each other). There are specific tests one can conduct to see if any of the assumptions have been violated. For instance, for autocorrelation, the test commonly used is the Durbin-Watson (D-W) test to see if the successive error terms, *e*'s, are correlated with each other. The DW statistic extends between 0 and 4 ($0 < d < 4$), where d stands for DW statistic. The rule of thumb for interpretation is that there is no

autocorrelation if DW statistic is around 2. (For a detailed discussion of the assumptions, see Chapter 3).

5. Besides Spearman's rho, there are other non-parametric tests that one can also use such as runs test, turning points test, sign test, Kendall's tau, Fischer's exact test, Mann-Whitney U test, Kruskal-Wallis test, among others. Of these, Spearman's rank correlation is considered the simplest yet useful. For a good summary of these tests, see Jaisal et al (2015).

6. The *t* test is considered the simplest among the parametric tests. There are other tests such as one, two, and three way ANOVA tests with repeated samples. Another test, the Mean Square Successive Differencing (MSSD) test can also be used for this purpose, but is considered more complex.

7. The following provides a brief description of the four phases: In the first phase, the monthly time series data are adjusted with the help of an adjustment factor to account for variations in the series. In the second phase, preliminary estimates are made of seasonal factors along with adjustments of the raw data, using a centered, 5-term moving average of the seasonal component for monthly series and a 4-term average for quarterly series. In the third phase, the seasonal factors calculated at the outset of Phase 2 are recomputed to adjust for extreme values. Also in this phase, the trend and cyclical components are estimated using a centered moving average of the original series. In the final phase, the method generates a set of summary statistics that can be used to determine how successfully the method has isolated the seasonal factors and to develop future estimates of the trend-cycle factor.

Chapter 2

Basic Time Series Models II

An important consideration in time series forecasts is that one must be able to capture the underlying pattern in the data and select a model that would be appropriate for forecasting. The time series models we discussed earlier are simple and relatively easy to use, but they have an inherent weakness in that they fail to adequately capture the underlying pattern in a series. This chapter discusses five additional time series models that are much better equipped to deal with this problem. They are Brown's double and triple exponential smoothing, Holt's two-parameter exponential smoothing, Winters' seasonal exponential smoothing, and time series with cyclical variations. Of these, the first four are extensions of exponential smoothing, and the fifth is a direct extension of the trend line, discussed earlier. Additionally, there is a whole range of other time series models, more advanced than those discussed here, that one can use, such as the well-known Box-Jenkins and transfer function models (Hyndman and Athanasopoulos, 2018).

Box-Jenkins model, discussed later in Chapter 4, deserves special attention because of the approach it uses which is significantly different from those discussed here and in the previous chapter. Also, as one would expect, both Box-Jenkins and transfer function models are analytically much more complex, as well as demanding on time and data requirements, than most conventional time series models.

BROWN'S DOUBLE EXPONENTIAL SMOOTHING

Exponential smoothing and the moving averages, as noted earlier, have an inherent weakness in that they tend to lag behind the actual observations, which makes it difficult to adequately capture the underlying trend. This

occurs because exponential smoothing, especially single exponential smoothing, assumes a random fluctuation around a constant value; as such, if there is a
linear trend in either direction (positive or negative), it cannot adequately capture it. Brown's double exponential smoothing corrects the problem by adding
the difference between the two values (single and double smoothed) to the
single smoothed value and adjusting for the trend in the series (Brown, 1956).

The following expressions are typically used for Brown's double exponential smoothing process:

$$Y_t^{'} = \alpha Y_t + (1-\alpha) Y_{t-1}^{'} \tag{2.1}$$

$$Y_t^{''} = \alpha Y_t^{'} + (1-\alpha) Y_{t-1}^{'} \tag{2.2}$$

where α is the smoothing constant, Y_t is the actual observation, $Y_t^{'}$ is the
single exponential smoothing value, $Y_t^{''}$ is the double exponential smoothing
value, and $Y_{t-1}^{'}$ and $Y_{t-1}^{''}$ are the most recent smoothed values.

To establish the linkage between a single and a double exponential smoothing, Brown's method uses an additional expression for forecasting, which
resembles a linear model, similar to double moving average, discussed in the
previous chapter but estimated differently, especially the slope coefficient, as
shown below:

$$\hat{Y}_{t+n}^{''} = a_t + b_t (T) \tag{2.3}$$

where a_t is the intercept, given by the expression 2Yt' - Yt'' [i.e., α = Yt' + (Yt'
– Yt'') = 2Yt' – Yt''], b_t is the slope, given by the expression, $\dfrac{\alpha}{(1-\alpha)}(Y_t^{'} - Y_t^{''})$,
and T is the number of periods into the future for which the forecasts are being
made (Makridakis and Wheelright, 1978).

Let us look at the parking meter revenue example we introduced in the
previous chapter to illustrate the application of the method. Table 2.1 shows
the data, as well as the forecasts. The calculations are based on $\alpha = 0.1$ and a
forecast, one period ahead. In general, low values are assigned to a smoothed
constant when there are frequent fluctuations in the data, and high values are
assigned when there is a trend. Low values indicate that recent observations
are weighted less heavily than distant observations and, vice versa. The last
column in the table shows the forecasts. For instance, to obtain the revenue
for the month of November, we plug in the values of a and b from the table
and apply them directly to Equation 2.3.

Table 2.1 Parking Meter Revenue: Brown's Double Exponential Smoothing

Month	Time	PMR ($1,000)	Y_t' $\alpha = 0.1$ ($1,000)	Y_t'' $\alpha = 0.1$ ($1,000)	a_t	b_t	$\hat{Y}_t''$ ($1,000)
January	t-10	250.00	250.00	250.00	--	--	--
February	t-9	200.00	245.00	249.50	240.50	-0.5000	--
March	t-8	225.00	243.00	248.85	237.15	-0.6499	240.00
April	t-7	275.00	246.20	248.59	243.81	-0.2655	236.50
May	t-6	300.00	251.58	248.89	254.27	0.2989	243.54
June	t-5	250.00	251.42	249.14	253.70	0.2533	254.57
July	t-4	225.00	248.78	249.10	248.46	-0.0356	253.95
August	t-3	200.00	243.90	248.58	239.22	-0.5199	248.42
September	t-2	175.00	237.01	247.42	226.60	-1.1566	238.70
October	t-1	200.00	233.31	246.01	220.61	-1.4110	225.44
November	t	250.00	234.98	244.91	225.05	-1.1032	219.20
December	t+1	-	-	-	-	-	223.95*
January	t+2	-	-	-	-	-	222.84*

*Forecasts.

The following shows how the values of the parameters, including the forecasts, were obtained for the revenue variable for the next three months— November, December, and January:

$$\hat{Y}''_{(November)} = a_{October} + b_{October}(T)$$

$$= 220.61 - 1.4110(1)$$

$$= 219.20$$

or \$219,200, which is the revenue for the month of November. The values of the parameters, a and b were obtained in the following way: $a_{October} = 2Y'_{Oct} - Y''_{Oct} = (2)(233.31) - 246.01 = 466.62 - 246.01 = 220.61$, and $b_{October} = [\alpha/(1-\alpha)](Y'_{Oct} - Y''_{Oct}) = [0.1/(1-0.1)](233.31-246.01) = (0.1111)$ $(-12.70) = -1.4110$.

To obtain the forecast for the month of December, $t+1$, we do the same so that

$$\hat{Y}''_{(December)} = a_{November} + b_{November}(T)$$

$$= 225.05 - 1.1032(1)$$

$$= 223.95$$

or \$223,950. As before, the values of the parameters, a and b were obtained the same way as for the month of October: $a_{November} = 2Y'_{Nov} - Y''_{Nov} = (2)(234.98)$ $- 244.91 = 469.96 - 244.91 = 225.05$, and $b_{November} = [\alpha/(1-\alpha)](Y'_{Nov} - Y''_{Nov})$ $= [0.1/(1-0.1)](234.98 - 244.91) = (0.1111)(-9.93) = -1.1032$.

However, for the month of January, $t+2$, we will need to multiply b by 2, since we will be forecasting two periods ahead, T = 2, so that

$$\hat{Y}''_{(January)} = a_{November} + b_{November}(2)$$

$$= 225.05 - 1.1032(2)$$

$$= 222.84$$

or 222.84 x \$1000 = \$222,840. Similarly, for the month of February, we will multiply b by 3 (T = 3), for March by 4 (T = 4), and so forth. It should be noted that in each of these cases, the coefficients will remain the same as they were for the month of November, since they are the most recent values we have for a and b.

HOLT'S TWO-PARAMETER EXPONENTIAL SMOOTHING

Holt's two-parameter exponential smoothing also deals with a linear trend in a series, but it uses a slightly different approach than the one used in Brown's double exponential smoothing. Structurally, the two models are quite similar, except that Holt's model uses a different smoothing constant than the smoothing constant generally applied to actual data, which gives it some flexibility. The flexibility also comes from the fact that it utilizes two smoothing parameters (α and γ), as opposed to one for Brown (α). Like all smoothing parameters, the values range between 0 and 1.

The basic equations used in Holt's two-parameter exponential smoothing for forecasting include the following:

$$\hat{Y}_t = \alpha Y_t + (1-\alpha)(Y_{t-1} + b_{t-1}) \tag{2.4}$$

$$\hat{b}_t = \gamma(Y_t - Y_{t-1}) + (1-\gamma)b_{t-1} \tag{2.5}$$

$$\hat{Y}_{t+T} = \hat{Y}_t + \hat{b}_t(T) \tag{2.6}$$

where γ is a new smoothing constant, and the rest of the terms of the equations (Y, α, and b) are the same as those used in Brown's double smoothing.

The equations above need a little elaboration: Equation 2.4 produces a smoothed value that adjusts for trend in the previous period, b_{t-1}, by adding it to the previous smoothed value, Y_{t-1}. This eliminates the lag that results when the single smoothed value is estimated. Equation 2.5 updates the estimate from the previous period, while Equation 2.6 is the forecasting equation, similar to Brown's double exponential smoothing (Makridakis and Wheelright, 1978).

To illustrate how the method works, we can use the same Parking Meter example. Table 2.2 shows the data and the results of the estimated equations. As can be seen from the table, Holt's exponential smoothing requires an initial value of Y_1, which is generally assumed to be the same as the initial value of the actual series, $Y_1 = \$250,000$ (Column 4). It also needs an initial value of b_1 in order to forecast the value of Y. The following shows the expression typically used for the coefficient, b_1:

$$b_1 = \frac{Y_2 - Y_1}{2} + \frac{Y_4 - Y_3}{2} \tag{2.7}$$

Table 2.2   Parking Meter Revenue: Holt's Two-Parameter Exponential Smoothing

Month	Time	Revenue Y_t ($000)	$\hat{Y}_t$ ($000)	b_t	$\hat{Y}_{t+n}$ ($000)
January	t-10	250.00	250.00	0	-
February	t-9	200.00	245.00	-0.50	250.00
March	t-8	225.00	242.55	-0.70	244.50
April	t-7	275.00	245.17	1.99	241.85
May	t-6	300.00	252.44	2.52	247.16
June	t-5	250.00	254.46	2.48	254.96
July	t-4	225.00	253.75	2.16	256.94
August	t-3	200.00	250.32	1.60	255.91
September	t-2	175.00	244.23	0.83	251.92
October	t-1	200.00	240.55	0.38	245.06
November	t	250.00	241.84	0.47	240.93
December	t+1	-	-	-	243.13*
January	t+2	-	-	-	244.42*

*Forecasts.

where the terms of the expression are the same as before. Thus, applying the equation (2.7) to the problem would produce a value of 0 for b_1 [((200-250)/2) + ((275-225)/2) = -25 + 25], for January, as shown in Table 2.2 (Column 5).

The application of the model is not difficult once we have the initial values, although the process is somewhat more involved than the double exponential smoothing method because of an added parameter, γ (Equation 2.5). For instance, to obtain the forecast value for December, t+1, we will first assign the values to the two-smoothed constants, α and γ (say, both at 0.1), then proceed to estimate the equations, as follows:

$$\hat{Y}_{(November)} = \alpha Y_t + (1-\alpha)(Y_{t-1} + b_{t-1})$$

$$= (0.1)(250) + (0.9)(240.55 + 0.38)$$

$$= 25 + (0.9)(240.93)$$

$$= 25 + 216.84$$

$$= 241.84$$

or $241,840; and

$$\hat{b}_{(November)} = \gamma(Y_t - Y_{t-1}) + (1-\gamma)b_{t-1}$$

$$= (0.1)(250 - 240.55) + (0.9)(0.38)$$

$$= 0.95 + 0.34$$

$$= 1.29$$

Now, adding the two values together, we get the forecast for the month of December, $t+1$

$$\hat{Y}_{(December)} = \hat{Y}_{(November)} + \hat{b}_{(November}(1)$$

$$= 241.84 + 1.29(1)$$

$$= 243.13$$

or \$243,130, obtained by multiplying b by 1, since T = 1.

As with double exponential smoothing, to forecast for the month of January, $t+2$, we will multiply $\hat{b}_t$ by 2, since T = 2, so that

$$\hat{Y}_{(January)} = \hat{Y}_{(November)} + \hat{b}_{(November)}(2)$$

$$= 241.84 + 1.29(2)$$

$$= 241.84 + 2.58$$

$$= 244.42$$

which will produce a revenue of \$244,420. For the month of February, we will multiply it by 3 (T = 3), for March by 4 (T = 4), and so forth, and repeat the process to forecast the value for any month in the future.

BROWN'S TRIPLE EXPONENTIAL SMOOTHING

While double exponential smoothing has an advantage over single exponential smoothing in that it can deal with a linear trend in a series, unfortunately, it cannot deal with a series that exhibits a non-linear trend. This is usually the case in a curvilinear trend where the data in a series tend to increase at an increasing or decreasing rate, or decrease at an increasing or decreasing rate. Brown's triple exponential smoothing, also called quadratic smoothing, corrects some of these problems by adding a third smoothing equation (2.8) to the two in double exponential smoothing (Equations 2.1 and 2.2),

The following presents the expressions for Brown's triple exponential smoothing:

$$Y_t' = \alpha Y_t + (1-\alpha)Y_{t-1}' \tag{2.1'}$$

$$Y_t'' = \alpha Y_t' + (1-\alpha)Y_{t-1}' \tag{2.2'}$$

$$Y_t''' = \alpha Y_t'' + (1-\alpha)Y_{t-1}''' \tag{2.8}$$

where Y_t' and Y_t'', respectively, are single and double exponential smoothing, and Y_t''' is the triple exponential smoothing, obtained by smoothing out the results of double smoothing in Equation 2.2'.

However, unlike the double exponential smoothing, which requires two coefficients, a and b, the triple exponential requires the estimation of three coefficients, a, b, and c, one for each, given by the expressions

$$a_t = 3Y_t' - 3Y_t'' + Y_t''' \tag{2.9}$$

$$b_t = \frac{\alpha}{2(1-\alpha)^2}[(6-5\alpha)Y_t' - (10-8\alpha)Y_t'' + (4-3\alpha)Y_t'''] \tag{2.10}$$

$$c_t = [\frac{\alpha}{(1-\alpha)}]^2(Y_t' - 2Y_t'' + Y_t''') \tag{2.11}$$

where the terms are the same as before, except that Y_t''' stands for triple-smoothed statistic.

As before, the equations need a little elaboration. Equation 2.9 determines the current value of data. Equation 2.10 determines the linear trend, while Equation 2.11 determines the quadratic trend. To do the forecast, the model combines all three equations—the current value of data, the linear trend, and the quadratic trend. The inclusion of a quadratic term allows it to better capture the underlying trend than either the single or double exponential smoothing (Makridakis and Wheelright, 1978).

The following provides the expression for forecasting with the three smoothing constants:

$$\hat{Y}_{t+1} = a_t + b_t T + \frac{1}{2}c_t T^2 \tag{2.12}$$

To apply the model, let us go back to the parking meter revenue data. As before, our goal is to forecast the revenue for the month of December, $t+1$. We will need the following data to obtain the initial estimates for the month of November for the three smoothed statistics based on previous calculations:

$$Y_{Nov} = \$250,000 \; (\text{Actual, Table 2.1})$$

$$Y'_{Oct} = \$233,310 \; (\text{Single-exponential, Table 2.1})$$

$$Y''_{Oct} = \$246,010 \; (\text{Double-exponential, Table 2.1})$$

$$Y'''_{Oct} = \$248,370 \; (\text{Triple-exponential, Table 2.3})$$

Assume for convenience that $\alpha = 0.1$, similar to what we used for single and double exponential smoothing. We can now use the above information to obtain the estimates for the month of November, t, using the expressions in Equations 2.1', 2.2', and 2.8, as follows:

$$Y'_{Nov} = \alpha Y_{Nov} + (1-\alpha)Y'_{Oct}$$
$$= (0.1)(250) + (0.9)(233.31)$$
$$= 25.00 + 209.98$$
$$= 234.98$$

$$Y''_{Nov} = \alpha Y'_{Nov} + (1-\alpha)Y'''_{Oct}$$
$$= (0.1)(234.98) + (0.9)(246.01)$$
$$= 23.50 + 221.41$$
$$= 244.91$$

$$Y'''_{Nov} = \alpha Y''_{Nov} + (1-\alpha)Y'''_{Oct}$$
$$= (0.1)(244.91) + (0.9)(248.76)$$
$$= 124.49 + 223.88$$
$$= 248.37$$

Next, we substitute the estimates of Y'_{Nov}, Y''_{Nov}, and Y'''_{Nov} into Equations 2.9-2.11 to obtain the values of the three smoothed coefficients—a, b, and c, as follows:

$$a_{Nov} = 3Y'_{Nov} - 3Y''_{Nov} + Y'''_{Nov}$$

$$= 3(234.98) - 3(244.91) + 248.37$$

$$= 704.94 - 734.73 + 248.37$$

$$= 218.58$$

$$b_{Nov} = \left[\frac{\alpha}{2(1-\alpha)^2}\right][(6-5\alpha)Y'_{Nov} - (10-8\alpha)Y''_{Nov} + (4-3\alpha)Y'''_{Nov}]$$

$$\left[\frac{0.1}{2(1-0.1)^2}\right][(6-5(0.1))(234.98) - (10-8(0.1))(244.91)$$

$$+ (4-3(0.1))(248.37)]$$

$$= (0.06)(1,292.39 - 2,253.17 + 918.97)$$

$$= (0.06)(-41.81)$$

$$= -2.51$$

$$c_{Nov} = \left[\frac{\alpha}{(1-\alpha)}\right]^2 (Y'_{Nov} - 2Y''_{Nov} + Y'''_{Nov})$$

$$\left[\frac{(0.1)^2}{(1-0.1)^2}\right][234.98 - 2(244.91) + 248.37]$$

$$= (0.12)(483.35 - 489.82)$$

$$= (0.12)(-6.47)$$

$$= -0.78$$

Now, using the estimated coefficients of a, b, and c from above, we can easily determine the revenue for the month of December, $t+1$, assuming the changes over time in the average level of the time series follow a quadratic pattern, as given below:

$$\hat{Y}'''_{(December)} = a_{Nov} + b_{Nov}T + c_{Nov}T^2$$

$$= 218.58 + (-2.51) + \left[(-0.78)(1)^2\right]$$

$$= 218.58 - 2.51 - 0.78$$

$$= 215.29$$

or \$215,290 and repeat the process for January, $t+2$, in the similar manner, but multiplying T by 2, since T = 2, so that

$$\hat{Y}'''_{(January)} = a_{Nov} + b_{Nov}T + c_{Nov}T^2$$

$$= 218.58 + (-2.51)(2) + \left[(-0.78)(2)^2\right]$$

$$= 218.58 - 5.02 - 3.12$$

$$= 210.44$$

or \$210,440, indicating a downward trend in revenues from \$215,290 to \$210,440.

Table 2.3 shows the data and related statistics for the model. The forecasts appear to be much lower than one would expect, given the general trend in the series. This could be partly because of the α-value used in determining the statistics and, in most likelihood, because the data used were arbitrarily selected. As noted before, the best way to select α is through a trial-and-error process until the one that produces the lowest forecast error.

As one would expect, a quadratic exponential smoothing is more complicated than a simple linear trend, which is more complicated than single smoothing, but, as it should become obvious, the application of the model is not as complicated since the principle of smoothing remains essentially the same. What makes the difference is the parameter in each case and how they are used to reduce the randomness in a series. Additionally, higher order models, such as quadratic exponential smoothing, does a better job of dealing with turning points, but they can also overreact to random fluctuations in the data (Makridakis and Wheelright, 1978). Nevertheless, it is a common problem that all forecasters have to deal with, regardless of the model used.

Table 2.3   Parking Meter Revenue: Brown's Triple Exponential Smoothing

Month	Time	Original Series ($000)	Y' α = 0.1 ($000)	Y'' α = 0.1 ($000)	Y''' α = 0.1 ($000)	a_t	b_t	c_t
January	t-10	250.00	250.00	250.00	250.00	-	-	-
February	t-9	200.00	245.00	249.50	249.60	-	-	-
March	t-8	225.00	243.00	248.85	249.53	-	-	-
April	t-7	275.00	246.20	248.59	249.44	-	-	-
May	t-6	300.00	251.58	248.89	249.39	-	-	-
June	t-5	250.00	251.42	249.14	249.36	-	-	-
July	t-4	225.00	248.78	249.10	249.33	-	-	-
August	t-3	200.00	243.90	248.58	249.26	-	-	-
September	t-2	175.00	237.01	247.42	249.07	-	-	-
October	t-1	200.00	233.31	246.01	248.76	-	-	-
November	t	250.00	234.98	244.91	248.37*	218.58	-2.51	-0.78
December	t+1	-	-	-	215.29*	-	-	-
January	t+2	-	-	-	210.44*	-	-	-

*Forecasts.

WINTERS' TREND AND SEASONAL
EXPONENTIAL SMOOTHING

Exponential smoothing models, in general, have an advantage over conventional time series models in that they assign greater weights to more recent observations, which allow them to compensate for recent changes in a series. Unfortunately, even with the assignment of weights, these models cannot effectively deal with seasonal variations that exist in a series. Winters' exponential smoothing corrects the problem considerably by taking into account both trend and seasonal variations in the forecast (Winters, 1960). As such, it does a better job of forecasting than the conventional forecasting models.

To ensure that both trend and seasonal variations are taken into consideration in the forecast, Winters' exponential smoothing combines the expression for a trend line, $Y = \alpha + bT$ (discussed in the previous chapter), with a seasonal adjustment factor (seasonal ratio) so that

$$\hat{Y}_{t+n} = \left(a_t + b_t T\right)S_{t-L+n} \qquad (2.13)$$

where $\hat{Y}$ is the estimated value of Y at time *t*+n, a and b are the respective intercept and slope coefficients, S is the seasonal ratio, L is the length of seasonality (i.e., the number of months or quarters in a year), and *n* is the number of time periods in a series.

The way the Winters' model works is that once the initial estimates of trend and seasonality have been made, it incorporates this information into an exponential smoothing process. This makes it possible to continuously update the estimates of the intercept, the slope, and the relevant seasonal factors. The uniqueness of the model lies in the fact that it applies the smoothing process three times: First, to estimate the average value of the series (stationarity); second, to estimate the trend component (linearity); third, to estimate the seasonal component (seasonality). Each of these stages has its own smoothing constants (α, β, and γ), which can be adjusted to accommodate the circumstances or as the situation demands. The constants are weights assigned by the forecaster that range between 0 and 1, such as $\alpha = 0.2$, $\beta = 0.05$, and $\gamma = 0.1$, and so forth, as long as they stay within that range. As noted previously, there are no hard and fast rules for assigning these weights, but the rule of thumb is to use a combination of weights that will produce the most accurate forecast; in other words, produce the least amount of error in the forecast value.

The following equations are generally used to estimate the values of a (intercept), b (slope), and S (the seasonal factor):

$$a_t = \alpha \frac{Y_t}{S_{t-L}} + (1-\alpha)(a_{t-1} + b_{t-1}) \tag{2.14}$$

$$b_t = \beta(a_t - a_{t-1}) + (1-\beta)b_{t-1} \tag{2.15}$$

$$S_t = \gamma \frac{Y_t}{a_t} + (1-\gamma)S_{t-L} \tag{2.16}$$

where Y is the actual observations, a is the intercept of the trend line, b is the slope of the trend line, S is the seasonal adjustment factor, t is the time, and α, β, and γ are the smoothing constants.

Each of the above equations has a specific purpose: Equation 2.14 deseasonalizes the series, Equation 2.15 smooths the trend, and Equation 2.16 produces a seasonal index. Interestingly, there are considerable similarities between these equations, especially the first two, and Holt's two-parameter model. For instance, Equation 2.14 is the same as Holt's Equation 2.4, except that the first term is divided by the seasonal value to remove any seasonal irregularities in Y, called deseasonalizing. Equation 2.15 is the same as Holt's Equation 2.5 used for smoothing the trend by updating the estimates from the previous period. Because of this apparent similarity, Winter's model is often treated as an extension of Holt's linear exponential smoothing, except that it includes an added equation to estimate seasonality. Finally, Equation 2.16 is the extra equation that produces a seasonal index by taking the ratio of the current value of the series, Y_t, and the current single smoothed value, a_t (Makridakis and Wheelright, 1978).

To give an example, let us say that we have four years of revenue data for the Water and Sewer (W&S) fund of a local government, each year containing four time periods (quarters). Although the two revenues are maintained separately for accounting purposes, for convenience, we have combined them into one. Table 2.4 shows the data for all 16 periods.

As can be seen from the table, the revenues tend to increase during certain times of the year when the water consumption goes up and then decrease when the consumption goes down. However, before the model can be fully applied, it is important that we have the initial estimates of trend and seasonality (discussed at length in Chapter 5). The trend estimates are obtained using the linear trend model, discussed earlier, Y = a + bT, as shown below:

$$\hat{Y} = 64.208 + 0.7116T$$

$$(50.7914)(5.4427)$$

$$MAPE = 2.6433 \ R^2 = 0.6791 \ F = 29.6234 \ DW = 2.3402$$

Table 2.4   Water & Sewer Revenue: Winters' Trend and Seasonal Exponential Smoothing

Year	Time (T)	Y_t ($1000)	Trend Value $\hat{Y}_t$ ($1000)	Seasonal Ratio Y_t / Y_t	Estimates of Seasonal Factors (S)
t-4	1	64,840	64,920	0.9988	1.0105
	2	65,970	65,631	1.0052	1.0148
	3	67,420	66,343	1.0162	1.0264
	4	62,350	67,054	0.9298	0.9483
t-3	5	68,370	67,766	1.0089	1.0105
	6	69,250	68,477	1.0113	1.0148
	7	71,470	69,189	1.0330	1.0264
	8	67,520	69,900	0.9659	0.9483
t-2	9	71,960	70,612	1.0191	1.0105
	10	72,680	71,324	1.0190	1.0148
	11	73,930	72,035	1.0263	1.0264
	12	69,480	72,747	0.9551	0.9483
t-1	13	74,560	73,458	1.0150	1.0105
	14	75,920	74,170	1.0236	1.0148
	15	77,130	74,882	1.0300	1.0264
	16	71,250	75,593	0.9425	0.9483
t	17	76,810*	-	-	-
	18	77,136*	-	-	-

*Forecasts.

As the results indicate, the t values for the intercept and slope, as well as the F value, respectively, were 50.7914, 5.4427, and 29.6234. All three turned out to be statistically significant at $p < 0.0001$, and there does not appear to be any serious autocorrelation problem, as given by the DW statistic.

Now, using the information above, we can obtain the trend value (estimates) for each of the 16 periods, starting with period 16 at time t-1, as

$$\hat{Y}_{16} = a + bT$$

$$= 64.208 + 0.7116T$$

$$= 64.208 + 0.7116(16)$$

$$= 75.593$$

or \$75.593 million. Similarly, for period 15 at time t-1, it will be

$$\hat{Y}_{15} = a + bT$$

$$= 64.208 + 0.7116T$$

$$= 64.208 + 0.7116(15)$$

$$= 74.882$$

or \$74.882 million and continue to repeat the process until we have estimated the values for all 16 periods (Table 2.4).

The seasonal factors for the model, on the other hand, are obtained using a two-step process: First, find the seasonal ratios; that is, take the ratio of actual observations to the trend values, and then estimate the factors by taking the average of the ratios for respective time periods. For instance, for period 1, taking into consideration all four time periods (t-1, t-2, t-3, and t-4), it will be (0.9988 + 1.0089 + 1.0191 + 1.0150)/4 = 4.0418/4 = 1.0105. For period 2, taken all four periods into consideration, it will be (1.0052 + 1.0113 + 1.0190 + 1.0236 = 4.0591)/4 =1.0148, and so forth (Column 6). Table 2.4 shows the trend values, the seasonal ratios, and the seasonal factors for all 16 periods.

We can now use the above information (the intercept, the slope, and the estimates of the seasonal factors) to forecast the W&S revenue for any period in the future. For instance, for period 17, at time t, it will be

$$\hat{Y}_{17} = [a + b(17)]S_{17}$$

$$= \left[64.208 + 0.7116(17)\right](1.0105)$$

$$= (76.3052)(1.0105)$$

$$= 77.1064$$

or \$77.1064 million, which appears reasonable, given the history of the revenue pattern for the same period. It is worth noting that since we do not have the actual value of S at time t for quarter 17, we have used 1.0105 as the best estimate for the respective period.

We can repeat the process for the next three periods - 18, 19, and 20, as

$$\hat{Y}_{18} = [a + b(18)]S_{18}$$

$$= \left[64.208 + 0.7116(18)\right](1.0148)$$

$$= (77.1068)(1.0148)$$

$$= 78.1566$$

or $78.157 million for period 18. Similarly, for period 19, it will be

$$\hat{Y}_{19} = [a + b(19)]S_{19}$$

$$= \left[64.208 + 0.7116(19)\right](1.0264)$$

$$= (77.7284)(1.0264)$$

$$= 79.7804$$

or $79.780 million. And for period 20, it will be

$$\hat{Y}_{20} = [a + b(20)]S_{20}$$

$$= \left[64.208 + 0.7116(20)\right](0.9483)$$

$$= (78.44)(0.9483)$$

$$= 74.3847$$

or $74.385 million and repeat the process for any number of periods into the future.

While the forecasts presented above take into consideration both trend and seasonal factors, it has an inherent weakness in that it treats time equally. In other words, it assigns equal weight to all time periods, including the most recent time period, which, given the conventional wisdom, should receive a higher weight. The Winters' model corrects this by assigning differential weights to each of the three smoothing constants—the intercept (α), the slope (β), and the seasonal factor (γ).

Assume, for convenience, that we have the following weights for each of the terms obtained through a trial-and-error process: $\alpha = 0.3$, $\beta = 0.1$, and $\gamma = 0.2$. We will use these weights to revise the estimates we obtained with undifferentiated weights. We will start with period 16, which is the most recent period in our series. Recall the notation L in Equation 2.13, which represents the length of seasonality. The expression t-L, in essence, represents the seasonal value four periods prior to the current period, t, or 16-4 = 12, since there are four periods or quarters for each year in our series. If we were dealing with monthly data, we will be subtracting 12 from the most recent period, and so forth.

The results of the estimates of the three smoothing constants for period 16 are given below:

[1] $a_{16} = \alpha \dfrac{Y_{16}}{S_{t-L}} + (1-\alpha)(a_{t-1} + b_{t-1})$

$\qquad = 0.3 \dfrac{71.250}{0.9483} + (0.7)(74.882 + 0.7116)$

$\qquad = (0.3)(75.1345) + (0.7)(75.5936)$

$\qquad = 22.5404 + 52.9155$

$\qquad = 75.4559$

[2] $b_{16} = \beta(a_t - a_{t-1}) + (1-\beta)b_{t-1}$

$\qquad = (0.1)(75.4559 - 74.882) + (0.7)(0.7116)$

$\qquad = 0.0574 + 0.4981$

$\qquad = 0.5555$

and

[3] $S_{16} = \gamma \dfrac{Y_{16}}{a_{16}} + (1-\gamma)S_{16}$

$\qquad = \gamma \dfrac{71.250}{75.4559} + (1-0.2)(0.9483)$

$\qquad = (0.2)(0.9443) + (0.8)(0.9483)$

$\qquad = 0.1889 + 0.7586$

$\qquad = 0.9475$

Using the revised estimates above, we can now forecast the W&S revenue for any number of periods in the future. Thus, for period 17, at time t = 1 (the first forecast period), the revenue will be

$$\hat{Y}_{17} = (a_t + b_t T)S_{t-L+n}$$

$$= \big[75.4559 + 0.5555(1)\big](1.0105)$$

$$= (76.0114)(1.0105)$$

$$= 76.8095$$

or $76.810 million. For period 18, at time t = 2 (the second forecast period), it will be

$$\hat{Y}_{18} = \left(a_t + b_t T\right) S_{t-L+n}$$

$$= \left[75.4559 + 0.5555(2)\right](1.0148)$$

$$= (76.0114)(1.0148)$$

$$= 77.1364$$

or $77.136 million and repeat the process for any number of periods in the future.

As with any forecasts, it is important to note that once the values of the forecast variable have been estimated for current, as well as all previous years (backcasts), the information is used to determine the amount of error the forecasts have produced for the model, using any of the methods suggested earlier in Chapter 1, such as MSE, RMSE, MAPE, etc. In general, high errors are associated with the incorrect assignment of weight to the smoothed constants, and vice versa. As noted earlier, the rule of thumb is to use a trial-and-error process until one finds a weight that would produce the least amount of error.

While the Winters' model has obvious advantages over other exponential smoothing models, it also has several disadvantages. For one, it does not incorporate the cyclical component. Part of the problem may lie in the difficulty in building it into the model; there are other methods such as trend line with cyclical variations that are better suited for that. Two, as with any exponential smoothing, the selection of the smoothing constants in the Winters' model requires a trial-and-error process or the judgment of the forecaster. Three, the constants are sensitive to the nature of the data, as one would expect with any forecasting model. Four, like most exponential smoothing models, it is based on the assumption of constancy in that it cannot be readily used to evaluate the effect of a policy change.

Regardless, as forecasting tools, exponential smoothing models, including Winter's model, have an advantage over most basic time series models in that they are parsimonious and relatively simple to use. Although it is possible to achieve greater accuracy with causal and more advanced time series models, savings in time and relative ease of use make these models an attractive alternative.

TIME SERIES WITH CYCLICAL VARIATIONS

Time series data often exhibit variations over time, such as cyclical, and if these variations are not taken into consideration in the forecasting equation, they can produce biased forecasts. This is particularly true when one is dealing with monthly or quarterly data where regular variations are fairly common. As noted earlier, a good example is sales tax revenue which shows an upward trend during certain times of the year, such as during the holiday season and a downward trend at other times. Another example is water consumption which, as noted earlier, increases during the summer months and decreases at other times, especially during the winter months. If one is to regress these data against time using the trend line, especially when there is a systematic variation in the data which is not accounted for in the model, say, for higher values, it would move the trend line upward. In other words, the intercept of the trend line for the month or quarter, α', when the values are high, would be higher than the intercept of the trend line for the data series, α. The same will be true if the data show a consistent decline during certain times of the year. Therefore, when these kinds of changes are explicit in the data, it is important that the forecasting equation reflects these trends.

One way to deal with a situation where there is a clear time trend is to define a term, say, δ, that takes into consideration the difference between the intercept of the trend line for the month or quarter in question, α', and the intercept of the trend line for the data series, α, ($\delta = \alpha' - \alpha$), so that the new equation for the trend line will be

$$Y_t = \alpha + \beta T + \delta \tag{2.17}$$

where δ is a positive number for the month or quarter in question and 0 for the rest.

Since the Equation 2.17 contains an additional term, δ, it can be estimated with the help of a dummy variable, as shown below:

$$Y_t = \alpha + \beta T + \delta D \tag{2.18}$$

where D is the dummy variable, and the rest of the terms are the same as in Equation 2.17.

A dummy variable takes on two values—0 and 1. Thus, if one is dealing with quarterly data, 1 would be assigned for the observations in the first quarter and 0 for the remaining three quarters. Assume that our observations vary from quarter to quarter; therefore, we will have four trend lines for four dummy variables - one for each quarter. In reality, we do not need four dummy variables; we basically need three, since the fourth one can be automatically determined from the three. In other words, we would estimate the equation

$$Y_t = \alpha + \beta T + \delta_1 D_1 + \delta_2 D_2 + \delta_3 D_3 \qquad (2.19)$$

where D_1 will be equal to 1 for the first quarter and 0 otherwise, D_2 will be equal to 1 for the second quarter and 0 otherwise, and D_3 will be equal to 1 for the third quarter and 0 otherwise. The intercepts are calculated slightly differently in a model with dummy variables. For instance, the intercept for quarter 1 will be $\alpha+\delta_1$, for quarter 2 it will be $\alpha+\delta_2$, for quarter 3 it will be $\alpha+\delta_3$, while for the missing quarter (quarter 4), it will be just α.

To give an example, let us say that we have four years of quarterly revenue data for a local government for local option sales tax (LOST), which is different from the revenue a government collects from the state for its share of state sales tax revenue. Table 2.5 shows the data for the government for all 16 quarters: $LOST_{t-4}$, $LOST_{t-3}$, $LOST_{t-2}$, and $LOST_{t-1}$. Our objective is to forecast the LOST revenue for the quarters at time t, $LOST_t$. As with the trend line, we convert the time (T) into a continuous variable.

Now, using the data in Table 2.5, we can estimate the extended equation with three dummy variables. The results of the estimated equation are shown below:

$$\hat{LOST_t} = 124{,}195.5 + 1{,}117.375T - 49{,}690.63D_1 - 47{,}999.5D_2 - 39{,}601.12D_3$$

$$(60.2487) \quad (7.2724) \quad (-24.8776) \quad (-24.3945) \quad (-20.3129)$$

$$MAPE = 1.7452 \quad R^2 = 0.9892 \quad F = 252.9970 \quad DW = 1.2207$$

Two things become obvious from the results: One, the trend for the LOST revenue is positive, given by $\beta > 0$ (1117.375). Two, the results appear to be reasonably good, as evidenced by low MAPE and high t values (within parentheses), all significant at $p < 0.01$, which can be easily checked against any standard t table. The R^2 also came out to be quite high and significant, as given by the high F-value. However, a cursory look at the DW statistic would indicate a slight positive autocorrelation (discussed at length in Chapter 3), but a more careful examination would indicate the result to be somewhat inconclusive[1] since the observed statistic lies between the lower and the upper limits of d, that is, $d_L < d < d_U$ (which can be easily checked against the standard DW table, found in any econometrics textbook). Overall, the model appears to be a good fit.

Table 2.5   LOST Revenue: Quarterly Data with Dummy Variables

Year	Quarter	LOST Revenue Y ($000)	Time	D_1	D_2	D_3
t-4	I	74,256	1	1	0	0
	II	78,415	2	0	1	0
	II	85,223	3	0	0	1
	IV	125,628	4	0	0	0
t-3	I	81,623	5	1	0	0
	II	83,450	6	0	1	0
	III	95,824	7	0	0	1
	IV	134,622	8	0	0	0
t-2	I	85,475	9	1	0	0
	II	87,129	10	0	1	0
	III	98,731	11	0	0	1
	IV	142,560	12	0	0	0
t-1	I	97,952	13	1	0	0
	II	91,546	14	0	1	0
	III	98,825	15	0	0	1
	IV	138,667	16	0	0	0
t	I	93,500*	-	-	-	-
	II	96,309*	-	-	-	-
	III	105,826*	-	-	-	-
	IV	146,543*	-	-	-	-

*Forecasts.

Let us try to interpret the intercept terms, since we have several dummy variables in the model. But, first, let us estimate the intercepts for each quarter. From our discussion on intercepts with dummy variables earlier, the estimated intercept of the trend line for the first quarter would be

$$\hat{\alpha} + \hat{\delta}_1 = 124,195.5 - 49,690.63$$

$$= 74,504.87$$

or $74,504.87. For the second quarter, it would be

$$\hat{\alpha} + \hat{\delta}_2 = 124,195.5 - 47,999.5$$

$$= 76,196.00$$

or $76,196.00. For the third quarter, it would be

$$\hat{\alpha} + \hat{\delta}_3 = 124,195.5 - 39,601.12$$

$$= 84,594.38$$

or $84,594.38. And for the fourth quarter, it would be

$$\hat{\alpha} = 124,195.50$$

or $124,195.50.

The estimates indicate that the intercepts vis-a-vis the LOST revenues are lower in the first three quarters than in the fourth quarter, which is consistent with the general pattern of sales tax revenue for time series data since consumer spending usually goes up during the holiday season, which mostly falls in the fourth quarter. From a forecasting point of view, the question is whether they are significantly low for the decision makers to be able to accept them as reliable. The t values corresponding to each of the dummy variables indicate that they are all statistically significant at less than 1 percent level of α, with $p < 0.01$ (which can be easily checked against any standard t table).

We can now proceed to forecast the LOST revenue by quarter for the current year, $LOST_t$. In the first quarter of t, $t+1$ will be quarter 17 with $D_1 = 1$, $D_2 = 0$, and $D_3 = 0$. Therefore, the forecast for LOST revenue in quarter I of t would be

$$L\hat{O}ST_{t+I} = \hat{\alpha} + \hat{\beta}(17) + \hat{\delta}_1(1) + \hat{\delta}_2(0) + \hat{\delta}_3(0)$$

$$= 124,195.5 + 1,117.375(17) + \hat{\delta}_1 + 0 + 0$$

$$= 124,195.5 + 18,995.375 - 49,690.63$$

$$= 93,500.245$$

or $93,500,245.

We can repeat the process to forecast the revenue for the next three quarters (II, III, andIV) in a similar fashion. That is,

$$(1)\ L\hat{O}ST_{t+II} = \hat{\alpha} + \hat{\beta}(18) + \hat{\delta}_1(0) + \hat{\delta}_2(1) + \hat{\delta}_3(0)$$

$$= 124,195.5 + 1,117.375(18) + \hat{\delta}_2 + 0 + 0$$

$$= 124,195.5 + 20,112.750 - 47,999.5$$

$$= 96,308.75$$

or $96,308,750 for Quarter II,

(2) $L\hat{O}ST_{t+III} = \hat{\alpha} + \hat{\beta}(19) + \hat{\delta}_1(0) + \hat{\delta}_2(0) + \hat{\delta}_3(1)$

$\qquad = 124,195.5 + 1,117.375(19) + \hat{\delta}_3 + 0 + 0$

$\qquad = 124,195.5 + 21,230.125 - 39,601.12$

$\qquad = 105,824.505$

or \$105,824,505 for Quarter III, and

(3) $L\hat{O}ST_{t+IV} = \hat{\alpha} + \hat{\beta}(20)$

$\qquad = 124,195.5 + 1,117.375(20)$

$\qquad = 124,195.5 + 22,347.5$

$\qquad = 146,543.000$

or \$146,543,000 for Quarter IV, and the process can be repeated for any number of quarters in the future.

It should be worth noting that although the focus here has been on quarterly variations, in reality, one could apply the procedure to any type of cyclical variations of data that exhibit variations at regularly spaced intervals in a time series.

FORECASTING IRREGULAR TIME SERIES

Forecasting with the time series data is relatively uncomplicated if the data have a trend or exhibit seasonal and regular cyclical variations, but it can be quite complicated if the series is irregular in that the data exhibit irregularities that cannot be explained by any of these three components. Irregularities occur in a series either because of random behavior of the data or caused by external factors. Although missing observations, reporting irregularities, and outliers can be considered a form of irregularity, they are usually treated as the intermediate stage between regular and irregular time series. Regardless, irregularities are a common occurrence in time series and, if not addressed properly, can produce significant forecast errors.

Conventional univariate time series models, such as those discussed here and in the previous chapter, while frequently used in forecasting because they are simple and relatively easy to use, do not have the ability to deal with major or frequent minor shocks. As such, these models are useful if the shocks are minor or a few, and there are no predictable shocks in the future.

However, variations of some of these methods, especially the exponentially smoothed methods, have been found to be quite effective in dealing with irregularities (Cipra, 2006; Cipra et al., 1995; Wright, 1986). For instance, there have been numerous applications of both univariate and multivariate time series models, in particular autoregressive integrated moving average (ARIMA), to deal with irregularities in time series (Duan and Zhang, 2020; Harvey et al., 1998; Cholette and Lamy, 1986) and the number, as well as the range of these methods, have been increasing over time.

SUMMARY

There has been significant growth in forecasting methods over the years—in number, complexity, and sophistication, along with an increase in the choices of methods available to a forecaster. This chapter has briefly discussed several additional time series models, in addition to those discussed in the previous chapter. This included Brown's double and triple exponential smoothing, Holt's two-parameter exponential smoothing, Winters' seasonal exponential smoothing, and time series with cyclical variations. Of these, the first three are extensions of exponential smoothing and the fourth a direct extension of the trend line discussed in the previous chapter. The chapter concluded with a brief discussion of forecasting with irregular time series.

NOTE

1. In general, the result is considered inconclusive if DW lies between the lower and upper critical values. More specifically, if DW > Upper critical value, which is 4, there is no statistical evidence of any positive autocorrelation. On the other hand, if 4-DW < Lower critical value, which is 0, there is statistical evidence of negative autocorrelation. (Note that d ranges between 0 and 4). Since our observed DW statistic is not greater than the upper critical value of 4; in other words, since 1.2207 < 4, we do not have a positive autocorrelation. By the same token, our observed DW is not less than 4-DW < Lower critical value of 0. In other words, since 4 − 1.2207 (2.7793) > 0, we do not have a negative autocorrelation. As such, we can safely assume that the result is inconclusive.

Also, as noted previously, DW statistic is one of the oldest, but useful, measures for testing if there is an autocorrelation problem in a series and usually needs a table to determine the significance level. These tables can be found in most econometrics textbooks, but are also available in most statistical software. Other measures, such as Ljung-Box Q test, have been found to be quite effective, especially for ARIMA models (discussed in some details in Chapter 4).

Chapter 3

Time Series Regression

In previous chapters, we have discussed models that use the information on a single variable that we are interested in forecasting, for example, data on revenues from a certain source. Our forecast models have therefore made the explicit assumption that all information that is important in understanding the past behavior of the variable and all information that is useful in forecasting the time path of that variable into the future are incorporated in that variable alone. In this chapter, we relax this assumption and consider situations where the information contained in other variables might be useful in understanding the dynamics of our variable of interest. It will highlight the basic structure of time series regression, the conditions, and assumptions that underlie a regression model, followed by examples of time series regression with single and multiple independent variables.

BACKGROUND DISCUSSION

Time series regression models are some of the oldest bivariate and multivariate forecasting methods. They work through analyzing relationships between key variables in the forecast over time. It seems natural to assume some sort of relationship between government revenues and spending and socioeconomic variables, to take one example. As personal income changes, personal spending is likely to change also, and along with that, sales tax revenues. Now, as we saw in the introductory chapter, some of the information about this relationship is embedded in the data generating process for the variable of interest. But the question is whether we can improve our forecast accuracy by deliberately modeling the relationship between the predictor and predicted variables. One can think of our approach here as figuring out whether adding variables to our model improves the fit of our forecast model.

One of the advantages of using multiple variables for forecasting is that our models become more explicit and transparent. Trying to address why a forecast is trending in a certain direction simply using coefficients of the conventional trend, cyclical, and seasonal components of a time series can be very difficult and may produce a sense of mysticism in non-forecasters. If one wants to try an exercise in frustration, one can try explaining something like how an exponentially weighted moving average works to an audience that has not taken a forecasting class. A sense that we may be chasing ghosts can take hold in the mind of the forecast audience. However, by being able to discuss what variables seem to be influencing a set of forecasts, the forecaster can relate more directly to his or her audience.

The limitations of using time series regression mainly deal with the numerous ways that the data or method may violate assumptions that must be met to produce the best unbiased estimate of future values of whatever variable we are trying to forecast. As we will see in this chapter, there are numerous assumptions that must be met in time series regression models. And although there are ways to "fix" issues with time series regressions, they add complexity to the models, reducing the transparency that is the benefit of using them.

BASIC STRUCTURE

One way to think about what we have studied before is to model the value of a variable now solely as a function of its own past values and errors, as in

$$y_t = f\left(y_{t-p}, \epsilon_{t-q}\right) \ \forall \ p, q > 0 \tag{3.1}$$

where p and q are periods in the past (for example, $p = 1$ is the value of y 1 period in the past—y_{t-1}, ϵ is the error term, and the notation $\forall$ indicates such that. Equation 3.1 says that the value of y at time t (now) is based on values in the past ($y_{t-1, t-2, \dots, t-p}$) and errors from the model ($\epsilon_{t-1, t-2, \dots, t-q}$). Thus, all information necessary to forecast to period $t+1$ is incorporated in the variable itself and errors in the past. In this chapter, we consider models that incorporate the current and past values of other variables X (bolded and capitalized x means a vector of variables, x_1, x_2, x_3, etc., where there is at least one x variable). Therefore, we will be examining models of the type

$$y_t = f\left(y_{t-p}, X, \epsilon_{t-q}\right) \ \forall \ p, q > 0 \tag{3.2}$$

where p and q once again indicate periods in the past.

The most common type of this model is the basic linear regression model

$$y_t = \alpha + \beta_1 x_{1t} + \upsilon_t \tag{3.3}$$

where the contemporaneous value of an independent variable x is used to predict the value of y. The α in Equation 3.3 is the intercept, interpreted as the estimated value of y when x is equal to zero, and the β term is the slope coefficient, the estimated change in y for a one unit change in x discussed earlier. The last term in the equation (υ) is the residual from the model, the amount of y_t that is left unexplained by the model.

AN ILLUSTRATIVE EXAMPLE

Let us look at an example with actual data from a major US city over a 35-year period (Appendix A.1)[1]. The city receives revenue from a number of sources, including sales tax revenues. There are two distinct sales tax revenue streams: For our purposes, we use data on the Taxable Retail Sales subject to the Home Rule Retailers' Occupation Tax (HRROT).[2] For this tax, retail sales outlets collect a tax on every sale in the city. The rate of the tax is currently 1.25 percent, having been raised from 1 percent in 2005. Dividing the sales tax revenues in a given year by the rate produces the estimates of Taxable Retail Sales, as shown in Figure 3.1. The figure also shows data for Population and Personal Income in the metropolitan statistical area (MSA), which are two potential predictors (x) variables for retail sales.

As can be seen from the figure, the two data series share some commonalities and have some differences. There is a positive trend in both receipts and income. And they both seem to share the cyclical pattern in the late 2000s, during the "Great Recession" period. However, the personal income data is much "smoother," exhibiting less volatility from year to year, especially during the period before 2008. Figure 3.2 shows the percent annual change in the data, which shows more clearly the relative changes are smaller in Personal Income until the Great Recession.

With that information in hand, we can begin to consider a formal statistical analysis of the relationship between personal income and retail sales. Equation 3.3 gives us the framework for the analysis. As long as a few conditions are met (discussed in the next section), estimation of the equation can be done through the method of *ordinary least squares* (OLS). This method involves choosing estimates of α and β_1 in equation 3.3 such that the error in the forecasted value of y_t minimizes the squared errors over all observations. If we define the residual sum of squares (RSS) as

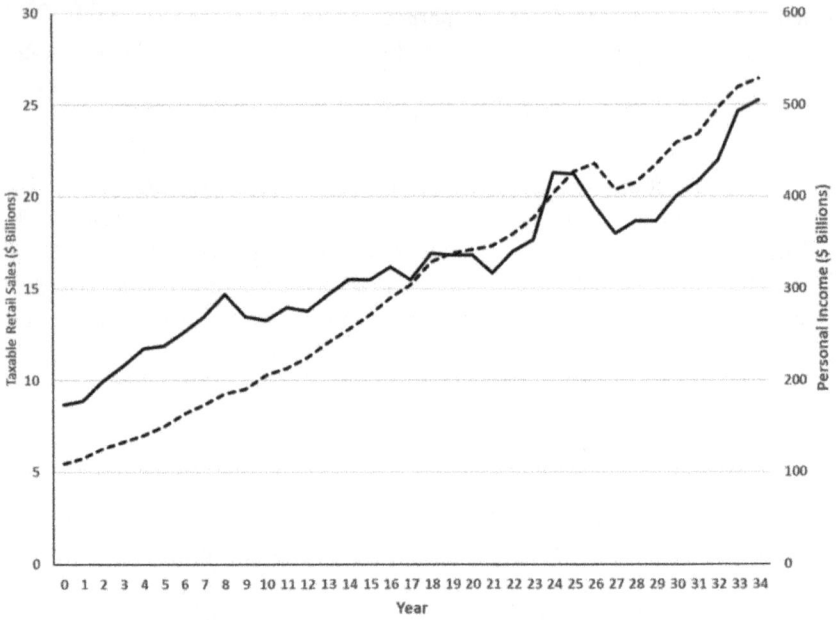

Figure 3.1   Taxable Retail Sales (solid line, left axis) and MSA Personal Income (dashed line, right axis).

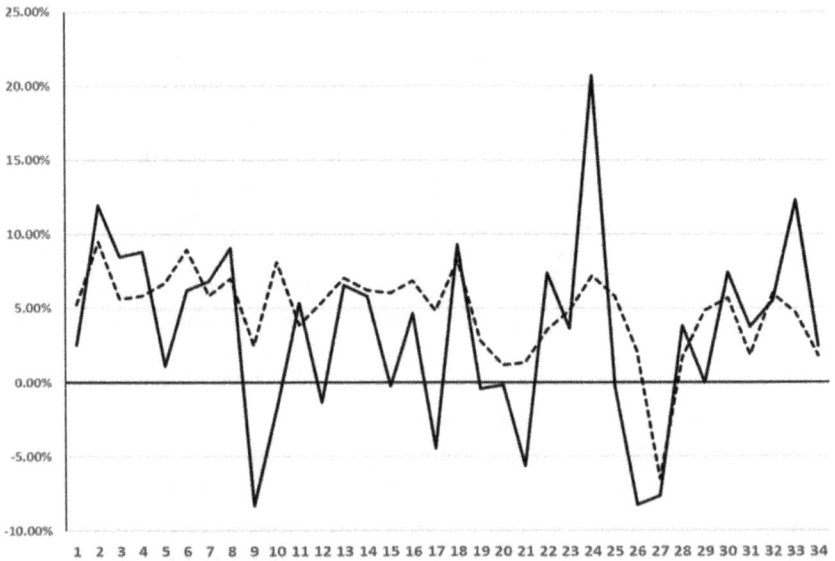

Figure 3.2   Annual Changes in Taxable Retail Sales (solid line) and MSA Personal Income (dashed line).

$$\sum_{t=1}^{T} \left(y_t - \alpha - \beta_1 x_{1t} \right)^2 \tag{3.4}$$

where T is the total number of time periods in the data, then minimizing this function with respect to β_1 will result in the predicted values that produce the lowest overall error.[3] While the mathematical notation here may seem daunting, there is actually a closed-form solution that can be obtained rather easily using regular or matrix algebra.[4]

The OLS results will consist of estimates for the intercept (α) and slope coefficient (β_1), along with estimates of the standard errors of those parameters. The standard error is calculated based on the error variance (how large the errors are compared to the predicted values) and the overall variation in the predictor variable x. The standard error is used in determining how precise the estimates of the intercept and slope coefficient are. The ratio of the coefficient estimate (intercept or slope) divided by the standard error is compared to known distributions of data to see how likely the parameter estimate is observed in the data strictly because of sampling variability.[5]

Returning to the taxable sales data, Equation 3.5 shows the results of a regression analysis of Taxable Retail Sales in each year (y_t) on MSA Personal Income in that year (x_t). The t-statistic (t ratio) in parentheses below the coefficient estimate is compared to the student's t-distribution in order to determine what is known as the statistical significance of the estimate. This test statistic is calculated using the error variance discussed above. Values in excess of 2.0 indicate that the coefficient estimate indicated is unlikely to have arisen strictly due to chance in obtaining the sample data. Therefore, that independent variable is important for forecasting the value of the y variable. We see in the results that the slope coefficient for Personal Income is statistically significant ($p < 0.001$), indicating that Personal Income is likely a good predictor of Taxable Retail Sales, subject to some caveats that we will discuss in the next section.

$$y_t = 6,822,000,000 + 30.8836 x_{1t} \tag{3.5}$$

$$(14.13) \qquad (20.98)$$

$$\text{MAPE} = 5.7115 \quad R^2 = 0.9281 \quad F = 439.9776 \quad DW = 0.7032$$

Conditions and Assumptions

Now that we have the basic results of an OLS regression analysis, it is appropriate to ask two questions: How do we know that these regression estimates produce unbiased estimates of the slope and intercept parameters? And, under what conditions will the standard errors used in calculating the tests of statistical significance be appropriate? In order to answer these questions, mathematicians and statisticians have worked out six assumptions under which OLS results will be unbiased, and the standard errors will be appropriate. The assumptions used to establish the unbiasedness of OLS regression and the appropriateness of the standard error calculations are called the *Gauss-Markov assumptions*, after the two mathematicians who established them.

Three of the assumptions apply to both OLS regressions with a single independent variable, called simple linear regression (SLR) and regressions with multiple predictor variables, called multiple linear regression (MLR). We denote these as SLR/MLR. One assumption only applies to SLR, and one applies only to MLR.

Assumption SLR/MLR1: Population Model is Linear in Parameters

In the population model (all possible time periods), the predicted variable y is assumed to be related to the predictor variables x1, x2, ..., in a linear (straight-line) fashion. What this means is that there are no nonlinearities in the relationship between y and the x variables, such as a quadratic ($y_t = \alpha + \beta_1 x_{1t} + \beta_2^2 x_{2t} + \upsilon_t$) or a cubic ($y_t = \alpha + \beta_1 x_{1t} + \beta_2^2 x_{2t} + \beta_3^3 x_{3t} + \upsilon_t$) relationship, as discussed in chapter 1. If there are these types of relationships, then the linear functional form will produce biased results. This assumption may be violated sometimes in time series data. As time progresses, a relationship may become stronger or weaker. In this case, we must use techniques called maximum likelihood estimation (MLE), beyond the scope of this textbook, to estimate our models.

Testing for this assumption in the time series context involves examining the residuals from linear regression plotted against time. Nonlinearities will show up as clear patterns in the data, with either positive or negative deviations consistently over time. An example of this is offered in the extended example section below.

Assumption SLR/MLR2: Random Sampling

The data in the regression model are assumed to be obtained through a random sampling of data from the population that follows the model in equation 3.3. This leads to regression with an error term that is random. If this condition does not hold, then the OLS estimates will also be biased. This assumption is the one that fails most often in time series analysis and forecasting. Serial correlation between observations (where the covariance between y_t and y_{t-1} is not equal to zero) and longer term trends (where the same relationship holds between y_t, y_{t-1}, y_{t-2}, ...) leads to a systematic pattern in errors from the regression. From a statistical perspective, this introduces bias into the OLS results, while from a forecasting perspective, those serial correlations and trends are information that could be integrated into the forecasting model to improve forecast model performance.

We can visualize this assumption and its violation by looking at the results from the OLS regression of Taxable Retail Sales on Personal Income (Figure 3.3). The solid line in the figure is the actual data, and the dashed line is the predicted values from the model. As one can see, the difference between the two lines (which are the residuals from the model) is not random. If it were, there would be no discernible pattern over time. However, if we look at consecutive years, such as t-25 through t-30 and t-11 through t-16, the residuals all have the same sign (if we define the residual as in the bracketed term in equation 3.4, they would all be positive for the earlier period and negative for the latter one). This would also be apparent in the plot of residuals against time described in the test for SLR/MLR1 above. This is a sign of serial correlation (also called autocorrelation) in the data, systematic information that could be gleaned from an analysis of the residuals to produce a better fit of the model.[6]

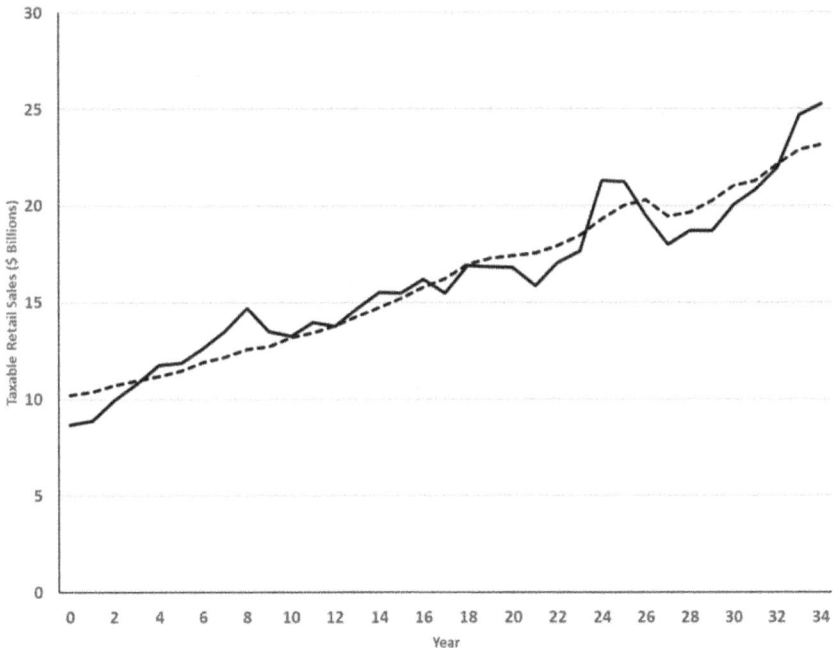

Figure 3.3 Predicted (dashed line) and Actual (solid line) Values from Estimation of Equation 3.5–Taxable Retail Sales Data.

There are at least two ways to deal with a serial correlation of this type within regression models. The first is to use an autocorrelation-consistent estimator. Such an estimator adjusts the OLS regression estimator to correct for the autocorrelation present in the data. The second approach, if one wants to get information about the serial correlation process from the estimator, is to directly enter lagged values of the dependent variable into the regression, as in:

$$y_t = \alpha + \phi_1 y_{t-1} + \beta_1 x_{1t} + \upsilon_t \qquad (3.6)$$

This form of the estimator is more direct for generating predictions from the regression results.[7]

Assumption SLR/MLR3: Zero Conditional Mean of the Error Term

This assumption states that the expected value (mean) of the error term, given any values of the predictor variable(s) or $E(\upsilon \mid x_1, x_2, \ldots, x_k) = 0$. This is actually a definition of unbiasedness. If the mean of the error term were not equal to zero at any point in the regression of y on x, this would imply that the regression line was not fitted in the middle of the data (returning to the discussion around Figure 3.3 to visualize this). This assumption works in conjunction with SLR/MLR2. Technically for this assumption to hold in the population, we have to assume that the x values are the same for any sample that we might take such that the same regression coefficients would be produced. In other words, it becomes impossible to have a set of predictor variables where the relationship between y and x differs substantially (causing the error to be not equal to 0. On face, this is an unrealistic assumption for most nonexperimental contexts (Wooldridge, 2006). However, if we can assume random sampling (SLR/MLR 2), then the error from any random sample will at least be unbiased, with a mean of 0.

There are at least two other situations where this assumption may not hold. The first is when the functional form of the model is incorrectly specified. This is related to Assumption SLR/MLR1. If there are nonlinearities in the relationship between y and x, they must be specified in the model, such as through the inclusion of a quadratic term. The other situation is where an important predictor variable is omitted. This is a common problem in cross-sectional (not time series) regressions. In time series analysis, this is not such an important assumption, as long as we can assume that the data generating process is incorporated in the time path of the y variable. In this case, the values of all variables not specifically modeled are reflected in the evolution of the variable of interest.

Assumptions SLR4: Sample Variations in the Predictor Variable

This is a relatively trivial assumption, with two exceptions. A regression analysis is meaningless if the values of the x variable are all the same. In most cases, if there is any variation in the population values of the predictor variable, then the x variable from a reasonably sized sample should have variation. There are only two situations where this may not be the case, when the population variation is low and when the sample size is small. The second situation is in the control of the analyst; they will need to get more data if they suspect this is a problem. The first situation is not directly observable, but all the analyst needs to do is inspect summary statistics for the x variable. If the variance of that variable is zero, then this assumption is suspect.

Assumption MLR5: No Perfect Collinearity

Assumption MLR5 builds upon Assumption SLR4 for cases of multiple regression (regression with more than one predictor variable). Not only must we ensure that there is variation in all predictor variables in multiple regression, but we must ensure that there are no perfect linear relationships between them. An example of this situation is if we thought that sales tax receipts were based on the industry composition of the metropolitan area. For simplicity, let's say that we thought the relationship was $y_t = \alpha + \beta_1 x_{1t} + \beta_2 x_{2t} + \upsilon_t$, where x_1 is the percentage of output in the metro area from manufacturing businesses, and x_2 is the percentage of output from nonmanufacturing businesses. If we attempt to run this regression, the results will be meaningless, as there is a linear relationship between the variables. The sum of the percentage from manufacturing and nonmanufacturing businesses will equal 1: $x_1 + x_2 = 1$. In other words, there will be a perfect negative correlation between x_1 and x_2. This correlation will confound the relationship between both variable and sales tax receipts.

Detecting violations of this assumption involve analyzing descriptive statistics for the sample data. Prior to running a regression, a correlation matrix should be generated. This shows the correlations between x variables and the y variable. If any of the correlations between x variables is equal to 1, this would be a situation of perfect correlation, and the model would need to be respecified.[8]

Assumptions SLR/MLR 6: Homoscedasticity

The last assumption is not a condition of unbiasedness for the OLS estimator. Rather, it has to do with simplifying calculations of the error variance for use in testing the effect of the predictor variables on the variable of interest. Earlier in this chapter, we discussed how the error variance was used in calculating test statistics for the statistical significance of relationships between the y and x variables. The homoscedasticity assumption states that the error of a regression equation has the same variance given any value of the independent variables: $Var(\upsilon|x_1,x_2,\cdots,x_n)=\sigma^2$. As long as this assumption holds, the derivation of the test statistics discussed earlier is relatively straightforward. But if the error variance is not constant, the appropriate test statistic will vary depending on where an observation lies in relation to the mean of the variable creating the heteroscedasticity problem.

An example of where this assumption may fail is in the regression of wages on education level. At low education levels, wages may vary dramatically among individuals due to the relatively larger role of chance in determining wages. However, with education, the variation in wages declines (Wooldridge, 2006). This causes a situation where the error variance is dependent on education level; therefore, test statistics are only valid at the mean of the education level variable.

Homoscedasticity can be assessed through certain tests that have been developed, which are largely beyond the scope of this work, or through analysis of residual plots from the regression, where the residuals (υ) are graphed against the predictor variables. If there are clear patterns in the residuals (increasing or decreasing with the values of the variables), then regression models should be used that correct for heteroscedasticity. These heteroscedasticity-consistent estimators correct the error variance in the calculation of test statistics for assessing the statistical significance of the predictor (independent) variables.

REGRESSION FORECASTS WITH SINGLE INDEPENDENT VARIABLE

Generating predictions from the regression model is a matter of "rolling the model forward" one period and using the model parameters and values of independent variables to generate predictions. To start our discussion, we note that the predicted (forecast) value of a time period within the sample ("in-sample") is given by the regression model less the error term:

$$\hat{y}_t = \alpha + \beta_1 x_{1t} \tag{3.7}$$

We denote the predicted value by placing a "hat" symbol over the y variable in Equation 3.7. This is read as "the predicted (forecast) value of y at time t is equal to the regression constant (α) plus the regression slope coefficient (β) times the value of the x variable at time t."

Returning to the sales tax receipt data, given the results in Equation 3.5 (and dropping the error term for now) and the value of MSA Personal Income at time t ($529,121,652), we can generate the forecast of sales tax receipts as:

$$\hat{y}_t = 6,822,000,000 + 30.8836\left(529,121,652\right) = \$23,163,181,451.71 \quad (3.8)$$

We note that this estimate is considerable under forecast, as one can see clearly in Figure 3.3. We will get better estimates in the full extended example shown below.

While this discussion is applicable to in-sample forecasts, how about out-of-sample forecasts, the heart of the forecasting question? Here we note that by rolling the regression equation forward one period, we would obtain:

$$\hat{y}_{t+1|t} = \alpha + \beta_1 x_{1t+1|t} \quad (3.9)$$

We note two things about Equation 3.9. First is the conditional term in the subscript for the forecasted value of y and the value of x at time $t+1$. We are generating forecasts of y at time $t+1$, conditional on information known at time t. So, the forecast at $t+1$ is only valid once we incorporate all information in the model up to time t. The second thing is to note that with regression-based forecasting, we need a value for the independent variables at time $t+1$. This is a major limiting factor in using regressions to forecast. These forecasts would likely come from either of two sources: An outside forecast generated by a third-party or an inside forecast using techniques similar to those discussed in Chapters 1 and 2 of this book. Let us say that we are forecasting five years into the future ($t+1$ through $t+5$) for sales tax receipts conditional on information known through time t. Our forecasts would be:

$$\hat{y}_{t+1} = 6,822,000,000 + 30.8836 \left(\overline{\text{MSA Personal Income}_{t+1}}\right)$$

$$\hat{y}_{t+2} = 6,822,000,000 + 30.8836 \left(\overline{\text{MSA Personal Income}_{t+2}}\right)$$

$$\hat{y}_{t+3} = 6,822,000,000 + 30.8836 \left(\overline{\text{MSA Personal Income}_{t+3}}\right)$$

$$\hat{y}_{t+4} = 6,822,000,000 + 30.8836 \left(\overline{\text{MSA Personal Income}_{t+4}}\right)$$

$$\hat{y}_{t+5} = 6,822,000,000 + 30.8836 \left(\overline{\text{MSA Personal Income}_{t+5}}\right)$$

Following the logic from the introduction, at this point, we only have forecasts or projections. We create a forecast by intentionally including estimates of the standard errors of the predicted values. Calculation of the standard errors of the forecast is beyond the scope of this book but can be found in most applied econometric or forecasting texts (see, e.g., Harvey, 1990, p. 51). The extended example below demonstrates this process.

REGRESSION FORECASTS WITH MULTIPLE INDEPENDENT VARIABLES

Extension of the method summarized in Equations 3.7 and 3.8 is direct; we simply add the number of independent variables estimated and their coefficients into the equation to find the predicted values:

$$\hat{y}_{t+1} = \alpha + \beta_1 x_{1t+1} + \beta_2 x_{2t+1} + \cdots + \beta_n x_{nt+1} \quad (3.10)$$

where n is the number of independent variables entered into the equation. The same logic applies to autoregressive estimators such as Equation 3.6, which includes lagged values:

$$\hat{y}_{t+1} = \alpha + \phi_1 y_t + \cdots \phi_p y_{t-p} + \beta_1 x_{1t+1} + \cdots + \beta_n x_{nt+1} + \upsilon_t \quad (3.11)[9]$$

where p is the number of lagged values of y needed to address serial correlation in the error terms. Otherwise, the calculations of the forecasted values and standard errors proceed in the same manner as with a single independent variable.

Steps in Creating a Time Series Regression Forecast

Throughout the chapter, we have used sales tax receipt data as an example. Now we will detail how analysis and forecasting of the data using an MLR would work. The analysis will proceed through six steps:

1. Perform an analysis of the descriptive statistics, looking for violations of the regression assumptions.
2. Perform an initial analysis of a regression model using data up to the most recent year of data available.
3. Examine the error characteristics of the data using measures from chapter 2.

4. Examine the residuals of the analysis for violations of regression assumptions.
5. Modify the model as necessary to produce the least in-sample error while controlling for violations of regression assumptions.
6. Forecast the data into the future, and examine the forecasts for credibility.

As pointed out earlier in the chapter, in order to forecast the data into the future, we need to have values of the independent variables. We will use the MSA Population and MSA Personal Income variables as potential predictor variables for our forecasts. For the sake of our example, we will assume that we have outside forecasts that the population is expected to grow at just 0.3 percent per year until $t+5$ and personal income is forecast to grow at 3.0 percent.[10]

Step 1: Examine Descriptive Statistics

The first step in the analysis is to examine descriptive statistics for the data. We look for two things during this step, violations of SLR/MLR1: Linearity, SLR/MLR2: Random Sampling and MLR5: Multicollinearity. We examine a time series plot and an autocorrelation function (ACF) for the dependent variable—Taxable Retail Sales, in order to assess linearity and random sampling. Described in greater details in Chapter 4, autocorrelation functions define how the observations in a time series, on average, are related to past observations. Figure 3.1 shows the time series plot of the taxable retail sales, and Figure 3.4 shows the ACF function for the data.

The time series plot does not suggest any nonlinearities. These would appear as "curves" in the data with consistently increasing or decreasing values. However, there do appear to be "cycles" in the data with periods of consistent downward or upward trends in values. This is suggestive of a positive serial correlation (a negative serial correlation would appear as a "sawtooth" pattern where there are abrupt upward and downward shifts around a mean). This is further suggested by the autocorrelation function in Figure 3.5. As can be seen from the lags of the autocorrelation function (the bars in the graph), they are statistically significant for the most part (the dashed lines show the 95% confidence interval, since the bars for the first several lags are outside of this they are significant). This suggests that autocorrelation will be an issue for our modeling.[11]

We examine multicollinearity (MLR5) through examining a correlation matrix for the variables in our dataset (Table 3.1). The correlation matrix

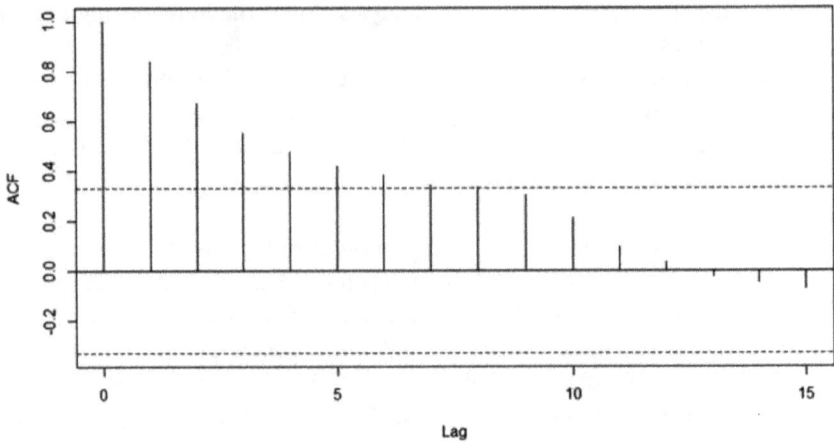

Figure 3.4   Autocorrelation Function for Taxable Retail Sales.

indicates that the two predictor variables have very high correlations, but they are less than 1. So, the model should be estimated, but we need to be careful in analyzing the statistical significance of the variables as the standard errors are likely to be miscalculated.

Step 2: Initial Regression Analysis

The next step is to perform an initial regression analysis. The resulting regression equation estimated using OLS is:

$$y_t = 44,393,700,000 - 4,958.61Pop_t + 52.0385PI_t \qquad (3.12)$$

$$\left(4.91\right) \qquad\quad \left(-4.16\right) \qquad\quad \left(9.96\right)$$

$$\text{MAPE} = 4.7882 \ \ R^2 = 0.9519 \ \ F = 337.4301 \ \ DW = 0.8405$$

where Pop_t is Population at time t, PI_t is personal income at time t, v_t is the residual term at time t. Both independent variables are statistically significant, indicating that they are significant predictors of Taxable Retail Sales. The

Table 3.1   Correlation Matrix for Variables in the Model

Variable	Taxable Retail Sales	Population	Personal Income
Taxable Retail Sales	1.0000	0.9024	0.9645
Population	0.9024	1.0000	0.9731
Personal Income	0.9645	0.9731	1.0000

t-statistics are much greater than 2.0; even with the caveat that there may be serial correlation, the predictor variables seem to be valid in our model. We next graph the outcome of the regression (Figure 3.5). As seen from the figure, the fitted model (dashed line) looks to reasonably fit the data (solid line).

Step 3: Examine Error Measures

The next step is to analyze error measures for the fitted model. For instance, the adjusted R^2 for the model is 0.95, indicating that changes in the independent variables predict 95 percent the variation in taxable retail sales, which is a good figure. The mean error for the model is 1,907,300. This indicates a very slight under forecast on average but no significant bias (the mean error is less than 0.01 percent of the average value of Taxable Sales). The root mean squared error is 862,940,000, and mean absolute percentage error (MAPE) is 4.7882 percent. This indicates that the model fit is good but not very strong. In general, it is expected that MAPEs are less than 5 percent at a minimum but 3 percent or less in the best case.

Step 4: Examine Regression Residuals

The next step is to examine the residuals from the regression for violations of assumptions and as a means to further refine our regression model. We

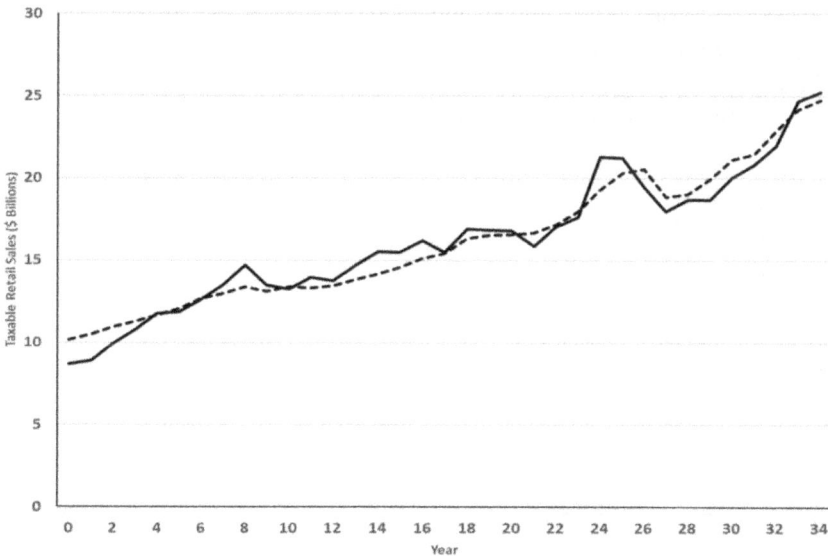

Figure 3.5 Actual (solid line) and Fitted (dashed line) Values from Estimation of Equation 3.12.

generate a graph of regression residuals over time (Figure 3.6) to assess assumptions SLR/MLR1: Linearity and SLR/MLR3: Zero Conditional Mean of the Error, an autocorrelation function for the residuals (Figure 3.7) to assess assumption SLR/MLR2: Random Sampling, and graphs of the regression residuals against Population and Personal Income (Figure 3.8) to assess assumption SLR/MLR6: Homoscedasticity. In addition, we conduct a test of homoscedasticity using the method of White (1980).

The graph of residuals over time (Figure 3.6) shows us two things. First, linearity is probably a valid assumption. If it were not, the pattern over time would show systematic and consistent differences from zero, such as an upward sloping curved pattern. But the graph instead seems to fluctuate around zero. And this also suggests that the Zero Conditional Mean Error assumption is met (this is also evident with the small value of the mean error calculation from the previous step).

The autocorrelation function for the residuals (Figure 3.7) confirms what the autocorrelation function in Step 1 suggests that serial correlation of the data is present. This is a violation of SLR/MLR2: Random sampling. This ACF indicates that one lag of the Taxable Retail Sales variable should be entered into the model to address this issue (one lag of the ACF is statistically significant, with a value of 0.53 indicating a strong one period—first order— serial correlation threat). In Step 5, we will address this through reestimating the model with the lagged value of the dependent variable.

The final two plots (Figures 3.8 and 3.9) show the relationship between the residuals and each of the predictor variables. In each case, there is no clear pattern where the residuals are higher at one point of the range of the variable. There may be a slightly smaller error in the middle of the range of each variable, but the magnitude is not significant. This is supported by the results of

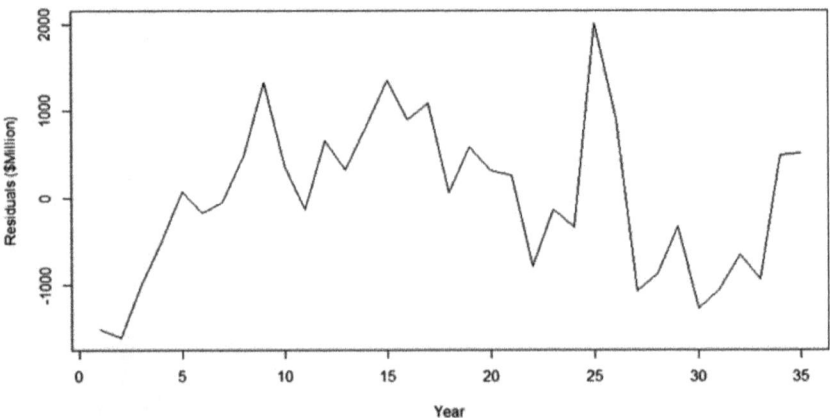

Figure 3.6   Residuals from Equation 3.12 over Time.

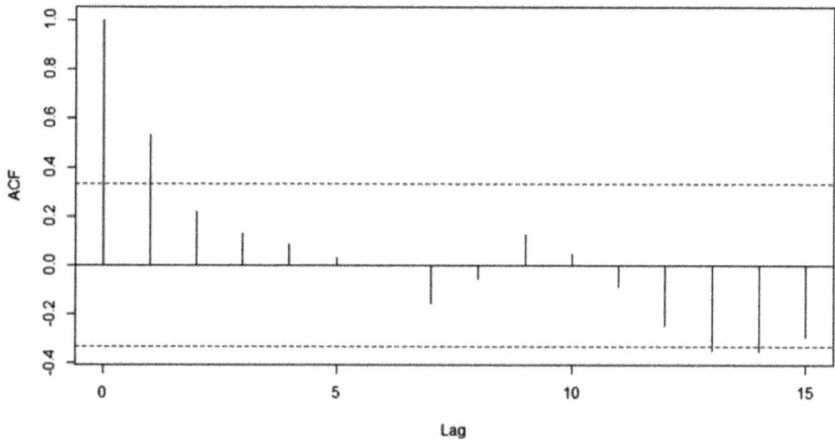

Figure 3.7   Autocorrelation Function for the Residuals from Equation 3.12.

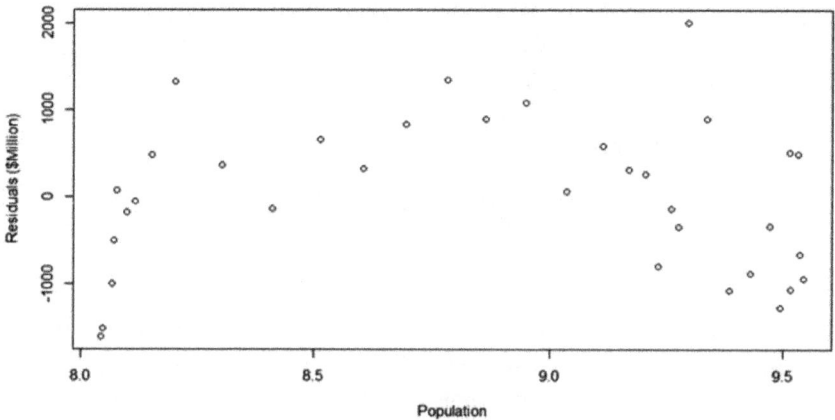

Figure 3.8   Residuals from Equation 3.12 and Population.

White's test, which is the test of the goodness of fit of the squared residuals from the original model (Equation 3.12) against the original predictor variables, the cross-product of those variables (Population*Personal Income) and the squared value of each variable (Population^2, Personal Income^2). The value of White's test statistic is 6.46, with a p-value of 0.26. This means that we cannot reject the null hypothesis, which is homoscedasticity. Therefore, with the evidence from the graphs and the test, we can surmise that Assumption SLR/MLR6: Homoscedasticity is likely to be a valid assumption.

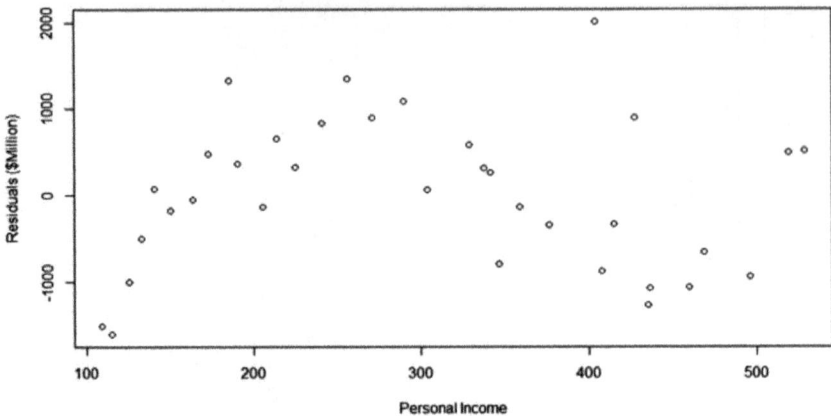

Figure 3.9   Residuals from Equation 3.12 and Personal Income.

Step 5: Modify and Reestimate the Regression Model

The primary threat to the validity of our regression model appears to be serial correlation. Therefore, we would add a lag of Taxable Retail Sales and reestimate the model, resulting in:

$$y_t = 35,330,200,000 + 0.3393y_{t-1} - 4,038.77POP_t + 37.5513PI_t \quad (3.13)$$

$$(3.93) \qquad (2.40) \qquad (-3.56) \qquad (5.04)$$

$$\text{MAPE}=3.6576 \quad R^2=0.9581 \quad F=252.3693 \quad \text{DW}=2.0943$$

A graph of the regression results (Figure 3.10) suggests that this model fits the data much better than the first model. This is further suggested by the error measures. The mean error now indicates an over forecast (-2,468,300) with a slightly higher magnitude, but the RMSE (761,970,000) and MAPE (3.66 percent) are significantly lower than from the model in Equation 3.12. The adjusted R^2 has improved slightly to 0.96. The autocorrelation function also shows no significant serial correlation remains in the model, and the remaining residual plots and tests show no violations of assumptions. Equation 3.13 thus becomes our final regression model for the relationships in the data.

Step 6: Forecast the Data Using the Final Regression Model

In the final step, we generate point estimates, standard errors, and confidence intervals for the forecast values. Using equations 3.13 for the model and 3.11 for the forecasts, we forecast the data from t+1 through t+5. Figure 3.11 and Table 3.2 show the forecast results. The left side of Figure 3.11

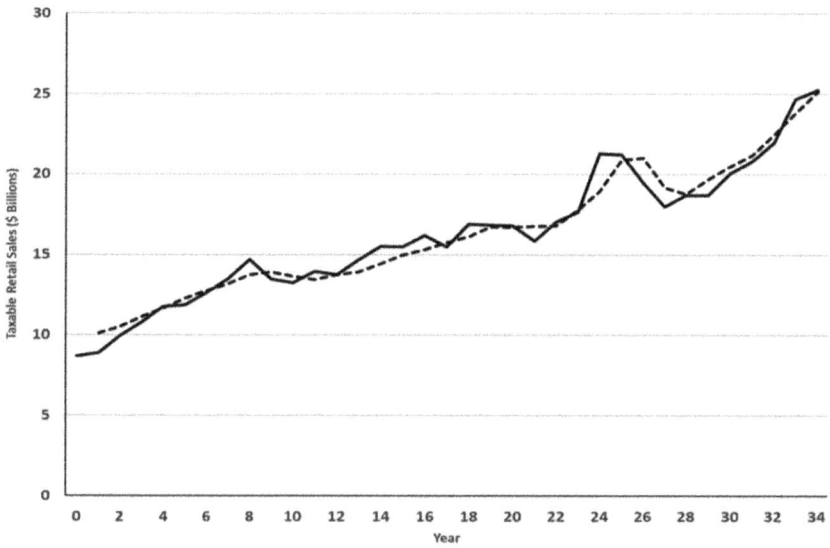

Figure 3.10 Actual (solid line) and Fitted (dashed line) Values from the Estimation of Equation 3.13.

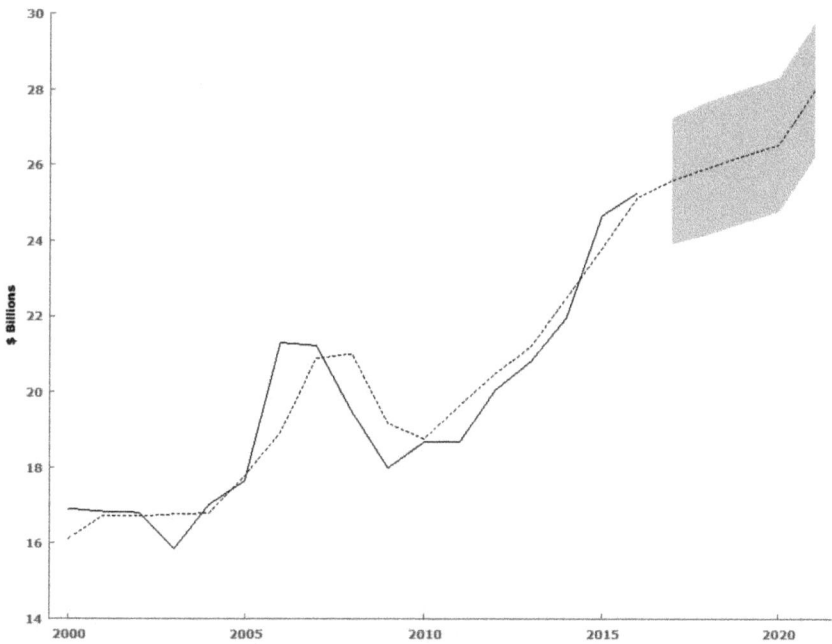

Figure 3.11 Forecast from Equation 3.13.

Table 3.2   Forecast Values from Equation 3.13

Fiscal Year	Prediction	Standard Error	95% Confidence Interval		
t+1 (Yr. 36)	25,594,900,000	811,178,000	23,937,400,000	–	27,250,700,000
t+2 (Yr. 37)	25,928,600,000	856,599,000	24,179,200,000	–	27,678,000,000
t+3 (Yr. 38)	26,249,700,000	861,674,000	24,489,900,000	–	28,009,500,000
t+4 (Yr. 39)	26,548,000,000	862,257,000	24,787,100,000	–	28,309,000,000
t+5 (Yr. 40)	27,980,800,000	862,324,000	26,219,700,000	–	29,741,900,000

shows the goodness of fit of the model and actual values up to time t. The right side shows the point estimate of the forecast value (dashed line) and the 95% confidence interval (gray shaded area). The forecast appears as an upward sloping line, with values ranging from $25.6 billion in t+1 to $27.8 billion in t+5. The 95% confidence interval is fairly wide; this area represents roughly two times the standard error, which is around 3.1 percent of the forecast value.

At face value, the estimates have credibility. It is plausible that given the past trends for growth in Taxable Sales and projected growth in both Population and Personal Income, Taxable Sales would continue to grow into the future. The growth rate of the forecast values does seem to be slightly less than the growth rate for the last few years of the actual data (from 2010 on). This may reflect lower projected Population or Personal Income growth rates.

Communication of this forecast should involve both the point estimates and the confidence interval. Decision makers need to know not only the best estimate of the future values of Taxable Retail Sales but also the amount of risk in relying on sales taxes linked to this revenue source. While a 3 percent error does not sound large, that equates to just over $10 million per year in city sales taxes.

SUMMARY

This chapter has provided a discussion and analysis of how to use time series regression analysis to forecast government revenue and spending variables of interest. The chapter began by developing the theory of regression analysis, then discussing the assumptions of regression analysis. This was done, first, for a single predictor (explanatory) variable, then expanded the discussion to cases with multiple predictors. In particular, it showed how to identify deviations from the assumptions of regression analysis and discussed how to address them. Finally, the chapter concluded with an extended example of forecasting sales tax data for a major US city using this methodology.

NOTES

1. The data were for the city of Chicago (retail sales) and the Chicago-Naperville-Elgin MSA (population and per capita income), from 1983 through 2016.
2. The other sales tax revenue stream comes from a portion of the state sales tax that is shared by local governments.
3. The errors must be squared as they are both negative and positive by definition and will result in biased results if not squared.

4. The math for this is somewhat beyond the scope of this text. Interested readers should consult Harvey (1990), Wooldridge (2006) or another introductory econometrics or statistics textbook.

5. This discussion is an oversimplification; readers are directed to the econometrics or statistics textbooks listed in note 3 for a full description of how standard errors and test statistics are calculated.

6. One can also test for the presence of serial correlation through running an autocorrelation function (ACF) on the residuals from the regression as described in an earlier chapter.

7. There is actually a third way to control for serial correlation that is frequently used in inferential statistics. That is to detrend the data through taking first differences. This eliminates trends in the data that are associated with longer-term serial correlation. However, this method sacrifices information on the serial correlation structure that is useful in building forecast models.

8. In inferential statistics, very high correlations (less than 1 but much more than 0) can present problems for calculating standard errors and traditional goodness of fit measures like R^2. But in forecasting applications, we care less for these calculations than the error measures described in Chapter 2.

9. Note that the autoregressive terms contain one through p periods of lagged values of y and thus start at time t for the time $t+1$ prediction. (See Chapter 5 for at length discussion of autoregressive models)

10. These are actually the compound growth rates for these variables since 2000.

11. Another thing that we look for in the autocorrelation function is the presence of long-term trends, a property known as *stationarity*, discussed in greater details in Chapter 4. In this case, the autocorrelation function will show all or most lags as being statistically significant, meaning that all or most lagged values are significant predictors of the current value. If this were the case, the best option is to take first differences of the values and use those differences in the regression model. Luckily for our model this is not the case.

Part II

ADVANCED TIME SERIES MODELS

Chapter 4

Box-Jenkins and ARIMA Models

The time series models we discussed earlier are relatively simple and uncomplicated, but they require the estimation of multiple coefficients that are limited in scope. Box-Jenkins (B-J) model (1976), named after the authors who developed the method, uses a different model-building structure than the conventional time series models that are versatile and efficient. In a typical time series model, the forecaster takes a specific model and proceeds to estimate the parameters, as we have in the chapters on basic time series models, but this creates two problems: One, when dealing with a data series, it is likely that one may observe not one but multiple different models that are statistically sound and, as such, should not be arbitrarily discarded. Two, when estimating a model, it is not always possible to find an explicit method of solution for determining the model parameters, which may require that we use a trial-and-error process until we find the right model.

B-J addresses both problems by suggesting a model-building approach that systematically eliminates inappropriate models and selects the one that is most appropriate (optimal) for a forecasting problem, given the nature of the data. This chapter presents a broad discussion of the B-J model and its essential characteristics in their bare essence.

BASIC STRUCTURE

Like all time series methods, B-J starts with a time series where each time period is treated as a separate observation. It builds a series of models based on these observations and their correlations and partial correlations (correlations between any two variables while controlling the effects of other variables). The models are built on the assumption that two sets of parameters

105

may exist within a historical series: An autoregressive (AR) parameter and a moving average (MA) parameter. The presence of an AR parameter in the model suggests that there is autocorrelation in the data. In other words, it means that the current level of the forecast variable (revenue, expenditure, etc.) can be explained by the past values of the variable, plus a random error that occurs in the present. For instance, a first-order AR model with lag one, AR(1), indicates a relationship among the successive observations of the time series for a period one year apart and can be written as

$$Y_t = \varphi_0 + \varphi_1 Y_{t-1} + e_t \qquad (4.1)$$

where Y_t is the forecast variable, φ is the model parameter whose value one is trying to estimate, Y_{t-1} is the lagged value of Y, and e_t is the error term assumed to be approximately normally distributed with 0 mean and constant variance, $e_t \sim n(0,\sigma^2)$.

Similarly, a second-order AR model with lag two, AR(2), indicates a relationship among the successive observations of the time series for a period two years apart and can be written as

$$Y_t = \varphi_0 + \varphi_1 Y_{t-1} + \varphi_2 Y_{t-2} + e_t \qquad (4.2)$$

and for the pth order AR model with lag p, AR(p), it will be

$$Y_t = \varphi_0 + \varphi_1 Y_{t-1} + \varphi_2 Y_{t-2} + \dots\dots\dots + \varphi_p Y_{t-p} + e_t \qquad (4.3)$$

On the other hand, the MA parameters indicate that the series values can be explained by the past random errors, plus a new random error that occurs in the present. One can think of these random errors as small shocks or disturbances, called "white noises," that set the process in motion initially and continue it afterward.[1] For instance, a first-order MA model with lag one, MA(1), can be written as

$$Y_t = \theta_0 + e_t + \theta_1 e_{t-1} \qquad (4.4)$$

where Y_t is the forecast variable, θ is the model parameter whose value we are trying to estimate, e_{t-1} is the lagged value of e_t, and e_t is the error term assumed to be approximately normally distributed with 0 mean and constant variance, $e_t \sim n(0,\sigma^2)$.

For a second-order MA model with lag two, MA(2), it can be written as

$$Y_t = \theta_0 + e_t + \theta_1 e_{t-1} + \theta_2 e_{t-2} \qquad (4.5)$$

and for the qth order MA model with lag q, MA(q), it will be

$$Y_t = \theta_0 + e_t + \theta_1 e_{t-1} + \theta_2 e_{t-2} + \ldots\ldots\ldots + \theta_q e_{t-q} \tag{4.6}$$

It is not unlikely to have both AR and MA parameters in the same model. If that is the case, it is called an autoregressive moving average (ARMA) model and can be expressed as

$$Y_t = \varphi_1 Y_{t-1} + \theta_0 + e_t + \theta_1 e_{t-1} \tag{4.7}$$

for a first order AR and MA, with lag 1. As a convention, the constant term in a mixed model is represented by θ instead of φ.

Equation 4.7 can be easily extended for multiple orders and time lags so that the new equation would appear as

$$Y_t = \varphi_1 Y_{t-1} + \varphi_2 Y_{t-2} + \ldots\ldots\ldots + \varphi_p Y_{t-p} + \theta_0 + e_t + \theta_1 e_{t-1}$$

$$+ \theta_2 e_{t-2} + \ldots\ldots\ldots + \theta_q e_{t-q} \tag{4.8}$$

where p and q are the orders of the model, and the rest of the terms are the same as before. It should be worth noting that the final model may not include both AR and MA parameters, as either of the φ and θ parameters can end up not being significant (i.e., not significantly different from zero).

Alternative Formulation

There is a term frequently used in ARMA models called backshift operator (B), which is a compact form of writing the equations in polynomials.[2] The backshift operators (B, B^2, B^3, ...) simply mean shifting back in time series or simply backing up by one-time unit (Nau, 2014). For instance, let us say that we have a time series Y at time t, Y_t, which, using the backshift operator, can be written as $Y_{t-1} = BY_t$, where B is the backshift operator. For Y_{t-2}, it can be written as the higher power of B or simply in terms of B raised to the power 2; that is,

$$Y_{t-2} = BY_{t-1} = B(BY_t) = B^2 Y_t \tag{4.9}$$

for $Y_{t-3,}$ it would be B raised to the power 3

$$Y_{t-3} = BY_{t-2} = B(BY_{y-1}) = B^2(BY_t) = B^3 Y_t \tag{4.10}$$

and for Y_{t-k}, it would be B raised to the power k

$$Y_{t-k} = B^k Y_t \tag{4.11}$$

Thus, for an ARMA model with p and q orders, the backshift operator, ignoring the constant terms in Equation 4.8, can be written as a combination of AR(p) and MA(q)

$$Y_t = \varphi_1 Y_{t-1} + \varphi_2 Y_{t-2} + \ldots\ldots + \varphi_p Y_{t-p} + e_t + \theta_1 e_{t-1}$$

$$+\theta_2 e_{t-2} + \ldots\ldots + \theta_q e_{t-q} \tag{4.12}$$

$$\left(1 - \varphi_1 B - \varphi_2 B^2 - \ldots\ldots - \varphi_p B^p\right) Y_t = \left(1 + \theta_1 B + \theta_2 B^2 + \ldots\ldots + \theta_q B^q\right) e_t \tag{4.13}$$

Put simply, the backshift operators are a convenient way to present the ARMA (as well as ARIMA) processes.[2]

Stationarity

The models described in Equations 4.7 and 4.8 are based on an important assumption that the series is "stationary," which means that the data fluctuate around a constant average (mean) and a variance that does not increase or decrease over time (time-invariant). In common sense terms, it means that when the data are plotted on a two-dimensional plane, they reflect a pattern that is roughly horizontal, although it may not be unusual to find some cyclical behavior in a series. Stationarity is generally an indication of a forecasting environment that is relatively stable, has a short forecasting horizon, and a transformable series, meaning that the data can be (mathematically) transformed into a stable series. A "nonstationary" time series, on the other hand, contains periodic variations and systematic changes in the average, known as "trend." It may also contain seasonal variations in the data (where the data fluctuate in a predictable fashion during certain times of the year, called "seasonality," although the trend is more frequently associated with the nonstationarity condition.[3]

For the most part, the trend is not permanent and, as noted earlier, can be easily removed with the help of simple transformation such as taking the square root, the natural log of the data, or using a simple process known as "differencing" (Makridakis and Wheelwright, 1978). In general, if initial differencing does not produce the intended result, it may be necessary to consider suitable data transformation, along with differencing, to make the series stationary (Hossain et al., 2019). Similarly, if nonstationarity is due to seasonality, it can be removed with the help of decomposition methods or method such as Census 11 (discussed briefly in Chapter 1), which is much more involved than simple log-transformation or differencing (Dagum and Bianconcini, 2016).

To give an example of how differencing works, suppose that we have a government whose revenue from sales tax for FY_{t-1} and FY_t were \$500,000 and \$525,000, respectively. For the purpose of de-trending the data, the value we will use for Y_t is not \$525,000 but rather the difference between the revenue for FY_t and FY_{t-1}, which is \$525,000 - \$500,000 = \$25,000. The transformation will allow us to achieve a reasonably stationary series. The number of times the original series is differenced to get a stationary series is called the "order" of the series. In general, the first difference will remove the linear trend in the data called the first order, the second difference will remove the quadratic trend called the second order, the third difference will remove the cubic trend called the third order, and so forth. If it is differenced d^{th} times, it is called d^{th} order. Models of these types are known as autoregressive integrated moving average (ARIMA) models.

The ARIMA models are essentially the same as the ARMA models, except that the original series Y_t is replaced by a differenced series, $\nabla^d Y_t$ meaning that Y_t has been differenced d times. The following presents the expression for an ARIMA model of order p, d, and q in regular form and backshift operator:

$$Y_t^{/} = \varphi_1 Y_{t-1}^{/} + \varphi_2 Y_{t-2}^{/} + \ldots\ldots + \varphi_p Y_{t-p}^{/} + \theta_0 + e_t + \theta_1 e_{t-1}$$

$$+\theta_2 e_{t-2} + \ldots\ldots + \theta_q e_{t-q} \tag{4.14}$$

where $Y_t^{/}$ is the differenced series, $\nabla^d Y_t$, and

$$\left(1 - \varphi_1 B - \varphi_2 B^2 - \ldots\ldots - \varphi_p B^p \right)(1 - B)^d Y_t$$

$$= \left(1 + \theta_1 B + \theta_2 B^2 + \ldots\ldots + \theta_q B^q \right)e_t \tag{4.15}$$

assuming the series has been differenced d times (if differenced once, it will be (1-*B*); if differenced twice, it will be (1-*B*)², and so forth), where e_t represents the white noise, p is the order (number) of AR terms, d is the number of times the series has been differenced, q is the order (number) of MA terms, and B is the backshift operator. Put simply, it is the transformed version of Equation 4.13.

It should be worth noting that while differencing is necessary to achieve stationarity in a series, over differencing can lead to unnecessary problems. The rule of thumb for differencing is to keep the order low, usually first or second order, which, in most cases, should yield a time series that will fluctuate around a constant mean producing stationarity. A common problem when over differencing occurs is that one may end up using additional AR or MA terms to minimize the problem, which could be unnecessary and time-consuming. While it is difficult to suggest a precise measure that will produce an optimal order of difference, the convention is to use differencing that will produce the lowest statistical errors, given by measures such as RMSE, MAE, MAPE, and so forth.

STEPS IN BOX-JENKINS

The application of the B-J model is not that complicated and can be presented in a four-step process: Identification, estimation, diagnostic checks, and forecasting. The first step involves identifying a tentative model by analyzing the past behavior of the forecasting variable. The second step involves selecting the initial parameters of the model and estimating the model parameters. The third step involves diagnostic checks of the estimated parameters to ensure that they are statistically significant. The fourth and final step involves the actual forecast. Although the steps are typical of any forecasting model, they are much more involved in B-J because of the nature of the model.

The following provides a detailed description of the steps:

Model Identification

Identification requires that before estimating the model, the data are carefully examined to determine the type of model that would be most appropriate: Pure autoregressive (AR), pure moving average (MA), or a mixed autoregressive moving average (ARMA)? This can be achieved with the help of autocorrelation (AC) and partial autocorrelation (PAC) analyses. Introduced briefly in Chapter 3, autocorrelations are measures of the correlations between the current values of a series with the series lagged for a certain number of periods. Partial autocorrelations, which are mostly used to supplement the autocorrelations, are similar to the regression coefficients in a causal model in the sense that they explain the strength of the relationship between time periods in a series after dependence on intervening time periods has been removed. In other words, they are the correlations between the current values of a variable and its previous values, holding the effects of all other time lags constant.

As with regular correlations, the correlation coefficients for both AC and PAC range between ±1, indicating the strength of correlation at different time lags. Figures 4.1 and 4.2 show the correlation plots, called correlograms, for a typical AR(p) and MA(q) process. Correlograms are extremely useful as visual tools for determining the behavior of AR and MA models. For instance, when a process extends infinitely, either from above or below, decaying relatively rapidly at higher lags, as in an AR(p) process (Figure 4.1), it is called attenuation, and when it suddenly changes after certain lags, say at lag k, as in an MA(q) process (Figure 4.2), it is known as truncation.

However, the process is not cut-and-dried in that the autocorrelation function (ACF) of an AR(p) process always attenuates (declines gradually), and the MA(q) process truncates (declines abruptly) in every situation. In reality, the relationship may reverse for a partial autocorrelation function (PACF), where it may truncate for an AR(p) process and attenuate for an MA(q) process. It should be worth noting that the PACF plays an important role in ARIMA, especially in situations where it is difficult to determine from the plots if the autocorrelation function (ACF) attenuates or truncates, in which case it is necessary to supplement the analysis with a partial autocorrelation function (PACF). Figures 4.3-4.6 show four examples of ACF and PACF for AR(1) and MA(1) models with different configurations (generated with random numbers for visual display).

As shown in Figures 4.3 and 4.4, for a first-order AR(1) model, correlations are high at shorter lags decaying gradually at higher lags for ACF and spiking at shorter lags with low correlations at higher lags for PACF, while the situation reverses for a first order MA(1) term (Figures 4.5 and 4.6). This means that if the ACF of a differenced series shows a sharp spike at lag 1 and the autocorrelation is negative, the series may be over differenced and, as common sense would suggest, a first order MA(1) should be considered.

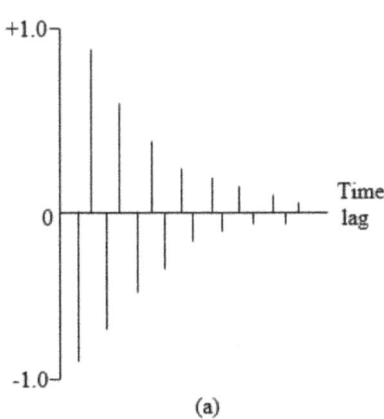

Figure 4.1 Hypothetical Autocorrelation Pattern for an AR(p) Model.

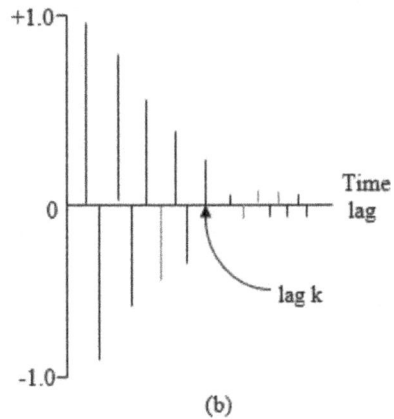

Figure 4.2 Hypothetical Autocorrelation Pattern for an MA(q) Model.

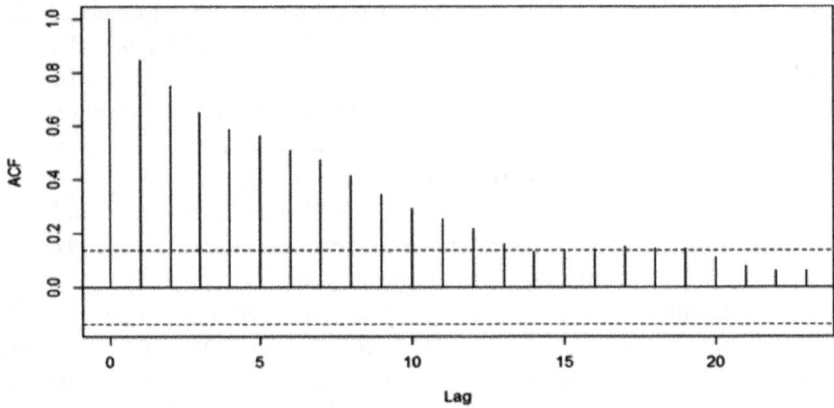

Figure 4.3   First-Order AR(1) Model—Decays (ACF).

Conversely, if the ACF of a differenced series shows a sharp spike at lag 1 and the autocorrelation is positive, the series may be under differenced and, by the same token, a first-order AR(1) should be considered.

In general, the order p (that of AR) is determined from the partial auto-correlations (PACs), and the order q (that of MA) is determined from the autocorrelations (ACs) of a differenced series. For instance, when the partial autocorrelations truncate after several lags, the last lag with the largest value should be used as the order of AR. Similarly, when the autocorrelations truncate after several lags, the last lag with the largest value should be used as the order of MA.

While these general guidelines make good sense when selecting the order of an AR or MA model, this may not be the case in every situation, much

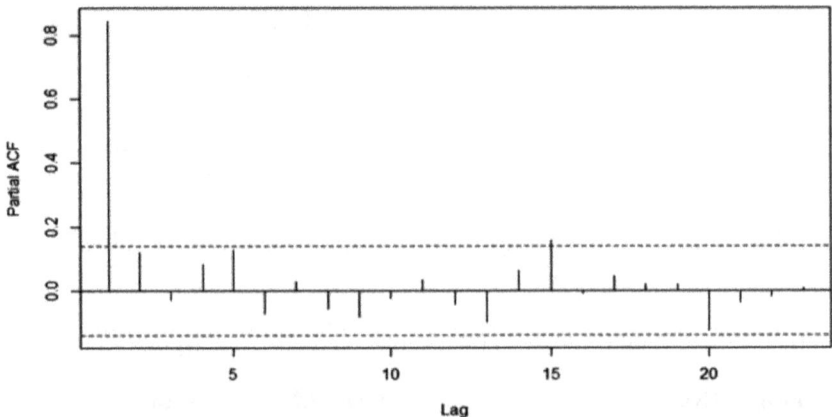

Figure 4.4   First-Order AR(1) Model—Truncates at lag 1 (PACF).

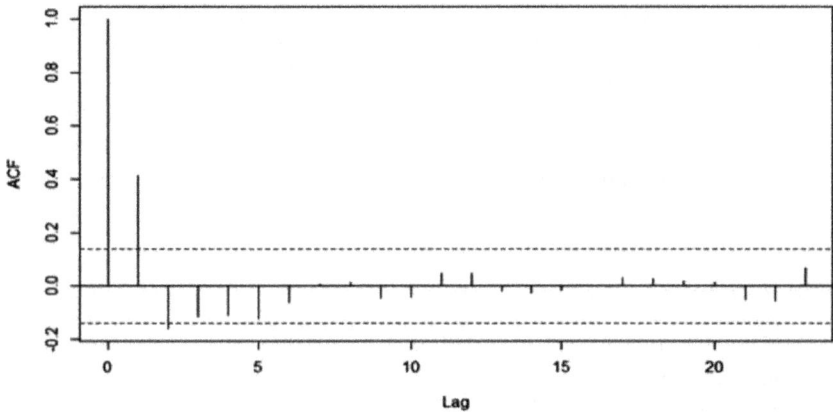

Figure 4.5 First-Order MA(1) Model—Truncates at lag 1 (ACF).

depends on the series in question, the length of the series, distribution of the data, and so forth. As such, the plots need to be carefully evaluated, for instance, with various error measurement statistics, such as RMSE, MAE, MAPE, and so forth, discussed in a previous chapter, to ensure the appropriate order of AR and MA models.

A mixed ARMA model involves a little more complicated process to identify. The rule of thumb for identifying an integrated ARMA process is to see how it decays in the tail for both ACF and PACF. In general, when the autocorrelation is very high for short lags and decays gradually for longer lags, it indicates the presence of an integrated component, meaning

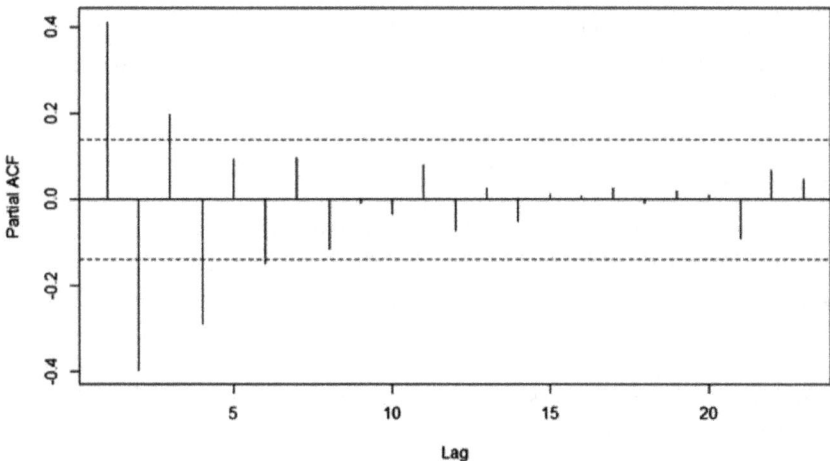

Figure 4.6 First-Order MA(1) Model—Decays (PACF).

that first differencing is necessary to detrend the series. On the other hand, if it is low or close to zero, it is possible that differencing once will leave an autocorrelation function that still decays slowly, in which case a second differencing will be necessary to detrend the series. Similarly, if the first partial autocorrelation is positive and very high, but the second is negative while the rest are quite small, it is an indication that the series contains an integrated component.

Unit Root Tests

Although autocorrelations and partial autocorrelations are the most convenient ways of detecting the presence of nonstationarity in a series, it is possible to have a series where it may be difficult to distinguish between a stationary and nonstationary series.[3] One way to correct the problem is to conduct formal statistical tests such as the unit root test (Maddala and Kim, 1998). A unit root means that the observed time series is not stationary. The test is done on a transformed version of the AR(1) model, in that the original model $Y_t = \varphi_0 + \varphi_1 Y_{t-1} + e_t$ is transformed into $Y_t = \delta_0 + \delta_1 Y_{t-1} + e_t$, where $\delta_1 = (\varphi_1 - 1)$ is the transformed coefficient. Thus, if $\varphi_1 = 1$, then $\delta_1 = 0$ and it becomes a test of $\varphi_1 = 1$, and so forth. There is a series of tests that can be conducted for this, but the two most frequently used for B-J are augmented Dickey-Fuller (ADF) and Phillips-Perron (PP) tests.[4] In fact, the latter is a refinement of Dickey-Fuller test (Newey and West, 1987).

To test the hypothesis that the observed series is not stationary, we would simply use the standard test procedure by setting the null hypothesis, H_0: $\delta_1 = 0$, or simply H_0: The series has a unit root and is nonstationary, and the alternative hypothesis, H_1: $\delta_1 \neq 0$, or simply H_1: The series does not have a unit root and, as such, is stationary. Most statistical software that deals with time series data, especially ARIMA models, include a variety of test statistics for unit root, including ADF and PP.

Model Estimation

The second stage of the process deals with estimation of the model parameters. For instance, to estimate the parameters of an autoregressive model with order p, AR(p), one would regress Y_t on Y_{t-1}, Y_{t-2}, ...,Y_{t-p}, but estimating the MA parameters is much more complicated. It would require a nonlinear, iterative least-squares procedure that consists of a complex combination of search routines and successive approximations, which makes it difficult to estimate them by hand. One would need a software program to estimate these parameters. In fact, the B-J models available on any standard statistical software usually include these routines.

The determination of the optimal value for the model parameters is a trial-and-error process that continues with backcasting (opposite of forecasting, i.e., estimating the past values rather than the future values) until the estimated values come as close as possible to the original series and the estimated coefficients are statistically significant. What this means in common sense terms is that since all ARIMA models are expressed as a function of past values of Y and e's, forecasts for the first few periods require the knowledge of the series for a few periods before t = 1.

Diagnostic Checks

Once the model has been determined through trial-and-error, the process requires that diagnostic checks are conducted to ensure that the model is statistically sound. Different methods and approaches are available for this purpose, based mostly on the distribution of the residuals. They fall into two broad categories: Visual and formal tests. This would range from simple residual histograms to residual plots, such as quintile-quintile (Q-Q) plots, to formal statistical tests, such as the Kolmogorov-Smirnov test, Shapiro-Wilk test, and Jarque-Bera test of goodness of fit for normality (discussed in Chapter 6), among others. Of these, the histogram is invariably the simplest yet, as a diagnostic tool, it provides a good eyeball impression of the distribution of the residuals that tells us if the series we are dealing with is a random, no-trend series.

Like the histogram, the residual plots provide useful information if their distribution is normal or approximately normal to lend support to the assumption of a random and no-trend series. The Q-Q plots, noted above, would be a good example where the quintiles of the residuals are plotted against the quintiles of the normal (theoretical) curve providing a convenient way to test for normality. If the plot is linear, the residuals are normally distributed. Points lying a significant distance from the linear relationship indicate the presence of outliers, in which case suitable measures such as transformation can be used to make the distribution of the residuals approximately normal.

As for autocorrelations, this would range from ACF and PACF plots, similar to those discussed earlier, to formal statistical tests such as Box-Pierce Q, also known as the Ljung-Box Q test, and so forth.[5] The ACF and PACF plots of the residuals serve as important diagnostic tools that allow us to see if additional structures (large correlations) are still present in the model. If all the autocorrelations and partial autocorrelations are small, the model is considered reasonably good. If some of the autocorrelations are large, the values of p and/or q need to be adjusted and the model reestimated; in other words, use a different order of the model. Convention suggests that if the residuals in the ACF and PACF plots are within $\pm 2 / \sqrt{n}$, a rule-of-thumb approach frequently used in residual analysis, one can assume a random, no-trend series.

Unlike the approaches suggested above, which are useful and visually attractive, the Ljung-Box Q test provides a formal approach that is frequently used to collectively test for the significance of autocorrelations, but not partial autocorrelations (Ljung and Box, 1978). It is essentially a chi-square (χ^2) test used for evaluating whether the overall correlogram of residuals exhibits any systematic error (for instance, due to a measurement problem). The following presents a typical expression for Q statistic:

$$Q_m = n(n+2)\sum_{k=1}^{m}\frac{r_k^2}{n-k} \tag{4.16}$$

where Q is the Q statistic, m is the number of coefficients being tested (equivalent to degrees of freedom in χ^2), n is the number of data points in a series, r is the autocorrelation coefficient, and k is the number of autocorrelation coefficients in the model at different lags ($k \leq m$). One quick point of observation about the degrees of freedom, m, since it plays an important role in χ^2 tests, especially when used in the context of B-J, the rule of thumb is that it should be no larger than one-quarter of the sample size, n.

To give an example, suppose that we have an AR(1) model for a series with 35 observations so that the model will include two parameters—one for the constant term and the other for the AR term; that is, $Y_t = \varphi_0 + \varphi_1 Y_{t-1} + e_t$. Let us further suppose that we were able to identify two autocorrelations from the correlogram with coefficients, say, of -0.165 and 0.217. We can now use this information to conduct a formal Ljung-Box Q test with appropriate test procedures, as given below:

H$_0$: The residuals are uncorrelated (i.e., the series is random and not trended)
H$_A$: The residuals are correlated (i.e., the series is not random and trended)

$$\text{Test Statistic:} Q_2 = 35(35+2)\left[\frac{(-0.165)^2}{34}+\frac{(0.217)^2}{33}\right]$$

$$=(1{,}295)[0.00223]$$

$$=2.8879$$

Decision Rule:
Reject H$_0$, if $Q_m > \chi^2$; otherwise, do not reject H$_0$

Conclusion: Since the observed χ^2 value of 2.8879 is less than its corresponding χ^2 value of 5.991 (which can be obtained from any χ^2 table) with 2 degrees of freedom (m = 2) that is significant at the 5 percent level of α, with $p < 0.05$, it means that the estimated model is not statistically significant. In other words, we cannot reject the null hypothesis that the residuals are uncorrelated. Put simply, there is support for the series being random (i.e., not correlated) and, as such, not trended.

Forecasts

The last step in the process is to generate the forecasts for the estimated model. The process can be complicated, especially if the model is integrated with higher lags and orders, in which case it will require the use of computers to do the forecast. However, for simpler problems it is possible to obtain them by hand, but the process can be tedious. It is also necessary during this stage to obtain the confidence intervals for the forecast values to provide the decision makers the flexibility to determine the budgetary decisions (revenue, as well as expenditure) in the event that the forecast values fall within these limits or intervals.

AN ILLUSTRATIVE EXAMPLE

Let us look at a simple example to illustrate the method. Suppose that we have the General Fund (GF) revenue of a local government, which includes revenues from all sources, except for those accounted for proprietary and fiduciary funds, of a hypothetical, relatively high-growth government for a period of 37 years (Table 4.1). In general, ARIMA models require a large data set, especially if the objective is forecasting (Box and Tiao, 1975), which may not be the case when, for instance, one is using time series data for pre- and post-comparison using models such as regression analysis (Linden, 2015).

A cursory examination of the data in the table would reveal that the government has experienced significant growth in revenue over the years, from $10.687 million at time t-36 to $195.24 million at time t. On the whole, the pattern shows sustained but very rapid growth in government revenues for recent years compared to the early years of the series. This is clearly reflected in the initial plot of the series (Figure 4.7).

As shown in Figure 4.7, there is an upward trend in the data indicating that the series is not stationary and that differencing is necessary. Unfortunately, the initial runs with the differenced series did not produce reliable results, in particular for repeated ADF tests (not shown here), so the data were transformed using a natural log (Figure 4.8). The log transformation of the data

Table 4.1 GF Revenue of a Local Government

Year	GF Revenue ($Million)	Log Transformed	Year	GF Revenue ($Million)	Log Transformed	Year	GF Revenue ($Million)	Log Transformed
t-36	10.687	2.369	t-23	22.450	3.111	t-10	88.650	4.485
t-35	11.934	2.479	t-22	23.860	3.172	t-9	95.691	4.561
t-34	12.895	2.557	t-21	25.761	3.249	t-8	95.840	4.563
t-33	13.230	2.582	t-20	27.661	3.320	t-7	102.891	4.634
t-32	14.271	2.658	t-19	30.438	3.416	t-6	125.677	4.834
t-31	15.150	2.718	t-18	35.183	3.561	t-5	137.770	4.926
t-30	16.369	2.795	t-17	39.972	3.688	t-4	153.966	5.037
t-29	16.883	2.826	t-16	45.871	3.826	t-3	167.965	5.124
t-28	17.141	2.841	t-15	49.690	3.906	t-2	186.880	5.230
t-27	18.100	2.896	t-14	54.483	3.998	t-1	189.131	5.242
t-26	19.293	2.960	t-13	60.673	4.105	t	195.240	5.274
t-25	20.452	3.018	t-12	66.582	4.198	--	--	--
t-24	21.163	3.052	t-11	76.961	4.343	--	--	--

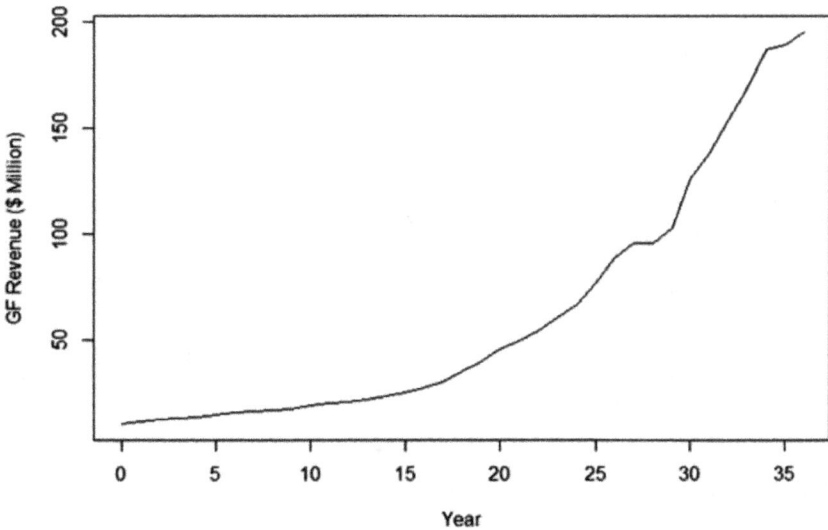

Figure 4.7   The Original Series Figure.

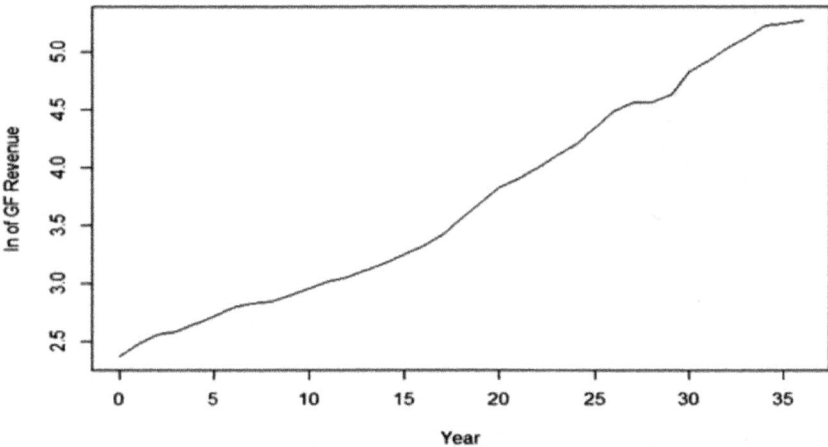

Figure 4.8   Series after Log Transformation.

appears to have improved the situation somewhat but not enough to detrend the data, indicating that differencing is necessary.

The first difference of the log-transformed series appears to have improved the result considerably (Figure 4.9), but on close observation, it appears that a little trend is still left in the series, indicating further that additional differencing would be helpful. The second differencing of the transformed series seems to have improved the result considerably, as the data appear to have achieved a good measure of stationarity (Figure 4.10).

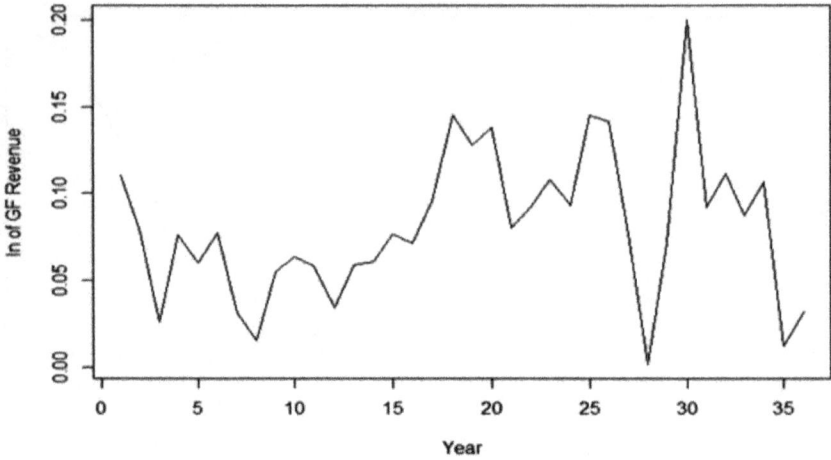

Figure 4.9   Series after First Differencing of Log-Transformed Data.

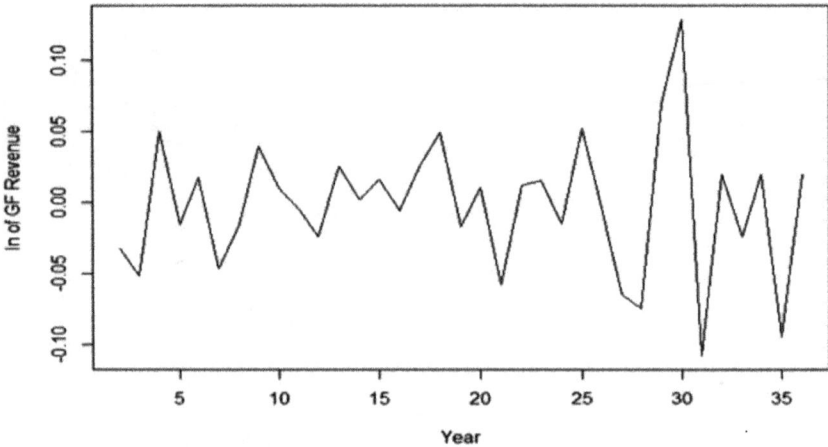

Figure 4.10   Series after Second Differencing of Log-Transformed Data.

However, to further ensure that the series is stationary, we do a hypothesis test similar to that suggested earlier (H_0: The series is not stationary, and H_1: The series is stationary) for both ADF and PP and look at the test results to draw appropriate conclusions. The following provides a brief summary of the test results for ADF and PP:

GF Revenue: Original Series
   Test Statistic (ADF): -1.8840, Lag order = 3, p-value = 0.6185
   Test Statistic (PP): -3.4744, Lag parameter = 3, p-value = 0.9092

GF Revenue: Series after first differencing of the log-transformed data
    Test Statistic (ADF): -1.6547, Lag order = 3, p-value = 0.7075
    Test Statistic (PP): -21.5450, Lag parameter = 3, p-value = 0.0216
GF Revenue: Series after second differencing of the log-transformed data
    Test Statistic (ADF): -3.7762, Lag order = 3, p-value = 0.0340
    Test Statistic (PP): -32.5710, Lag parameter = 3, $p < 0.01$

As the results show, both ADF and PP statistics appear to be high and insignificant for the original series, indicating that differencing is necessary to detrend the series. The first differencing improved the results for PP but not for ADF, suggesting that additional differencing is necessary to detrend the series. Accordingly, we conducted a second differencing of the data to see if it would further improve the results. The second differencing appears to have improved the results for both ADF and PP, as both appear to be statistically significant at 5 and 1 percent levels of α, with p-values at 0.0340 and <0.01, respectively. We can, therefore, reject the null hypothesis and safely conclude (i.e., accept the alternative hypothesis) that the series is stationary.

Model Identification

Once the series has been detrended, the next step in the process is to select the best possible model that will be suitable for estimation and forecasting. To ensure that we retain the model that is optimal, we proceed in three steps: First, look at the ACF and PACF plots to determine the order of the AR and MA processes. Second, look at the combination of AR and MA terms and various error measurement statistics such as RMSE, MAE, MAPE, AIC[6], and so forth. Third, select the model with the lowest errors.

Unfortunately, as before, the ACF and PACF plots before and after the differencing, with and without log transformation, did not produce any clear picture of the order combination that would be optimal. Since none of the autocorrelations and partial autocorrelations appeared to be significant at any lag, with the exception of the partial autocorrelation at lag 3 (not shown here), the question then is which terms to select to determine the final order of the model. As noted earlier, when plots do not reveal a clear order, we can still find the best model by looking at the combination of AR and MA terms that would best meet the diagnostic checks. As for the combination of orders, it is possible to have any number of combinations, but the convention is to keep the order low to maintain parsimony.

As with most statistical models, parsimony is helpful in Box-Jenkin not because the simpler models are easier to fit and explain but because parsimonious models help avoid the problem of parameter redundancy (Pankratz, 1983). Redundancy occurs when a higher order model is used that does not

Table 4.2   Order Combination of Ar And Ma Terms and Error Measurement

Order Combination	RMSE	MAE	MAPE	AIC
ARIMA(1,2,1)	0.0383109	0.0285186	0.7678886	-118.3676
ARIMA(1,2,2)	0.0387818	0.0293144	0.7678886	-116.8267
ARIMA(1,2,3)	0.0366204	0.0284775	0.7458262	-116.8779
ARIMA(2,2,1)	0.0386961	0.0291576	0.7648822	-117.4525
ARIMA(2,2,2)	0.0359091	0.0282415	0.7368634	-116.6984
ARIMA(2,2,3)	0.0337608	0.0270198	0.7124371	-119.1062
ARIMA(3,2,1)	0.0384197	0.0284545	0.7470752	-115.9734
ARIMA(3,2,2)	0.0381963	0.0287251	0.7545165	-114.3454

produce significantly more information than a model with fewer terms. Table 4.2 shows ARIMA models with different order combinations and their corresponding errors.

As shown in the table, the fifth model, ARIMA(2,2,2), has one of the smallest RMSE, MAE, MAPE, and a reasonably good AIC. Although ARIMA(2,2,3) appears to have better accuracy, albeit marginally, two of its MA coefficients, MA(1) and MA(2), were found statistically insignificant and, as such, it was excluded from consideration. We could have tried higher order models, but it is unlikely they would have produced any better results. Thus, among the eight models, ARIMA(2,2,2) appears to be the best for model estimation.

Model Estimation

Having identified the model, the next step in the process is to estimate the model parameters. The estimation process requires the use of both least squares and nonlinear least squares criteria to obtain the estimates. The least squares criterion is generally used for AR(p) models since the parameters of the model could be found by regressing Y_t on Y_{t-1}, Y_{t-2}, ..., Y_{t-p}, while for MA(q), as well as mixed models are a little more complicated since the MA terms contain the powers of θ; as such, the convention is to use nonlinear least squares. And the method commonly used for this purpose is Maximum Likelihood Estimation (MLE), which is much more suitable for dealing with nonlinear functions than the conventional least squares method. In fact, most statistical software have built-in provisions that allow for maximum likelihood estimation (MLE).[7]

The following presents the estimated model for ARIMA(2,2,2):

$$\left(1 - 1.1505B + 0.4260B^2\right)\left(1 - B\right)^2 Y_t = \left(1 - 1.885B + 1.00B^2\right)e_t$$

where Y_t is the log of GF budget at time t, and e_t is the error term at time t.

Table 4.3   **Final Estimation of the Model Parameters: ARIMA (2,2,2)**

Number Number	Model Type •	Estimated Coefficients	Std. Errors	t-Ratios*	p-value
1	AR(1)	0.9839	0.1316	7.47644	<0.0001
1	AR(2)	-0.7307	0.1329	-5.49812	<0.0001
1	MA(1)	-1.5355	0.1346	-11.40788	<0.0001
1	MA(2)	1.0000	0.1622	6.16523	<0.0001

*df = 36-4-2 = 30

As with most statistical models, once a model has been estimated, it is important to determine how good the model is by looking at the significance of the estimated parameters. Accordingly, we look at the standard errors, t ratios, and the p-values associated with the estimated parameters to determine their significance. Table 4.3 shows the estimated coefficients for the AR and MA terms and their corresponding t ratios and p-values.

As can be seen from the table (4.3), all the terms used in the model came out to be significant at $p < 0.0001$, indicating that the model is statistically sound and can be used for forecasting. However, as is customary with B-J, before continuing with forecasting, it is important that we conduct some diagnostic checks to ensure further that our model is statistically sound.

Diagnostic Checks

Two sets of diagnostic checks are generally conducted once the model has been estimated: t-ratios, such as those presented in Table 4.3, and residual analysis. The t ratios tell us if the model is statistically sound, while the residual analysis tells us if we are dealing with a random, no-trend series.

We already know from the results presented in Table 4.3 that all four estimated parameters of our model have significant t ratios, indicating that the model is statistically sound. Let us now look at the residual plots to further establish the soundness of the estimated model. Figure 4.11 presents the residual histogram, the residual plot, and the ACF plot for normality. As can be seen from the residual histogram, the distribution appears to be approximately normal. The residual plot also appears to be normally distributed with approximately zero mean. The ACF plot turns out to be normal as well, as expected. This can be easily corroborated by the fact that the autocorrelations are within $\pm 2 / \sqrt{n} = \pm 2 / \sqrt{37} = \pm 2 / 6.0828 = \pm 0.3299$, indicating that the residuals are uncorrelated, which is consistent with the assumption of a random, no-trend series.

Additionally, to ensure that the residuals are uncorrelated and came from a no-trend series, we look at the Q-Q plot (Figure 4.12). As noted earlier, these

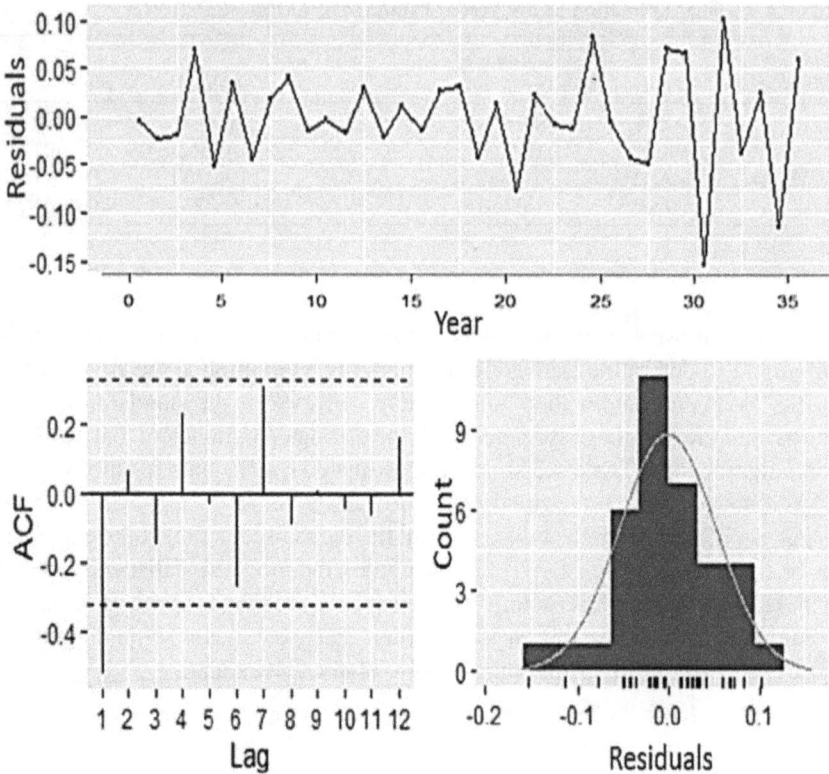

Figure 4.11   Residual Plots of ARIMA(2,2,2).

plots are visually simple and also easier to interpret than most residual plots. All the residuals clustered around the line of normality with a few outliers noticeably away from the line, indicating a random and no-trend series.

Finally, the Ljung-Box Q test produces a χ^2 value of 8.1503 with 7 degrees of freedom ($m = 7$), much lower than the corresponding critical χ^2 value of 18.5 (found in any χ^2 table). The test also produces a p-value of 0.3195, which is much higher than the significance level of α at 0.01 and 0.05; as such, we cannot reject the null hypothesis that the residuals are uncorrelated. In other words, the results provide support for the series to be random and not trended.

Forecasts

The last step in the process, once the diagnostic checks confirm the soundness of the model, is to do the forecast. Table 4.4 shows the GF revenue forecasts for the government for the next five years, along with 95% confidence

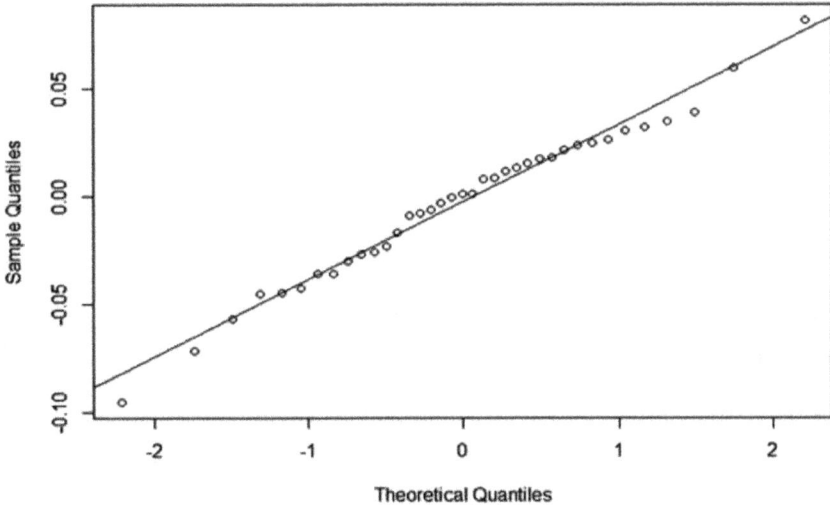

Figure 4.12   Q-Q Plot of ARIMA(2,2,2) Residuals.

intervals (CIs). The intervals are based on the assumption that the residuals are uncorrelated and normally distributed, as ARIMA requires them to ensure their validity. In general, the intervals tend to increase as the forecast time horizon increases. This is particularly true for stationary series with d > 1 (Hyndman and Athanasopoulos, 2018).

It should be worth noting that for a stationary series, in particular the series that does not require initial differencing, d = 0, the forecasts tend to converge to the estimated mean of the series. What this means is that any forecast at time t+i (where i = 1, 2, ..., T) will eventually approach a constant. This makes sense because the stationary models primarily use the information contained in the recent years of Y_t and e_i; as such, the contribution of these terms is mostly realized in the first few years of forecasts (Pankratz, 1983).

Table 4.4   GF Revenue Forecast (in Original Terms)

Year	Point Forecast ($Million)	95% CI Lower Bound	95% CI Upper Bound
t+1 (Yr. 38)	212.0152	196.8526	228.3455
t+2 (Yr. 39)	230.3890	201.7177	263.1355
t+3 (Yr. 40)	241.4238	201.142	289.7725
t+4 (Yr. 41)	243.9826	192.9928	308.4442
t+5 (Yr. 42)	244.3313	180.5225	330.6945

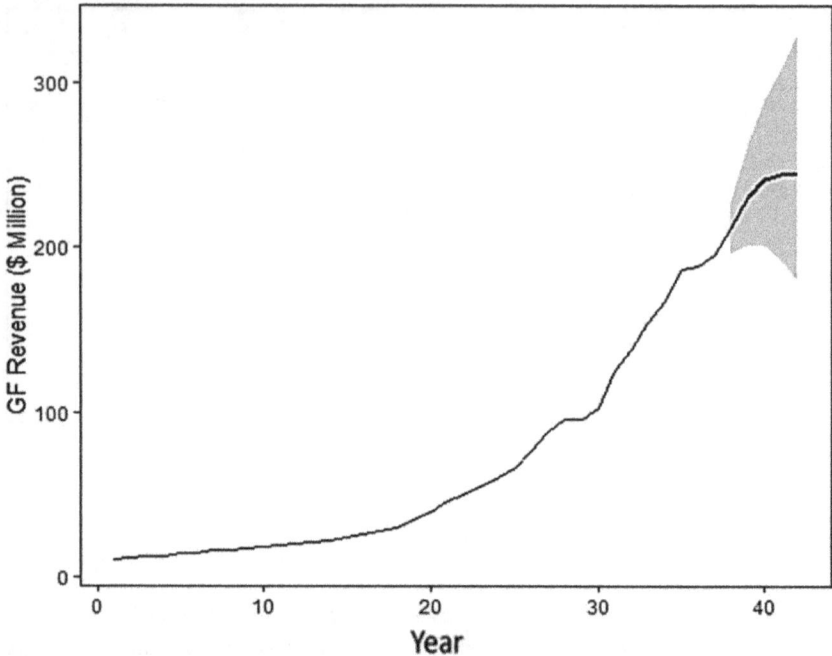

Figure 4.13   Five-Year Forecasts with 95% Confidence Bands (Shaded Area).

Figure 4.13 presents the forecast plot, including the 95% confidence bands (highlighted by the shaded area). Overall, the forecasts appear to be reasonable in light of the pattern observed in the original data that show a consistent increase in revenue over time.

Although we could have extended the forecasts to a much longer term, the ARIMA models are particularly suitable for forecasting short and intermediate terms due to the convergence of the model to the mean of the series, as noted earlier. While long-term forecasts are useful for long-term planning and developing strategies, the accuracy of the forecasts remains a question as one goes further into the time horizon. As such, and as is customary with all forecasts, short-term or long-term, it is important that the data are periodically updated and the model reestimated, as new data become available to ensure the accuracy of the forecasts, regardless of how good or sophisticated the models are, including ARIMA.

SUMMARY

This chapter has provided an overview of the well-known Box-Jenkins (B-J) method, including a broad discussion of the concept that underlies the method. To illustrate how the method is used, the chapter looked at a simple example of General Fund revenue forecast for a hypothetical local government. Unlike most conventional time series models of forecasting, B-J provides a systematic method of identifying, estimating, diagnosing, and forecasting. It has been extensively used in the private sector, as well as in government, especially for forecasting government budgets. The method is suitable for time series of medium to higher lengths, preferably 50 or more observations, but it can be used for time series of shorter lengths depending on the specific purpose for which it is used. As for forecasting, like most time series models, it is suitable for short and intermediate-term forecasts, although long-term forecasts involving five to seven years have become fairly common.

NOTES

1. There is a term frequently associated with white noise, called random walk, although the two terms are not the same. Random walk means that each successive value in a series is equal to the value in the previous period plus a random (non-systematic) term, e_t's, that is a white noise, $Y_t = Y_t \text{-} 1 + e_t$, where e_t, are independent and come from normal distribution. If the random walk includes a constant (intercept) plus the white noise term, e_t, that is, $Y_t = \alpha + Y_{t-1} + e_t$, it is known as random walk with a drift. If, instead of Y_{t-1}, it is regressed on a time trend, β_t, that is, $Y_t = \alpha + \beta_t + e_t$, it is known as random walk with a deterministic trend. On the other hand, if it contains both a drift (α) and deterministic trend (β_t), along with the white noise term, e_t, that is, $Y_t = \alpha + Y_{t-1} + \beta_t + e_t$, it is known as random walk with a drift and a deterministic trend. Interestingly, a random walk with or without a drift can be transformed into a stationary process by differencing. Differncing is one way to minimize the problem in time series regression with results that are significant, but spurious (Granger and Newbold, 1986).

2. Formally, we can write the backshift operator for AR(1), ignoring the constant term, φ_0 and with slight algebraic manipulations as

$$Y_t = \varphi_1 Y_{t-1} + e_t$$

$$Y_t = \varphi_1 B Y_t + e_t$$

$$Y_t - \varphi_1 B Y_t = e_t$$

$$(1 - \varphi_1 B) Y_t = e_t \qquad [4.1]$$

For AR(2), it would. be

$$Y_t = \varphi_1 Y_{t-1} + \varphi_2 Y_{2-1} + e_t$$

$$Y_t = \varphi_1 B Y_t + \varphi_2 B^2 Y_t + e_t$$

$$Y_t - \varphi_1 B Y_t - \varphi_2 B^2 Y_t = e_t$$

$$\left(1 - \varphi_1 B - \varphi_2 B^2\right) Y_t = e_t \qquad [4.2]$$

and, for AR(p). , it would be

$$\left(1 - \varphi_1 B - \varphi_2 B^2 - \ldots\ldots\ldots - \varphi_p B^p\right) Y_t = e_t \qquad [4.3]$$

Similarly, the backshift operator for MA(1), ignoring the constant term, θ_0 and with slight algebraic manipulations, can be written as

$$Y_t = \theta_1 e_{t-1} + e_t$$

$$Y_t = \theta_1 B e_t + e_t$$

$$Y_t = \left(\theta_1 B + 1\right) e_t$$

$$Y_t = \left(1 + \theta_1 B\right) e_t \qquad [4.4]$$

For MA(2), it would be

$$Y_t = \theta_1 e_{t-1} + \theta_2 e_{t-2} + e_t$$

$$Y_t = \theta_1 B e_t + \theta_2 B^2 e_t + e_t$$

$$Y_t = \left(\theta_1 B + \theta_2 B^2 + 1\right) e_t$$

$$Y_t = \left(1 + \theta_1 B + \theta_2 B^2\right) e_t \qquad [4.5]$$

and, f. or MA (q), it would be

$$Y_t = \left(1 + \theta_1 B + \theta_2 B^2 + \ldots\ldots\ldots + \theta_q B^q\right) e_t \qquad [4.6]$$

Finally, the backshift operator for the ARMA model with p and q orders can be written as a combination of AR(p) and MA(q)

$$Y_t = \varphi_1 Y_{t-1} + \varphi_2 Y_{t-2} + \ldots\ldots + \varphi_p Y_{t-p} + e_t + \theta_1 e_{t-1} + \theta_2 e_{t-2}$$

$$+ \ldots\ldots + \theta_q e_{t-q} \qquad [4.7]$$

$$\left(1 - \varphi_1 B - \varphi_2 B^2 - \ldots\ldots - \varphi_p B^p\right) Y_t = \left(1 + \theta_1 B + \theta_2 B^2 + \ldots\ldots + \theta_q B^q\right) e_t \quad [4.8]$$

3. In general, if a time series is stationary the observed data points will fluctuate around constant mean, whi. le for non-stationary series they will fluctuate around a trend path. The Box-Jenkinks methodology generally assumes the data being studied are stationary.

4. The augmented Dicky-Fuller test, also known as ADF test, is generally used to test the null hypothesis that a unit root is present in a series, i.e., the series is non-stationary; the alternative hypothesis indicates that the series is stationary. The ADF statistic is a negative value. In general, the larger the negative value, the less the likelihood that the series is non-stationary, i.e., reject the null hypothesis that a unit root is present.

Like the augmented Dickey-Fuller test, the Phillips-Perron test is a unit-root test and is used to test the null hypothesis that the time series is integrated of order 1. The advantage of using Phillips-Peron is that it corrects for any serial correlation and heteroskedasticity in the error term by modifying the Dickey-Fuller test statistic. The modification, which makes it more robust than Dickey-Fuller, is done using Newey-West (1987) heteroskedasticity and autocorrelation-consistent covariance (matrix) estimator. However, some believe that under certain circumstances, such as limited sample, it may not be as effective as the augmented Dickey-Fuller test (Davidson and McKinnon, 2004). Besides ADF and Phillips-Peron, there are other tests one can use such as KPSS (Kwiatkowski-Phillips-Schmidt-Shin), Harris-Tzavalis, Levin-Lin-Chu, and Breitung and Das, among others.

5. Also known as modified Box-Pierce test, Lejung-Box Q test is used to examine the residuals in a time series, in particular, from an observed ARMA model to see if the underlying population autocorrelations for the residuals (errors) are zero, as specified by the forecaster. Put differently, the null hypothesis for the test indicates that the data are independently distributed, meaning that the population correlations (autocorrelations in the case of ARMA) for the residuals from which the sample has been drawn are zero in that any observed correlation or autocorrelation, as the case may be, in the data are due to randomness of the sampling process. The alternative hypothesis obviously means that the data are not independently distributed, i.e., they indicate the presence of serial correlation.

6. AIC (Akaike Information Criterion) is frequently used in ARIMA models to measure the efficiency of the order combination of AR and MA models. Given a range of models for a time series, AIC estimates the efficiency, i.e., the quality of each model relative to other models. In general, a lower value indicates efficiency. In other words, the lower the value of AIC the more efficient, i.e., the better is the quality of the model.

7. The maximum likelihood estimation (MLE) method is used for estimating the parameter of a probability distribution by maximizing the likelihood function, i.e., finding the parameter values that maximize the likelihood of the observed data in a statistical model. In other words, MLE finds the probability of obtaining the data we have observed. For ARIMA models, it is similar to the OLS estimates that we obtain by minimizing the sum of the squared errors, i.e., minimize $\sum_{t}^{T} e_t^2$, for t ranging from 1,2,.......,T (Hyndman and Athanaspoulos, 2018).

Chapter 5

Seasonal ARIMA Models

Seasonal behavior of budgetary activities, especially those related to revenues and expenditures, is a common occurrence in government. As noted previously, local governments collect most of their property tax revenue at the beginning of the calendar year and the utility revenue more during the months when the utility consumption is high. While the state governments collect sales tax revenue throughout the year, it tends to increase during the holiday season than at other times. Income tax revenue, on the other hand, is not seasonal but reflects the changes in the business cycle. Similarly, government expenditures also reflect seasonal patterns, especially at the local level, when expenditures tend to increase during the holiday season or during the summer months when the level of outdoor activities tends to increase, while remaining more or less the same at other times.

Although somewhat more complicated than forecasting with regular, non-seasonal series, it is important that budget forecasts take into consideration these changes in the data to produce good and reliable forecasts. This chapter extends the discussion on time series models to include ARIMA models with seasonal data.

SEASONAL TIME SERIES

When the data in a time series exhibit a pattern of behavior that repeats at regular time intervals, such as those described above, they are called seasonal data. The intervals within which the data exhibit these patterns of behavior during a season, called seasonal periods, can be for any length of time—a week, a month, a quarter, or any other time length. Thus, a season of one year with weekly data has 52 periods, monthly data has 12 periods, quarterly data has 4 periods, and so forth.

While the seasonal behavior has a tendency to exhibit a certain basic pattern that is consistent across seasons, the basic pattern itself can change over time, from season to season and over the entire length of the series. For instance, the peaks at the height of the season may change from one season to the next, just as troughs can change from one season to the next. Also, it is not uncommon for a seasonal series to contain other patterns of behavior, such as those related to special events or activities that take place periodically but not necessarily at regular intervals, in which case the seasonal models should be able to reflect these patterns in the series in some fashion (Makridakis and Wheelright, 1978).

In general, seasonal behavior in a series means that there exists a relationship among the series values separated by the number of periods in a season. For instance, if we are dealing with a monthly series, then the value of one month, say, September, will be related to the values of all September in the series. The same will be for all the months in the series and, in each case, it will be separated by 12 months, s = 12, which is the number of periods in a season. If we are dealing with a quarterly series, s = 4, the same pattern of behavior will be reflected for the same quarter among the successive seasons in the series, and so forth.[1]

Basic Structure

Structurally, a seasonal ARIMA process is very similar to regular, nonseasonal ARIMA, with the difference that the seasonal periods are treated as a supplement to the regular ARIMA process since they take place within the same annual time series. What this means is that a seasonal ARIMA process has both nonseasonal and seasonal components, but to distinguish between the two, the seasonal model uses upper cases for autoregressive parameters (P), differencing (D), and moving average parameters (Q). In other words, a typical seasonal ARIMA model with both autoregressive (AR) and moving average (MA) parameters is characterized by (p,d,q) for the regular component and (P,D,Q) for the seasonal component of the model. That is,

$$Seasonal\ ARIMA(p,d,q)(P,D,Q)_s$$

where s is the number of terms or periods in a season.

Like a regular, nonseasonal ARIMA model, the presence of a seasonal AR parameter in the model would suggest that there is autocorrelation in the data, meaning that the current level of the forecast variable for a given period in the series, Y_t, say, a month or quarter can be explained by the past values of the variable for the same month or quarter for successive seasons, plus a random error that occurs in the present. Thus, for a seasonal autoregressive (SAR) model with one AR parameter (P = 1); that is, SAR(1), the relationship among the first period of successive seasons, can be written as

$$Y_t = \Phi_1 Y_{t-s} + e_t \tag{5.1}$$

where Y_t is the forecast variable, Φ is the model parameter, s is the seasonal component (i.e., number of observations or periods in a season), and e_t is the error term, assumed to be approximately normally distributed with 0 mean and constant variance, $e_t \sim n(0, \sigma^2)$, similar to the basic ARIMA model, discussed earlier.

Similarly, for a SAR model with two AR parameters (P = 2); that is, SAR(2), the relationship between the second period of successive seasons can be written as

$$Y_t = \Phi_1 Y_{t-s} + \Phi_2 Y_{t-2s} + e_t \tag{5.2}$$

and for a SAR model with P AR parameters; that is, SAR(P), it will be

$$Y_t = \Phi_1 Y_{t-s} + \Phi_2 Y_{t-2s} + \ldots\ldots\ldots + \Phi_p Y_{t-ps} + e_t \tag{5.3}$$

As with SAR models, the presence of seasonal moving average (SMA) parameters would indicate that the series values can be explained by the past random errors for successive seasons, plus a new random error that occurs in the present. Thus, a SMA model with one MA parameter (Q = 1); that is, SMA(1), would indicate the past random errors related to period 1 of successive seasons, plus a new random error that occurs in the present, and can be written as

$$Y_t = \Theta_1 e_{t-s} + e_t \tag{5.4}$$

where Y_t is the forecast variable, θ is the model parameter, and the rest of the terms are the same as before. Also, as noted before, the random errors are small shocks or disturbances, called "white noise," that initially set the process in motion and continue it afterward.

Similarly, an SMA model with two MA parameters (Q = 2); that is, SMA(2), would indicate the past random errors related to period 2 of successive seasons, plus a new random error that occurs in the present and can be written as

$$Y_t = \Theta_1 e_{t-s} + \Theta_2 e_{t-2s} + e_t \tag{5.5}$$

and for an SMA model with Q MA parameters; that is, SMA(Q), it will be

$$Y_t = \Theta_1 e_{t-s} + \Theta_2 e_{t-2s} + \ldots\ldots\ldots + \Theta_Q e_{t-Qs} + e_t \qquad (5.6)$$

If both SAR and SMA are present in the same model, for a first-order seasonal ARIMA model, it can be written as

$$Y_t = \Phi_1 Y_{t-s} + e_t + \Theta_1 e_{t-s} \qquad (5.7)$$

Likewise, for a second-order seasonal ARIMA model with both parameters, it can be written as

$$Y_t = \Phi_1 Y_{t-s} + \Phi_2 Y_{t-2s} + e_t + \Theta_1 e_{t-s} + \Theta_2 e_{t-2s} \qquad (5.8)$$

and for a seasonal ARIMA model with P and Q orders, equation 5.8 can easily be extended to include the new orders so that the new equation will be

$$Y_t = \Phi_1 Y_{t-s} + \Phi_2 Y_{t-2s} + \ldots\ldots\ldots + \Phi_P Y_{t-Ps} + e_t + \Theta_1 e_{t-s}$$
$$+ \Theta_2 e_{t-2s} + \ldots\ldots\ldots + \Theta_Q e_{t-Qs} \qquad (5.9)$$

where all the terms are the same as before.

Seasonal Differencing

Seasonal time series, like regular nonseasonal series, often exhibit strong fluctuations in the data that are nonstationary. As mentioned earlier, nonstationarity is usually due to the presence of trends resulting from periodic and systematic changes in the data, which can be easily removed with measures such as log transformation or differencing, or both. Thus, if a series is differenced once, it is a seasonal ARIMA model of order one with first nonseasonal differencing; if it is differenced twice, it is a seasonal ARIMA model of order two with second nonseasonal differencing, and so forth.

Formally, a seasonal ARIMA(1,1,1)(1,1,1)$_s$ model of order 1 can be written as

$$(1 - \Phi_1 B)(1 - \Phi_1 B^s)(1 - B^s)(1 - B)Y_t = (1 + \Theta_1 B)(1 + \Theta_1 B^s)e_t \quad (5.10)$$

where s stands for season.

Likewise, a seasonal ARIMA(2,2,2)(2,2,2)$_s$ model of order 2 can be written as

$$\left(1-\Phi_1 B - \Phi_2 B^2\right)\left(1-\Phi_1 B^s - \Phi_2 B^{2s}\right)\left(1-B^s\right)^2\left(1-B\right)^2 Y_t$$

$$=\left(1+\Theta_1 B+\Theta_2 B^2\right)\left(1+\Theta_1 B^s+\Theta_2 B^{2s}\right)e_t \qquad (5.11)$$

and for a seasonal ARIMA(p,d,q)(P,D,Q)$_s$ model of order D, it can be written as

$$\left(1-\Phi_1 B - \Phi_2 B^2 - \ldots\ldots - \Phi_P B^P\right)\left(1-\Phi_1 B^s - \Phi_2 B^{2s} - \ldots\ldots - \Phi_P B^{Ps}\right)$$

$$\left(1-B^s\right)^D\left(1-B\right)^d Y_t = (1+\Theta_1 B+\Theta_2 B^2 + \ldots\ldots + \Theta_Q B^Q)$$

$$\left(1 + \Theta_1 B^s + \Theta_2 B^{2s} + \ldots\ldots + \Theta_Q B^{Qs}\right)e_t \qquad (5.12)$$

where s is the number of observations or periods in a season. Note that the seasonal part of the model consists of terms similar to the nonseasonal components of the model but involves backshifts of the seasonal period.

Seasonal ARIMA Process

Operationally, a seasonal ARIMA model follows the same basic steps as the regular, nonseasonal ARIMA model: Identification, estimation, diagnostic checks, and forecasting. The process begins once the model has been detrended for stationarity, followed by identification—the most important step in the process since everything else follows from it. As with regular, nonseasonal models, identification allows us to determine the best model for estimation based on the most appropriate SAR, SMA, or a mixed seasonal ARMA structure. This is done with the help of correlation plots (correlograms) showing the autocorrelation (AC) and partial autocorrelation (PAC) for SAR and SMA processes, similar to regular ARIMA models, discussed earlier.

In general, correlations tend to be smaller at higher lags for both AR and MA processes as additional parameters are added to the model. The conventional wisdom for the regular ARIMA model, which also applies to seasonal models, is to keep the model parsimonious; in other words, keep the number of parameters vis-a-vis the order of the AR and MA processes as low as possible.

The next set of steps are pretty much the same as those discussed earlier: A range of statistical tests, such as the augmented Dickey-Fuller (ADF) and Phillips-Peron (PP) tests on the original and differenced or log-transformed series, or both, to ensure that the series has been properly detrended for stationarity. This is followed by measures to determine the appropriate order

of the model. Finally, once the model has been properly identified, it is estimated, followed by a series of statistical tests to ensure that it is statistically
sound. This typically includes measures such as *t* ratios, residual histogram,
Q-Q plot, Ljung-Box Q test, and so forth, as discussed earlier. The process
completes with the forecasts.

SEASONAL ARIMA WITH QUARTERLY DATA

To illustrate, let us look at a couple of examples involving the general
sales tax revenue of a state government. We will look at both quarterly and
monthly data, starting with quarterly revenues. Let us say that we have the
quarterly sales tax revenue data for the government for the last 65 quarters
(Table 5.1).[2] Sales tax revenue constitutes the single most important source
of revenue for most state governments; in some cases, by as much 50 percent
or more of the total revenue, especially for states that do not have an income
tax to supplement the sales tax revenue.

Table 5.1   Sales Tax Revenue: Quarterly Data

N of Qtrs. (Quarter)	Sales Tax Rev. ($Million)	N of Qtrs. (Quarter)	Sales Tax Rev. ($Million)	N of Qtrs. (Quarter)	Sales Tax Rev. ($Million)
1-Q1	3676.314	23-Q3	5547.248	45-Q1	7151.766
2-Q2	3835.809	24-Q4	5007.777	46-Q2	7248.544
3-Q3	3964.583	25-Q1	4974.838	47-Q3	7367.274
4-Q4	3883.405	26-Q2	4686.458	48-Q4	6998.104
5-Q1	3904.886	27-Q3	4903.542	49-Q1	7173.469
6-Q2	3913.394	28-Q4	4909.866	50-Q2	7071.422
7-Q3	4094.585	29-Q1	5060.191	51-Q3	7075.589
8-Q4	4011.545	30-Q2	5033.583	52-Q4	6931.030
9-Q1	4236.440	31-Q3	5385.575	53-Q1	7058.524
10-Q2	4283.424	32-Q4	5422.183	54-Q2	6918.111
11-Q3	4681.717	33-Q1	5559.179	55-Q3	7274.981
12-Q4	4486.350	34-Q2	5699.471	56-Q4	7151.123
13-Q1	4749.354	35-Q3	5988.986	57-Q1	7452.506
14-Q2	4851.322	36-Q4	6038.661	58-Q2	7576.926
15-Q3	5095.817	37-Q1	6373.034	69-Q3	8001.233
16-Q4	5053.431	38-Q2	6327.128	60-Q4	7893.054
17-Q1	5182.774	39-Q3	6371.577	61-Q1	8360.016
18-Q2	5171.403	40-Q4	6389.221	62-Q2	8341.699
19-Q3	5485.482	41-Q1	6754.232	63-Q3	8501.957
20-Q4	5220.188	42-Q2	6554.858	64-Q4	8471.729
21-Q1	5639.003	43-Q3	6754.461	65-Q1	8708.532
22-Q2	5405.531	44-Q4	6813.039	---	---

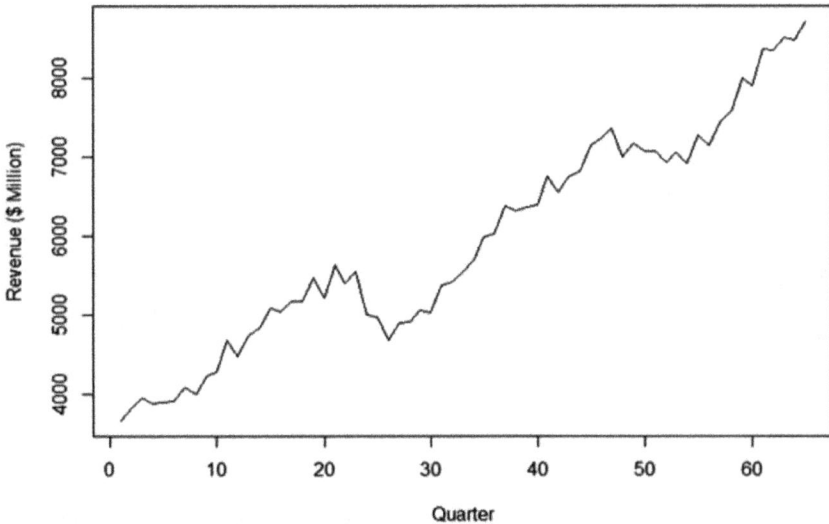

Figure 5.1   The Original Series.

Figure 5.1 shows the growth trend of sales tax revenue for the state. A quick glance at the figure would indicate that the government has been experiencing considerable growth in revenue over the years, for instance, from roughly $3676 million in Quarter-1, to about $8709 million in Quarter-65, a 136.88 percent increase over a little over 16-year period. However, there were some downward trends in the data for several quarters, for instance, from Quarter-24 through Quarter-32, and again from Quarter-48 through Quarter-56, with an occasional dip or two in between. Interestingly, each dip was followed by a period of continuous growth. On the whole, the pattern shows a sustained increase in revenue during the entire period.

As the figure shows, there is an upward trend in the data indicating that the series is not stationary and that differencing is necessary. The initial (first) seasonal differencing of the series does not appear to have significantly detrended the data (Figure 5.2), indicating that a nonseasonal differencing would be helpful. In general, seasonal differencing tends to remove the seasonal trends, as well as any seasonal random walk that may be due to nonstationarity. If the trend is still present in the data, a nonseasonal differencing may be necessary to remove the trend (since our model consists of both seasonal and nonseasonal components). The nonseasonal differencing of the series after the initial first seasonal differencing seems to have considerably improved the results, as the series appears stationary (Figure 5.3).

To further ensure that the series is stationary, we conduct a hypothesis test, similar to the test for the regular nonseasonal ARIMA in the previous chapter

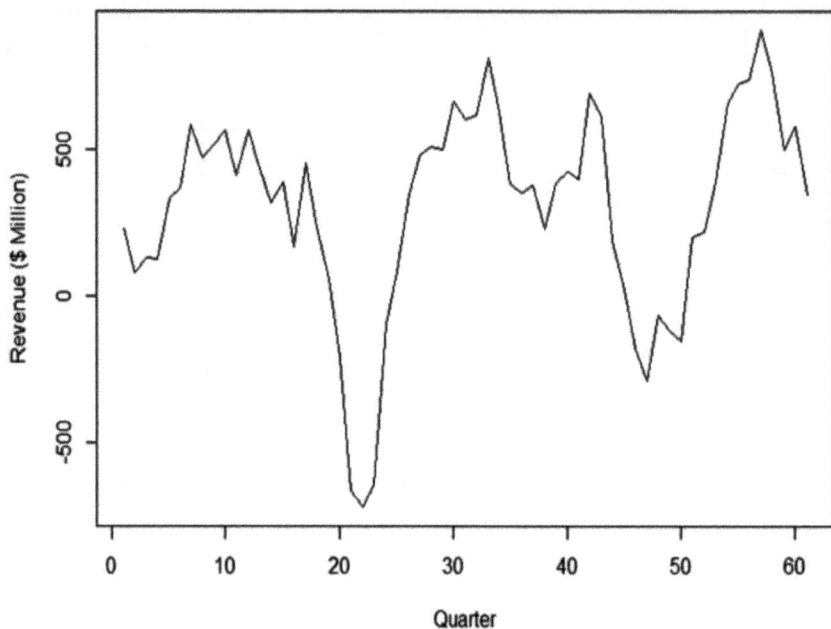

Figure 5.2 Series after First Seasonal Differencing.

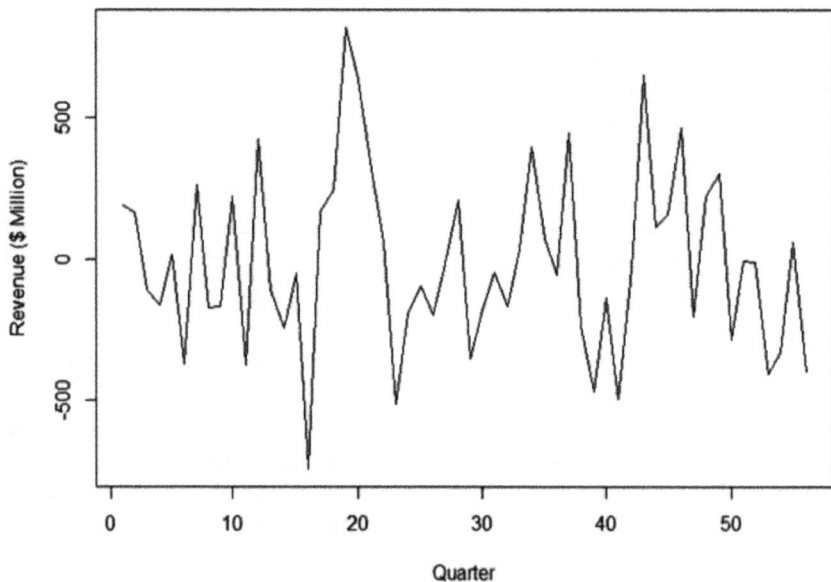

Figure 5.3 Series after (First) Non-seasonal Differencing of the (First) Differenced-Seasonal Data.

(H_0: The series is not stationary, and H_A: The series is stationary), using both ADF and PP, and examine the test results to draw the appropriate conclusion. The following provides a brief summary of the test results for ADF and PP, before and after differencing:

Sales Tax Revenue: Original series
 Test Statistic (ADF): -2.2525, Lag order = 3, p-value = 0.4726
 Test Statistic (PP): -10.8840, Lag parameter = 3, p-value = 0.4683
Sales Tax Revenue: Series after (first) seasonal differencing
 Test Statistic (ADF): -4.0597, Lag order = 3, p-value = 0.0123
 Test Statistic (PP): -14.0270, Lag parameter = 3, p-value = 0.2762
Sales Tax Revenue: Series after (first) nonseasonal differencing of the (first) differenced-seasonal data
 Test Statistic (ADF): -5.6463, Lag order = 3, $p < 0.01$
 Test Statistic (PP): -49.1930, Lag parameter = 3, $p < 0.01$

As the results show, the p-values for both ADF and PP appear to be high and insignificant for the original series, indicating that differencing is necessary to detrend the series. The first differencing seemed to have improved the result for ADF but not for PP, suggesting that additional differencing is necessary to detrend the series. Accordingly, we do a nonseasonal differencing of the first differenced-seasonal series to see if it would further improve the results. As expected, the additional differencing of the series improved the results for both ADF and PP, as both appear to be statistically significant at $p < 0.01$. We can, therefore, reject the null hypothesis and safely conclude (i.e., accept the alternative hypothesis) that the series is stationary.

Model Identification

With the data thus detrended, the next step is to examine the various ACF and PACF plots to determine the order of AR and MA processes, together with various error measurement statistics to ensure that the selected model is the best possible for estimation and forecasting. Interestingly, no clear order emerges from the plots for the original series (not shown here), indicating the need for both regular and seasonal differenced plots of the data. Figures 5.4 and 5.5 show the ACF and PACF plots after the first seasonal difference. As the plots show, the first seasonal difference in the data does not reflect any significant improvement. Interestingly, while the ACF plot shows some decay (Figure 5.4), the PACF plot does not depict any clear order (Figure 5.5).

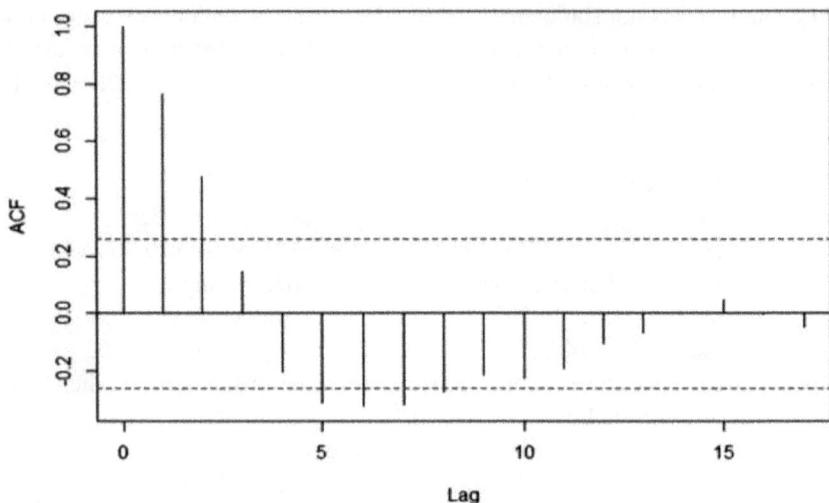

Figure 5.4   ACF Plot after First seasonal difference.

Since none of the ACF and PACF plots provide clear evidence of dis-cernible orders at any lag, with the exception of partial autocorrelations at lags 4 and 8, after the seasonal and regular nonseasonal difference, we look

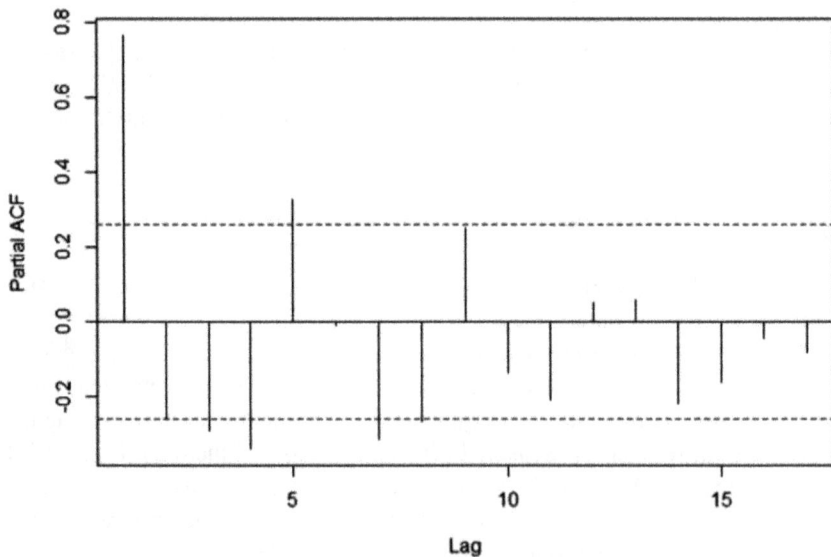

Figure 5.5   PACF Plot after First Seasonal Difference.

Table 5.2   Order Combination of AR and MA Terms and Error Measurement

Order Combination	RMSE	MAPE	MASE	AIC
ARIMA(1,1,1)(0,1,1)4	132.2064	1.78524	0.5965948	780.0195
ARIMA(1,1,1)(1,1,1)4	132.3988	1.80774	0.6044132	781.5795
ARIMA(2,1,1)(1,1,1)4	131.5350	1.786385	0.5984314	782.8360
ARIMA(2,1,1)(0,1,1)4	164.7012	2.185501	0.7376637	798.2432

at the various error measurement statistics, such as those discussed earlier (e.g., RMSE, MAPE, MASE, and AIC) to determine the final order of the model.[3] Table 5.2 shows the ARIMA models with different order combinations and corresponding errors. In fact, several other models were also run with different order combinations, but we included here only the ones with small errors.

As can be seen from the table, the first model, ARIMA(1,1,1)(0,1,1)4, has the smallest MAPE, MASE, AIC, and a reasonably good RMSE. Although ARIMA(2,1,1)(1,1,1)4 appears to have a slightly better RMSE, two of its MA coefficients do not appear to be statistically significant and, as such, it was excluded from consideration. As before, we could have used higher order models, but there is no guarantee that higher order models would necessarily produce better results. Also, as noted earlier, parsimony is an important consideration is selecting the order in a time-series model, especially for ARIMA. Therefore, of the four models, ARIMA(1,1,1)(0,1,1)4 appears to be the best for model estimation and forecasting.

Model Estimation

As before, once the model has been identified, the next step in the process is to estimate the model parameters. The estimation process requires the use of both least squares and nonlinear least squares criteria to obtain the estimates. As discussed previously, the least squares criterion is generally used for AR(p) models since the parameters of the model could be obtained by regressing Y_t on Y_{t-1}, Y_{t-2}, ..., Y_{t-p}. On the other hand, for MA(q), as well as mixed models, the convention is to use the nonlinear least squares method, as noted earlier, such as the maximum likelihood estimation (MLE), which is much more suitable for dealing with nonlinear functions than the conventional least squares method.

The following presents the estimated model for ARIMA(1,1,1)(0,1,1)4:

$$(1 - 0.6866B)(1 - B)(1 - B^4)Y_t = (1 - 1.4913B)(1 - 1.00B^4)e_t$$

Once a model has been estimated, as we did for the regular nonseasonal model, it is important to determine how good the model is by looking at the significance of the estimated parameters. Therefore, we look at some of the same statistics we looked at for the regular nonseasonal model, namely standard errors, *t* ratios, and the *p*-values, to determine the significance of the estimated parameters.[4] Table 5.3 shows the estimated coefficients for the AR, MA, and SMA terms and their corresponding standard errors, *t* ratios, and their corresponding *p*-values.

As the table shows, all the terms used in the model came out to be significant, with *p*-values ranging between <0.001 and <0.05, indicating that the model is statistically significant. However, as is customary with ARIMA models, before doing the forecasts, it is important that we conduct some diagnostic checks to further ensure the statistical soundness of the model and the series used for model estimation.

Diagnostic Checks

In general, diagnostic checks are conducted to ensure that the residuals are uncorrelated in that they have zero mean with constant variance and are normally distributed. As we noted previously, two sets of checks are generally conducted: *t* ratios and residual analysis. The t ratios tell us if the model is statistically sound, while the residual analysis tells us if we are dealing with a random, no-trend series. We already know from the results presented in Table 5.3 that all three estimated parameters of our model have significant *t* ratios, indicating that the model is statistically sound. The residual analysis, which typically includes the residual histogram, the residual plot, and the ACF plot, also indicates the soundness of the estimated model (Figure 5.6).

As can be seen from the residual histogram, the distribution of the residuals appears to be approximately normal. The residual plot by quarter also appears to be normally distributed with approximately zero mean. Similarly, the ACF plot gives the impression of no correlation among the residuals. And as can be seen from the plot, autocorrelations are within $\pm 2 / \sqrt{n} = 2 / \sqrt{66} = \pm\, 2 / 8.1240 = \pm\, 0.2462$,

Table 5.3   Final Estimation of the Model Parameters: ARIMA(1,1,1)(0,1,1)4

Order Number	Model Type	Estimated Coefficients	Std. Errors	t Ratios*	p-value
1	AR1	0.6866	0.2219	3.0942	<0.001
1	MA1	-0.4913	0.2443	-2.0111	0.0486
1	SMA1	-1.0000	0.1824	-5.4825	<0.001

*df = n-(p+q+P+Q+1) = 65-(1+1+0+1+1) = 61

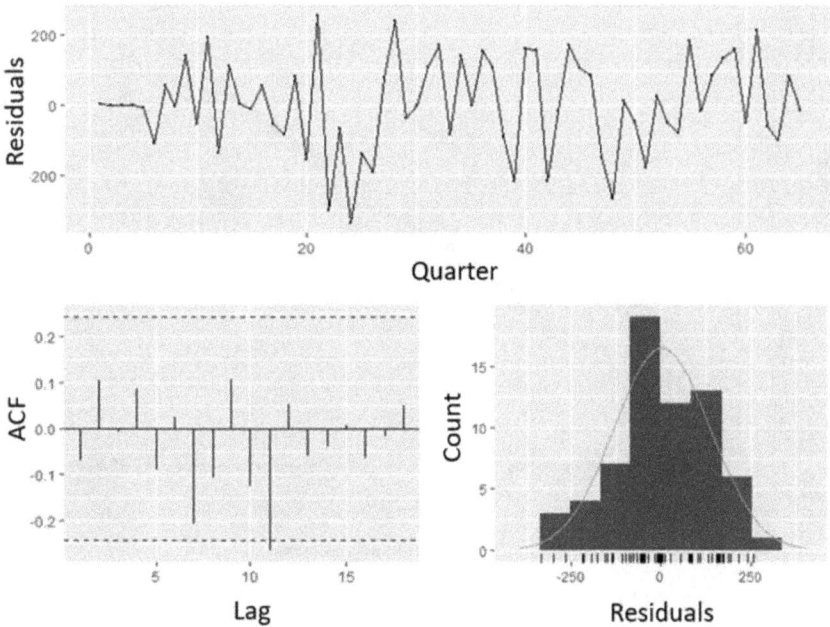

Figure 5.6   Residual Plots for ARIMA(1,1,1)(0,1,1)4.

indicating that the residuals are uncorrelated, which is consistent with the assumption of a random and no-trend series. Additionally, the Q-Q plot of the residuals also shows that they are uncorrelated and came from a no-trend series (Figure 5.7).

Finally, the Ljung-Box Q test produces a χ^2 value of 8.5229, with 7 degrees of freedom (m = 7) and a *p*-value of 0.2887, which is lower than the critical χ^2 value of 18.5 (found in any χ^2 table). Also, the observed *p*-value of 0.2887 is much higher than the conventional significance levels of α at 0.01 and 0.05, indicating that there is not sufficient evidence to reject the null hypothesis that the residuals are uncorrelated. In other words, there is strong and significant support for the series to be random and not trended.

Forecasts

The diagnostic checks confirm that the model, as a whole, is statistically sound, thus setting the stage for forecasting. Table 5.4 shows the revenue forecasts for the government for the next eight quarters, with 95% confidence intervals (CIs). Overall, the forecasts appear reasonably good, given the seasonal pattern observed in the original series.

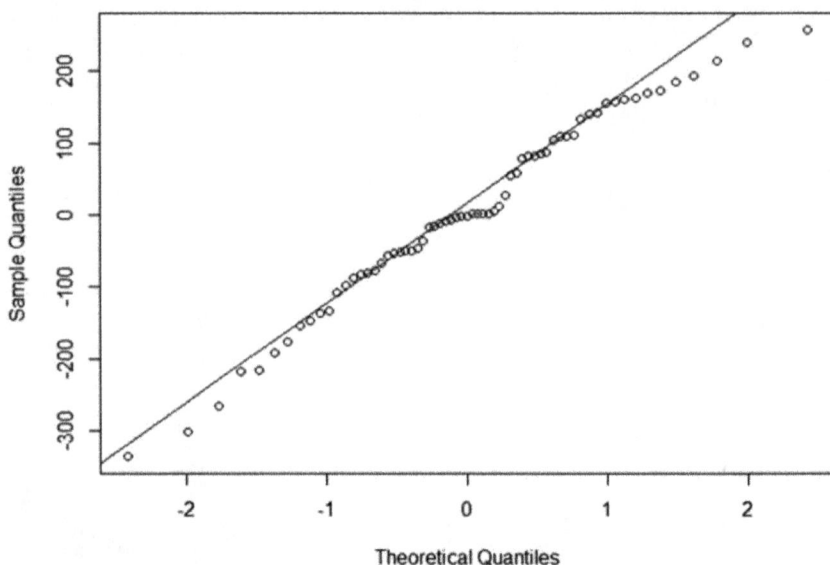

Figure 5.7   The Q-Q Plot of Residuals for ARIMA(1,1,1)(0,1,1)4.

As noted earlier, seasonal data, including those for sales tax revenue, are directly related to factors such as demand for goods and services in a regular annual cycle. In other words, it will increase during certain times of the year when demand is high and decrease when the demand is low, assuming no changes in the purchasing power, the general condition of the economy, and so forth. This is clearly reflected in the forecasts. As the table shows, the revenue is projected to increase for six of eight forecast quarters, except for Quarter-68, t+3, and Quarter-72, t+7, when they will decline by a small percentage from the previous quarter and then going back up in the next quarter.

Table 5.4   Quarterly Forecasts for State Sales Tax Revenue

Time (t) Period-Qtr.	Point Forecast ($Million)	95% CI Lower Bound	95% CI Upper Bound
t+1 (66-Q2)	8695.253	8493.637	8973.199
t+2 (67-Q3)	8926.698	8493.637	9359.758
t+3 (68-Q4)	8819.484	8250.433	9388.534
t+4 (69-Q1)	9053.326	8360.939	9745.712
t+5 (70-Q2)	9032.610	8218.658	9846.562
t+6 (71-Q3)	9258.949	8332.269	10185.629
t+7 (72-Q4)	9148.229	8116.701	10179.757
t+8 (73-Q1)	9379.664	8250.295	10509.034

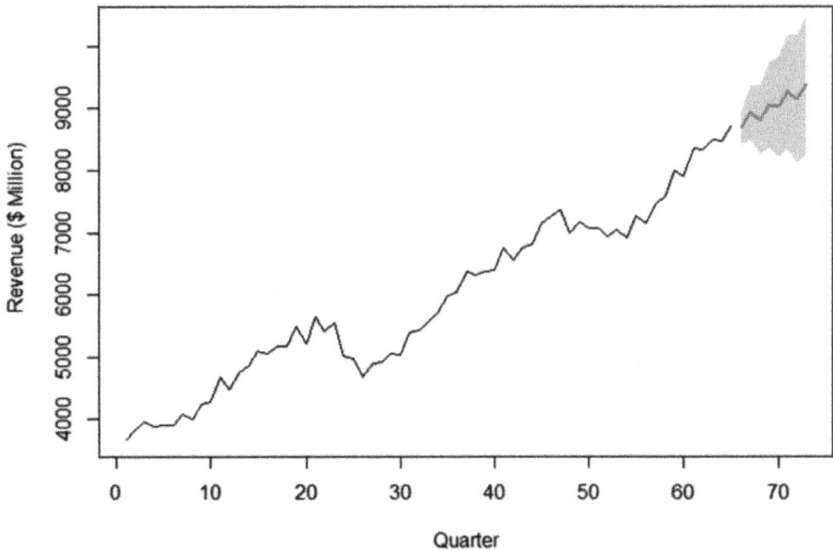

Figure 5.8 Quarterly Forecasts with 95% Confidence Bands (Shaded Area).

Figure 5.8 shows the forecasts, including the 95% confidence bands (highlighted by the shaded area). As can be seen from the figure, the revenue is expected to continue to increase for the forecast period, with a couple of dips in between, consistent with the general growth pattern of the series.

Theoretically, we could have extended the forecasts to a much longer term. But, as noted earlier, time-series models in general and ARIMA models, in particular, are suitable for forecasting short and intermediate terms due to the convergence of the model to the series, indicating very little improvement in the forecasts afterward.

SEASONAL ARIMA WITH MONTHLY DATA

In the example presented above, we looked at the quarterly sales tax revenue, but, as noted earlier, seasonal time series also applies to monthly data. To illustrate, let us go back to the state sales tax revenue data we used for quarterly forecasts, but for months. To keep the discussion and analysis consistent, we will use the same time length for the series we used for the quarterly data (Appendix 3).[5] We thus have a total of 180 months, instead of 65 quarters, beginning with the month of September for period 1 and ending with the month of August for period 180. Interestingly, since we are using the

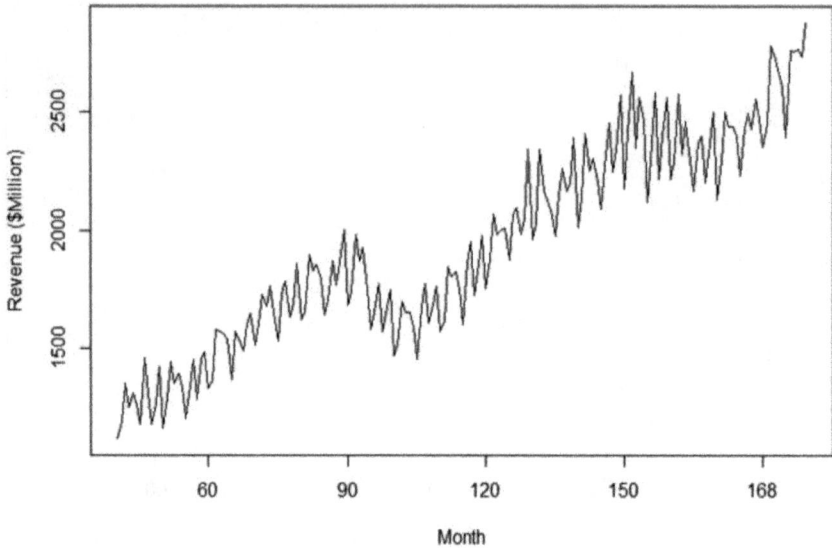

Figure 5.9   The Original Series.

same revenue data for the same time length, except that they are in months, we should expect the data to exhibit a similar seasonal growth pattern that we observed for the quarterly series.

It should be worth noting that unlike property tax revenue or revenue from user fees and charges, sales tax revenue is particularly vulnerable to the general condition of the national economy that can get easily reflected in the revenue trend. For instance, the downward trend observed in the series was about the time in 2008–2009 when the country as a whole was going through a major recession. The effect of the economic downturn was felt by most states in the country, especially those that rely heavily on sales tax revenue. Interestingly, the state was able to bounce back faster than most other states in the country, reflecting a growth pattern that is reasonably strong, although there was a slight downward trend for a short period toward the tail-end of the series before it began to climb-up again. On the whole, the pattern shows a sustained and consistent increase in revenue during the entire period with some dips in between. Figure 5.9 shows this growth pattern in revenue.

Looking at the figure, it is clearly evident that there is an upward trend in the data indicating that the series is not stationary and that differencing is necessary. Also, since we are using the same data we used for the quarterly series, but for months, it is expected that the initial (first) seasonal differencing will not fully detrend the series (Figure 5.10), indicating that nonseasonal

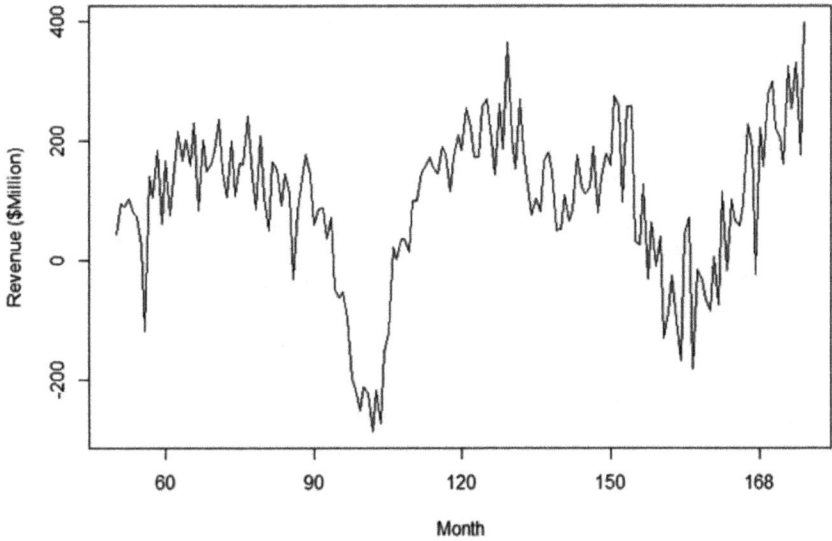

Figure 5.10   Series after First Seasonal Differencing.

differencing is necessary. The nonseasonal differencing of the data, which is the (first) nonseasonal differencing of the (first) differenced-seasonal series, appears to have significantly improved the results, as the series appears to have achieved considerable stationarity (Figure 5.11).

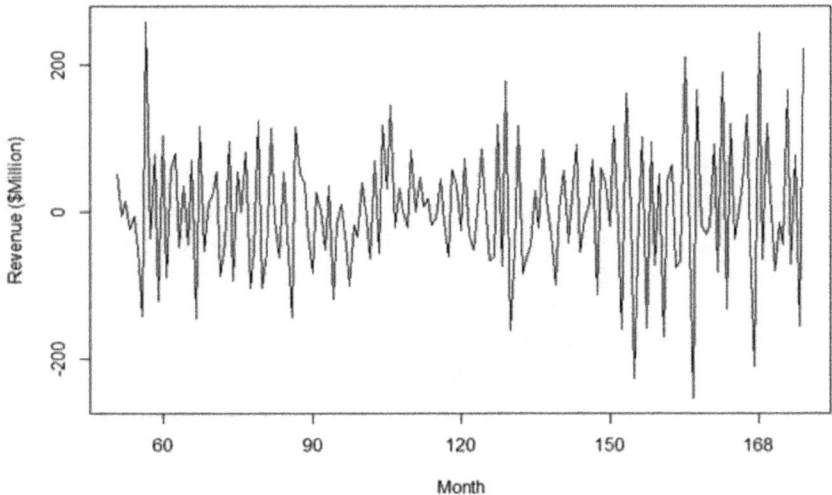

Figure 5.11   Series after (First) Non-seasonal Differencing of the (First) Differenced-Seasonal Data.

As before, we conduct a hypothesis test after each differencing to further ensure that the series is stationary (H_0: The series is not stationary, and H_1: The series is stationary). The results of the tests are presented below:

Sales Tax Revenue: Original series
    Test Statistic (ADF): -1.3554, Lag order = 5, p-value = 0.8456
    Test Statistic (PP): -125.62, Lag parameter = 4, $p < 0.01$
Sales Tax Revenue: Series after (first) seasonal differencing
    Test Statistic (ADF): -1.8649, Lag order = 5, p-value = 0.6327
    Test Statistic (PP): -33.0350, Lag parameter = 4, $p < 0.01$
Sales Tax Revenue: Series after (first) nonseasonal differencing of the (first) differenced-seasonal data
    Test Statistic (ADF): -5.5919, Lag order = 5, $p < 0.01$
    Test Statistic (PP): -219.12, Lag parameter = 4, $p < 0.01$

As expected, since we are using the same time length for both series, the initial differencing gives a mixed signal, indicating that while it improved the situation somewhat, it has not achieved the needed stationarity. This is clearly evident in the p-value for ADF, which was rather high at 0.6327, but turned out to be quite low for PP at $p < 0.01$; hence, the mixed signal. The results further suggest that additional differencing is necessary to detrend the series. The second differencing appears to have considerably improved the results for both ADF and PP, as the p-values for both appear to be quite low at <0.01, indicating that the results are statistically significant. This allows us to reject the null hypothesis and, as before, safely conclude (i.e., accept the alternative hypothesis) that the series is stationary.

Model Identification

As with the quarterly data, once the series has been detrended for stationarity, we construct the ACF and PACF plots to see if we are able to determine the order combination for the model. This is necessary to determine the AR and MA processes that would be most appropriate for model selection and estimation. As before, the ACF and PACF plots do not show any clear order (not shown here), indicating the need for differencing for seasonality.

Since the seasonal models contain both seasonal and regular, nonseasonal components, we take one seasonal difference and one regular, nonseasonal difference and construct the ACF and PACF plots for the first-order seasonal differenced data. Unfortunately, both plots appear to decay gradually with significant values at different lags (not shown here), indicating that additional plots are necessary to determine the order of AR and MA processes for the model.

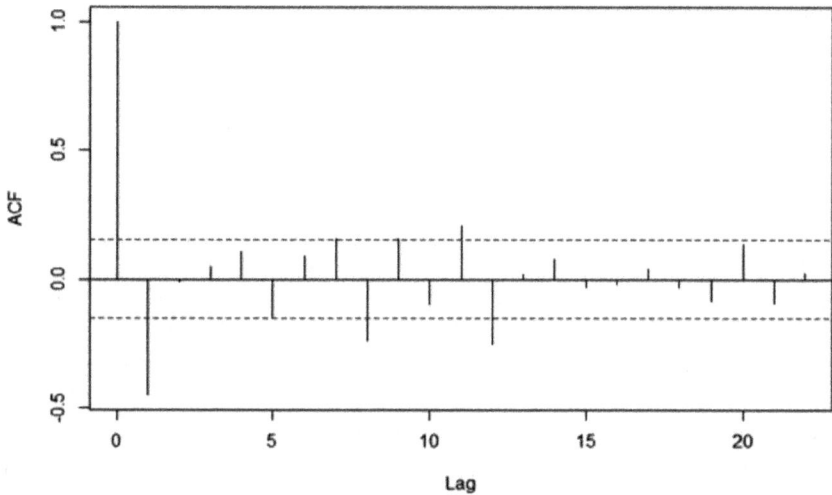

Figure 5.12   ACF Plot after Seasonal and Regular Non-seasonal Differencing.

Figures 5.12 and 5.13 show the ACF and PACF plots after the regular, non-seasonal and seasonal differencing of the series. As can be seen from the PACF plot, it has two clear spikes—one at lag 1 and the other at lag 13 that clearly appear significant, indicating a regular AR with order 1 and a seasonal AR of order 1. We can now look at the ACF plot to determine the order of the MA component of the model. A cursory look at the plot would indicate that it is significant at lag 1 and also at lags 8 and 12, then decaying gradually at higher lags.

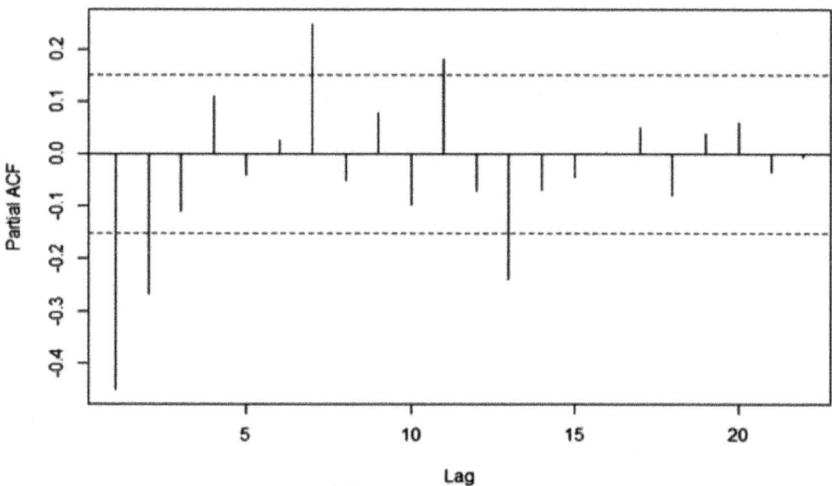

Figure 5.13   PACF Plot after Seasonal and Regular Non-seasonal Differencing.

Table 5.5 Order Combination of AR and MA Terms and Error Measurement

Order Combination	RMSE	MAPE	MASE	AIC
ARIMA(1,1,1)(1,1,1)12	62.38959	2.386095	0.3374084	1892.987
ARIMA(1,1,2)(1,1,1)12	61.42778	2.316166	0.3269179	1888.206
ARIMA(2,1,1)(1,1,1)12	62.19224	2.378336	0.3356702	1892.999
ARIMA(2,1,2)(1,1,1)12	61.01002	2.304543	0.3256999	1889.667

The results of the plots also tell us that although some autocorrelations and partial autocorrelations appear significant, the plots do not give us a clear and precise picture as to the order of AR and MA that would best describe the model. Accordingly, we look at various efficiency measures similar to those discussed earlier to determine the best possible model. Table 5.5 shows the ARIMA models with different order combinations and their corresponding errors.[6] As before, several other models were also run with different order combinations, but, for convenience, we included here only the ones with small errors.

As the table shows, of the four models, the second model, ARIMA(1,1,2) (1,1,1)12 appears to be the most efficient. It has the lowest AIC, the second lowest RMSE, MAPE and MASE, and all its t ratios came out to be significant (discussed in the next section). Although ARIMA(2,1,2)(1,1,1)12 gives the impression of being somewhat more efficient since it has the lowest RMSE, MAPE, and MASE, it also has a higher AIC than the second model. Overall, ARIMA(1,1,2)(1,1,1)12 appears to be the best possible model for estimation and forecast.

Model Estimation

Having identified the appropriate order combination for regular and seasonal AR and MA processes, we can now estimate the model. In fact, each of the four models described in Table 5.5 was individually run to estimate the model parameters and tested for their statistical significance to ensure that the final model selected was the best possible model.

The following provides the estimated model:

$$\left(1-0.7706B\right)\left(1-0.2561B^{12}\right)\left(1-B\right)\left(1-B^{12}\right)Y_t$$

$$= (1-0.8972B^{12})\left(1-1.1420B+1.6179B^2\right)e_t$$

To determine that the model is statistically sound, we look at some of the same statistics we used for the regular nonseasonal and the seasonal model with the quarterly data—standard errors, t ratios, and the associated p-values to ensure that the estimated coefficients are statistically significant. Interestingly, the t ratio for AR(2), in ARIMA(2,1,2)(1,1,1)12 was quite low at -0.7291 (not shown here); as such, it turned out to be not statistically significant. This, in part, explains why it was excluded from consideration. Table 5.6 shows the estimated coefficients for the AR1, MA2, SRA1, and SMA1 terms of the selected model, their corresponding standard errors, t ratios, and associated *p*-values.

As the table shows, all the terms used in the model came out to be significant with *p*-values ranging between <0.001 and <0.05, indicating that the model as a whole is statistically significant, similar to what we observed for the quarterly series, as expected.

Diagnostic Checks

As before, we need to conduct some diagnostic checks to further ensure the statistical soundness of the model and the series used for model estimation. To do so, we look at the various residual plots for the estimated model to see if the residuals are uncorrelated; in other words, if they are normally distributed (Figure 5.14). As can be seen from the figure, in particular the residual histogram, the distribution of residuals appears to be approximately normal. Similarly, the residual plot for months also appears to be normally distributed with approximately zero mean. The ACF plot for residuals further tells us that there is no autocorrelation among the residuals. In the same vein, the autocorrelations appear to be within $\pm 2 / \sqrt{n} = 2 / \sqrt{66} = \pm\, 2 / 8.1240 = \pm\, 0.2462$,

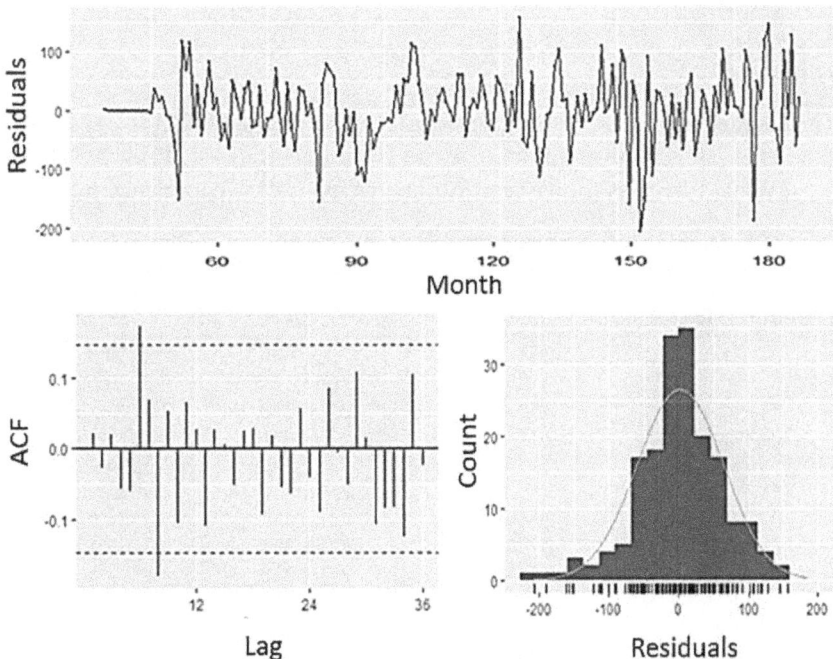

Figure 5.14 Residual Plots for ARIMA(1,1,2)(1,1,1)12.

Table 5.6   Final Estimation of the Model Parameters: ARIMA(1,1,2)(1,1,1)12

Order Number	Model Type	Estimated Coefficients	Std. Errors	t Ratios*	p-value
1	AR1	0.7706	0.1150	6.7009	<0.001
2	MA2	0.6179	0.0767	8.0561	<0.001
1	SRA1	0.2561	0.1094	2.3410	0.0204
1	SMA1	-0.8972	0.1126	-7.9680	<0.001

*df = n-(p+q+P+Q+1) = 180-(1+2+1+1+1) = 174

indicating that the residuals are uncorrelated, consistent with the assumption of a random and no-trend series.

As expected, the Q-Q plot (not shown here) corroborates that the residuals are mostly clustered around the line of normality, indicating that they are random, which is understandable since we are using the same revenue data we used for the quarterly series. And, finally, the Ljung-Box Q test produces a χ^2 value of 25.383, with 19 degrees of freedom (m = 19) and a p-value of 0.1483. The observed χ^2 of 25.383 is considerably lower than the critical χ^2 value of 34.8 (found in any χ^2 table). On the other hand, the observed p-value of 0.1483 is small but not lower than the significance levels of α at 0.01 and 0.05; as such, we cannot reject the null hypothesis that the residuals are uncorrelated. Put simply, there is strong and significant support for the series to be random and not trended.

Forecasts

The diagnostic checks further confirmed that the model overall is statistically significant, thus allowing us to go ahead and do the forecast. Table 5.7 shows the revenue forecasts for the next 12 months, with 95% confidence intervals.

Table 5.7   Monthly Forecasts for State Sales Tax Revenue

Time (t) Period-Month	Point Forecast ($Million)	95% CI Lower Bound	95% CI Upper Bound
t+1 (181-Sept)	2633.082	2507.608	2758.555
t+2 (182-Oct)	2738.979	2607.297	2870.661
t+3 (183-Nov)	3008.305	2866.876	3149.734
t+4 (184-Dec)	2918.941	2765.091	3072.790
t+5 (185-Jan)	2926.135	2758.142	3094.128
t+6 (186-Feb)	2859.886	2676.802	3042.969
t+7 (187-Mar)	2685.524	2486.952	2884.096
t+8 (188-Apr)	2938.076	2723.980	3152.172
t+9 (189-May)	2993.138	2763.708	3222.568
t+10 (190-Jun)	2892.798	2648.358	3137.237
t+11 (191-Jul)	2952.321	2693.271	3211.371
t+12 (192-Aug)	3083.620	2810.394	3356.845

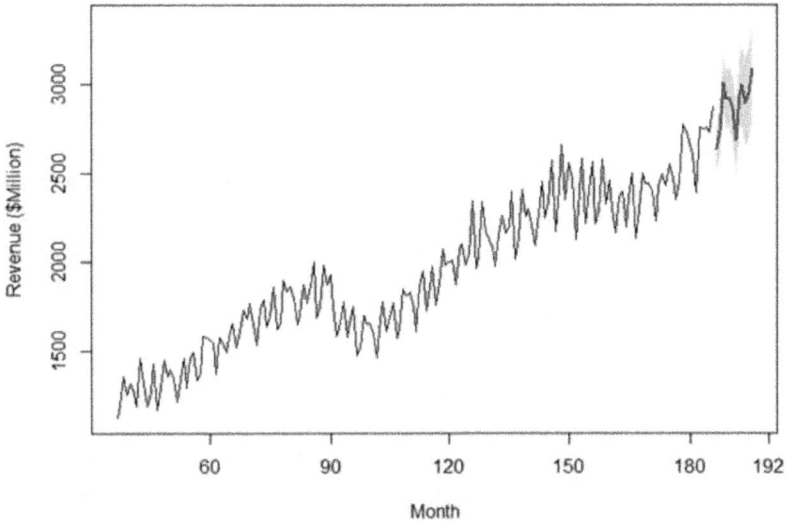

Figure 5.15   Monthly Forecasts with 95% Confidence Bands (Shaded Area).

As the table shows, the revenue will continue to increase for the forecast period, from \$2633.082 million at t+1, to \$3083.620 at t+12, with some dips in between, consistent with the growth pattern for the series, as a whole.

To be more specific, there will be months of slow growth when it will decline and then pick up again. For instance, it will decline by a small percentage from the projected growth of \$3.008 billion in November, t+3, to \$2.919 billion in March, t+7, and then again in June, t+10, to \$2.893 billion, from \$2.993 billion in May, t+9. Figure 5.15 shows the forecasts, with 95% confidence bands (highlighted by the shaded area), reflecting a growth pattern that is consistent with the general pattern of the series.

Since we used the revenue data for the same time length as the quarterly series, it would be interesting to see how the quarterly and monthly forecasts compare. Table 5.8 shows the comparison. As can be seen from the table, the forecasts compare well with an average difference of less than 2.5 percent for the first three of the four quarters and less than 1.5 percent for the last quarter.

Table 5.8   Comparison of Quarterly and Monthly Forecasts

Quarter-Month	Quarterly Forecasts ($Million)	Monthly Forecasts ($Million)	Percentage Difference
Q-66 (Sept–Nov)	8695.253	8380.366	0.0376
Q-67 (Dec–Feb)	8926.698	8704.962	0.0255
Q-68 (Mar–May)	8819.484	8616.738	0.0235
Q-69 (Jun–Aug)	9053.326	8928.739	0.0139

Although they are negligible, several factors may have contributed to the differences, such as aggregation of data (converting the monthly data to quarterly series, since the quarterly data were not readily available, which could have resulted in some information loss), selection of the order combination for AR and MA processes, time length of forecasts, and so forth. Overall, both ARIMA models produce forecasts that appear reasonably good in light of the general growth pattern of the data. As for which forecasts the government should use, quarterly or monthly, it depends on the forecasting objective.

SUMMARY

Seasonality is a common occurrence in government. Seasonality occurs when revenues and expenditures experience regular and predictable changes that recur every calendar year. Understanding the seasonal behavior in the data is critical for a government to be able to carefully plan its expenditure activities. This chapter extended the discussion on regular ARIMA models in the previous chapter to ARIMA models with seasonal data. As highlighted in the chapter, the forecasting process is essentially the same for both regular and seasonal ARIMA. To illustrate how the seasonal models are used, the chapter looked at quarterly, as well as monthly sales tax revenue data for a state government.

NOTES

1. For time series models, seasonality is typically introduced multiplicatively. What this means intuitively is that if a month, say, September is related to the preceding month, which is August, and to the previous September a year ago, then it is also related to August of the previous year, 13 months ago. The same would apply to the remaining months of the season. The convention is to use the backshift operator to show this relationship between s points time periods apart, where s is the number of observations or periods in a season. For example, a seasonal ARIMA model of order P and Q, differenced D times, it will be

$$\Phi_P(B^s)(1 - B^s)^D Y_t = \Theta_Q(B^s)e_t \qquad [5.1]$$

where B is the backshift operator.

2. The data used in the example were the actual sales tax revenue for the State of Texas, from September 2003 (the beginning of the 1st quarter of the fiscal year 2003), through August 2018 (the end of the 4th and last quarter of the fiscal year 2018). The original data were in terms of monthly sales tax revenue; we converted them into

quarterly series to run the model (Appendix A.2). To provide a little background about the data, they are presented according to the fiscal year of the government which starts on September 1 and ends on August 31. Thus, Q1 of year 1, which represents the 1st quarter of the series beginning on September 1, 2003; Q2 represents the 2nd quarter of the series beginning on December 1, 2003; Q3 represents the 3rd quarter of the series beginning on March 1, 2004; Q4 represents the 4th quarter of the series beginning on June 1, 2004, and so forth.

3. Since the ARIMA models typically use MLE for estimating the model parameters, it is expected that the log likelihood value should be used for model selection. The loglikelihood value is the value of the negative logarithmic value of the likelihood function. Usually, the smaller the value of the likelihood function the better the model. Interestingly, however, for time series modeling we do not use the likelihood value for model selection. Instead, we use RMSE, MASE, MAPE and AIC values for selecting the best model for model selection and forecast.

4. The rule of thumb for determining the significance of the estimated parameters is that if the absolute value of the estimated coefficient is greater than the twice the corresponding standard error it is considered statistically significant. However, once we know the standard errors the calculation of *t*-ratios (t values) is straightforward since it is obtained be simply dividing the estimated coefficient by the corresponding standard error.

5. The data used are the same sales tax revenue for the State of Texas, except that they are by months, from September 2003 through August 2018, and came from the Office of Comptroller, Texas, Monthly State Revenue Watch, Transparency: State Revenue and Spending, Associated Data Files; https://comptroller.texas.gov/transparency/revenue/watch/

6. In fact, the actual number of order combinations we looked and analyzed was much higher, but we present here only the ones that compare well with the final model.

Chapter 6

Advanced Time Series Models

Time series models, such as simple moving average, exponential moving average, trend line, and the ARIMA models discussed in the previous chapters, are known as univariate models because they deal with past observations or past errors of a single (dependent) variable. Some consider this unrealistic because they do not take into account the causal relationship that may affect the forecast variables. While causal models, in particular econometric models, take this into consideration, they have an inherent weakness in that they are built incrementally, equation by equation, called "structure." Also, they have a strict requirement that they must be correctly identified before estimating the parameters to produce reliable forecasts. Identification is a problem of model formulation, not estimation, thus, often contributing to the difficulties in determining the exact structural relationship between the variables under consideration.

This is where multivariate time series models such as transfer function models have an advantage in that they provide a fairly unrestricted approximation to the structural model because identification in these models is not based on the standard parametric tests such as t-tests; instead, they are based on autocorrelation and cross-correlation (Makridakis and Wheelwright, 1978). This chapter looks at two well-known multivariate time series models, vector autoregression (VAR) and vector error correction (VEC) that considerably addresses the problem.

VECTOR AUTOREGRESSION

Developed by Sims (1972), VAR provides an alternative to the structural approach to time series modeling. The structural approach, where some variables are treated as endogenous and some as exogenous (predetermined with lags), requires that the equations in the model are correctly identified. Identification is achieved by assuming the presence of some predetermined variables only in some equations, but not all, which is often subjective. According to Sims, if simultaneity among a set of variables is pure, then they should be treated exactly the same (Sims, 1980). In other words, there should not be any a priori distinction between endogenous and exogenous variables.

Operationally, it creates two major problems: One, it does not provide a clear dynamic (time-variant) specification that identifies the relationship among the variables of interest, and two, since the endogenous variables in these models can appear on both sides of the equation, it can complicate the process of estimation and inference. VARs avoid the problem by treating every endogenous variable in the system as a function of the lagged values of all the endogenous variables in the system.

VARs and their derivatives, such as VEC, discussed later in the chapter, which use a somewhat different approach such as autoregressive distributed lag[1] to conventional structural modeling, are often treated as a special case of multivariate autoregressive moving average (MARMA) models. As such, they are often called vector autoregressive moving average (VARMA) models. There are other more complex forms of MARMA models that have been developed in recent years which can deal with even more complex problems than the ones discussed here.

Basic Structure

An important difference between conventional econometric models and MARMA is that the latter includes additional independent variables that do not suffer from the difficulties of the structural models described above. As noted earlier, this is due to the fact that model specification vis-à-vis identification in both ARMA and MARMA is not based on the *t*-tests, but rather on autocorrelation and partial autocorrelation coefficients (for determining the degree to which two series are correlated). Although ACF and the PACF do not directly tell us the order of an ARMA or MARMA model, they can provide good visual impression about the order to suggest that the model would be a good fit for the time series data.

The following provides a simple expression for a VAR model with two-time series variables, X and Y:

$$Y_t = \alpha_1 + \beta_1 Y_{t-1} + \beta_2 Y_{t-2} + \ldots\ldots + \beta_m Y_{t-m} + \gamma_1 X_{t-1} + \gamma_2 X_{t-2}$$

$$+ \ldots\ldots + \gamma_m X_{t-m} + v_{1t} \tag{6.1}$$

$$X_t = \alpha_2 + \lambda_1 Y_{t-1} + \lambda_2 Y_{t-2} + \ldots\ldots + \lambda_m Y_{t-m} + \delta_1 X_{t-1} + \delta_1 X_{t-2}$$

$$+\ldots\ldots + \delta_m X_{t-m} + v_{2t} \tag{6.2}$$

where Y_t and X_t are the dependent variables, and Y_{t-j} and X_{t-j} are the past values of Y_t and X_t (for j = 1, 2, ..., m) when they are treated as exogenous or lagged endogenous variables, α, β, γ, λ, and δ are the parameters of the model, and v_t's are the stochastic random terms, called innovations (i.e., shocks or impulses).[2]

For three time series variables, X, Y and Z, this would be

$$Y_t = \alpha_1 + \beta_1 Y_{t-1} + \beta_2 Y_{t-2} + \ldots\ldots + \beta_m Y_{t-m} + \gamma_1 X_{t-1} + \gamma_2 X_{t-2} + \ldots\ldots$$

$$+\gamma_m X_{t-m} + \zeta_1 Z_{t-1} + \zeta_2 Z_{t-2} + \ldots\ldots + \zeta_m Z_{t-m} + v_{1t} \tag{6.3}$$

$$X_t = \alpha_2 + \lambda_1 Y_{t-1} + \lambda_2 Y_{t-2} + \ldots\ldots + \lambda_m Y_{t-m} + \delta_1 X_{t-1} + \delta_2 X_{t-2} + \ldots\ldots$$

$$+\delta_m X_{t-m} + \zeta_1 Z_{t-1} + \zeta_2 Z_{t-2} + \ldots\ldots + \zeta_m Z_{t-m} + v_{2t} \tag{6.4}$$

$$Z_t = \alpha_3 + \varphi_1 Y_{t-1} + \varphi_2 Y_{t-2} + \ldots\ldots + \varphi_m Y_{t-m} + \theta_1 X_{t-1} + \theta_2 X_{t-2} + \ldots\ldots$$

$$+\theta_m X_{t-m} + \xi_1 Z_{t-1} + \xi_2 Z_{t-2} + \ldots\ldots + \xi_m Z_{t-m} + v_{3t} \tag{6.5}$$

and so forth, meaning that as more time series variables are added to the system, the number of equations will also increase. The objective of VAR is to facilitate the determination of *m* in Equations 6.3-6.5 and estimate the values of the parameters α, β, γ, λ, δ, φ, θ, ζ, and ξ.

Types of VAR

Operationally, all VAR models fall into two broad categories—unrestrictive and restrictive. Depending on how the variables are included in a model, a VAR can be defined as unrestrictive or restrictive. In an unrestrictive VAR, all the variables in an equation are included in the model, whereas in a restrictive VAR, some variables in one equation and other variables in another equation are included in the model. The restrictions and specifications are mostly derived from the theory or theories that underlie the models. Restricted models typically include multiequation models, as one would expect. Good examples of restricted models are early macroeconomic models, especially those used in the 1950s through the 1970s, but over time, especially following

Chapter 6

the works of Sims and others, there has been a consistent growth in the use of unrestricted models.

Steps in VAR

Although structurally different, the application of VAR is not much different from regular nonseasonal or seasonal ARIMA models in that it follows the same basic steps: Checking for stationarity, model identification (selecting the order of the model), model estimation, diagnostic checks, and forecasting. However, VARs have several distinguishing features that separate them from the ARIMA models, two of which are worth noting: One, it is important to determine that there is a causal relationship between the variables before estimating the model. It makes very little sense to estimate a model only to discover that there was no causal relationship between the variables. Although causality is implicit in both single and multiequation (regression) models, this is particularly important where forecasting is concerned.

Two, it is important to determine if there is a significant relationship (correlation) in the long-run behavior of the series to avoid the potential for spurious results. The behavior often serves as a precursor to determining whether a VAR model can be run with or without differencing. We will look at it in some detail at the end of the chapter.

AN ILLUSTRATIVE EXAMPLE

To illustrate, let us look at the annual budget of a state government with multiyear revenues and expenditures over a 28-year period (Appendix 4).[3] A cursory look at the data would indicate that there has been a consistent increase in both state revenue and expenditure during the study period. However, as one would expect, there were fluctuations in the data for some years to reflect the general condition of the state economy. Figure 6.1 shows the general growth pattern for the state.

As the figure shows, while the revenue has been increasing consistently during the entire period, at times by a significant margin, with occasional dips, the growth in expenditure has also been consistent. In other words, both variables have been moving upward in the same direction, although not at the same rate. Overall, the budget of the state reflects a relatively healthy and expanding economy.

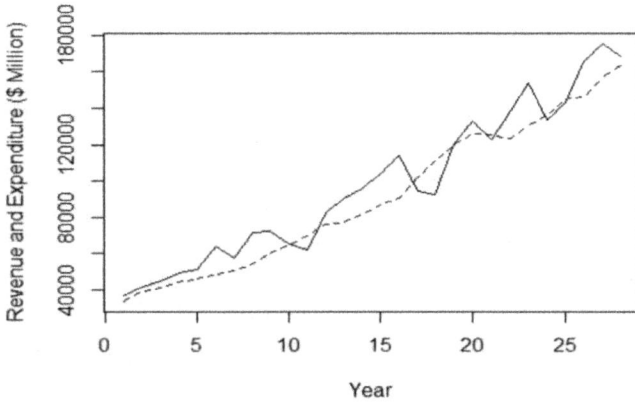

Figure 6.1 Government Revenue (solid line) and Expenditure (dashed line).

VAR and Causality

An important concern in all causal models, including regression analysis, which also applies to VAR, is that while they deal with the dependence of one variable on other variables, they do not necessarily establish causation. In other words, the mere presence of the relationship between variables does not prove causality or the direction of influence. In regression analysis with time series, the situation is different because only the past can cause what happens today, but not the other way round. Future events cannot cause what happens today. According to Koop (2000), time does not run backward. The question then is: Does variable X cause variable Y, or variable Y cause variable X? Therefore, before a causal relationship can be established, it is important to do a test of causality and the test commonly used for this purpose is the well-known Granger-Causality test (Granger, 1969).

The test involves running regressions on all possible pairs of time series. For a two-variable case, it will be similar to the example in Equations 6.1 and 6.2

$$Y_t = \alpha_1 Y_{t-1} + v \alpha_2 Y_{t-2} + \ldots\ldots + \alpha_n Y_{t-n} + \beta_1 X_{t-1}$$

$$+ \beta_2 X_{t-2} + \ldots\ldots + \beta_m X_{t-m} + v_{1t} \tag{6.6}$$

$$X_t = \gamma_1 X_{t-1} + \gamma_2 X_{t-2} + \ldots\ldots\ldots + \gamma_m X_{t-m} + \delta_1 Y_{t-1} - + \delta_2 Y_{t-2}$$

$$+ \ldots\ldots + \delta_n Y_{t-n} + v_2 \tag{6.7}$$

where X_t is the presumed causal variable and Y_t is the effect or response variable, both at time t, v_t is the stochastic random term, and α, β, γ, and δ are the respective parameters of the model.

In its bare essence, what it means is that determining the causal relationship involving, say, two time series, X_t and Y_t, where X is the presumed causal variable and Y is the response variable, the Granger-Causality allows us to see how much of the current value of Y can be explained by the past values of Y and whether adding the past values of X can improve the explanation. If it does, one can safely assume that X has caused Y, *ceteris paribus*. In other words, Y is said to be Granger-caused by X if it helps in the prediction of Y, provided that the coefficients of the lagged X's are statistically significant. However, it should be worth noting that X Granger-causes Y does not mean that Y is the effect of X. What it means is that it measures the presence of a causal relationship but does not, by itself, indicate the existence of causality in the conventional sense of the term.

The procedure for the causality test is essentially the same as the procedure in typical hypothesis testing with null and alternative hypothesis:

H_0: Y does not Granger-cause X
H_A: X Granger-causes Y
Test Statistic: F
Statistical Decision:
Reject H_0, if F statistic is not statistically significant; otherwise, do not

However, unlike the conventional hypothesis tests, the Granger-Causality test uses two-way causation between X and Y, given by two distinct hypotheses, with the statements that X Granger-causes Y and Y Granger-causes X to ensure that the relationship is not two-way. On the other hand, it is possible that the results are such that we cannot reject either hypothesis, thereby, indicating that there is no one-way causation. From a practical point of view, eliminating the likelihood of one-way causation early in the study saves time in that it is better to find early in the study than after the model has been estimated that there was no causal relationship. This is particularly important when one is dealing with a large number of variables and needs to decide a priori how many variables to include in a model and, more importantly, which endogenous variables to include in the model. Since we are dealing with only two endogenous variables, the discussion is somewhat moot; nevertheless, we will go ahead and test for the causality of the variables in our model.

Granger-Causality Test

There is an underlying notion in all causal models, which includes VAR, that when there are multiple time series in a system, they tend to influence each other, which makes it possible to forecast a series with its own past values, as well as the past values of the other series in the system. As noted earlier, the Granger-Causality test determines whether the series cause each other. The test produces an F statistic[4] with a corresponding p-value. Depending on where the significance level (α value) is set, if the p-value is less than the α value, one can reject the null hypothesis and conclude that there is sufficient evidence to support that the time series in question causes the other series.

Table 6.1 shows the test results for the two series, Y_t (revenue) and X_t (expenditure), at lags 1, 2, and 3, along with their corresponding F statistics and p-values. As the table shows, given the F statistics and the corresponding p-values, we cannot reject the null hypothesis at all three lags that Y does not Granger-cause X, but we can reject the hypothesis that X does not Granger-cause Y. What this means is that since the p-values are less than 0.05 in all three cases, we can reject the null hypothesis that expenditure is relevant in predicting the future revenues of the government. In other words, based on the test results, it appears that Granger causality runs one way from X (expenditure) to Y (revenue), where X Granger-causes Y, and not the other way.[5]

Interestingly, at higher lags, the relationship tends to reverse somewhat. For instance, at lag 3, the F statistic for the null hypothesis Y does not Granger-cause X appears to increase considerably, along with a much lower p-value than at lags 1 and 2. Although additional tests were not conducted at higher lags, given the trend, it seems likely that the relationship will eventually reverse where Y will Granger-cause X and not the other way. Interestingly, this is consistent with how budget decisions are made in government. While the expenditure budget is prepared based on the needs of the government for the upcoming budget year, it has to be matched by the availability of revenue to fund the expenditures. This is particularly important for state and local governments where, by law, their proposed budgets have to be balanced. For

Table 6.1   Granger-Causality Tests

Null Hypothesis			
(Lag 1; Order 1; n = 28)	*F-Value*	*Probability*	*Statistical Decision*
Y does not Granger-Cause X	0.2032	0.6562	Do not reject
X does not Granger-Cause Y	15.0330	0.0007	Reject
(Lag 2; Order 2; n = 28)			
Y does not Granger-Cause X	0.7959	0.4643	Do not reject
X does not Granger-Cause Y	15.5070	0.0007	Reject
(Lag 3; Order 3; n = 28)			
Y does not Granger-Cause X	2.4019	0.1014	Do not reject
X does not Granger-Cause Y	4.8827	0.0018	Reject

instance, in Texas, as noted earlier, the State Comptroller must certify that the revenue needed to finance the proposed budget will be available before the Governor can sign it into law.

Checking for Stationarity

An important consideration in ARIMA models is that they must be stationary before estimating the models if the original series are non-stationary. This is usually achieved by differencing the series, but the guiding principles are not quite as precise when it comes to VAR. There is a general understanding in VAR modeling that if the objective is hypothesis testing, either singly or jointly, in order to examine the statistical significance of the coefficients, then it is essential that all components of VAR are stationary, but differencing may throw some information on long-run relationships between the series away (Brooks, 2014). The alternative is to run VAR in levels (without differencing), but the problem with running VAR in levels when the series are nonstationary is that standard errors may not be reliable, meaning that it will be difficult to make inferences about the value of the estimated coefficients.

On the other hand, it is possible to estimate VAR models in levels if the nonstationary data are cointegrated (move in the same direction in the long run).[6] According to Fanchon and Wendel (1992), if the series is nonstationary, but cointegrated, then there is enough evidence to support the argument that estimation with such data in levels will yield consistent parameter estimates. This is further corroborated by Hamilton (1994), Duy and Thoma (1998), Gujarati and Porter (2009), and others that it is possible to estimate the model in levels if the variables are nonstationary but cointegrated. This is because they tend to produce consistent parameter estimates, although it may contribute to loss of efficiency due to the presence of cointegration.

Additionally, the conventional wisdom among the practitioners is that differencing is not necessary if the primary objective of VAR is forecasting. This is in part because forecasting is essentially a conditional expectation[7] and, as such, it relies on parameter estimates of the model rather than on the standard errors, although the latter is important to establish the reliability of the estimates. Accordingly, we will estimate the model without differencing and look at the cointegration issue later in the chapter.

Determining the Order of the Model

The first and foremost step in VAR modeling is to select the order of the model before it could be estimated. In order to do so, we need to decide first the maximum number of lag lengths (usually at the discretion of the researcher) and then select from this maximum the number of lag terms to determine the order, which will be optimal. The idea behind optimal lag is to select the lag that would produce the lowest residual correlation and, as such, will be most efficient. However, there is no definitive rule for selecting the optimal lag. Since this is an empirical question, it is often achieved through trial and error.[8] For instance, if we include too many lags, it will use up too many degrees of freedom which may increase the likelihood of multicollinearity. By the same token, if we include too few lags, it may contribute to specification error (Gujarati and Porter, 2009). One way to address the question is to use efficiency criteria, such as AIC, HQ, SIC, FPE, and so forth, we used earlier for the ARIMA models, and select the lag that would be most efficient. Put simply, select the one that would produce the least amount of information loss.

Table 6.2 shows the order of VAR at different lags under different criteria. As shown in the table, the values tend to decrease at higher lags but do not seem to produce a lag that will be optimal under all four criteria. Lag 6 appears to have the lowest error or information loss on all four and, as such, should be considered a good option, but as noted earlier, including too many lags, especially when dealing with a small sample, could contribute to statistical problems. The next best lag at which all four criteria have the lowest error is lag 2. It also happens to be that "optimal" lag that produces the lowest error for multiple maximum lag lengths—lag 5, lag 4, and lag 3, as well as lag 2, thereby, making it the preferred order for the model.

However, to further ensure that the selected order is optimal, we do an error check for different lags to cross-validate the order, but unlike the default measures we used for the ARIMA models, we use a procedure frequently used in time series analysis for causal models, called holdout sample. Used primarily for model validation, a holdout sample randomly withholds a fraction of data (holdout) that is not used in model fitting to help produce an unbiased assessment of how well the model would perform if applied to the holdout data. The sampling partitions the data into two sets—training set (main data) and test set (holdout data).[9] The way the process works is that after the model is fitted to the training data, it is then applied to the holdout sample. The results are then compared to determine the accuracy of the model for estimation and forecasting.

Tables 6.3 and 6.4 show the accuracy of different VAR models for the training and test data set, based on the same set of error measures we used previously—ME, RMSE, MAE, and MAPE. As the tables show, VAR(2) produces the least error on all four measures for the majority of the models, indicating that it is the best order for model estimation and forecasting. The result appears to be consistent with the optimal lag we obtained from the VAR selection process under different criteria in Table 6.2.

Model Estimation and Diagnostic Checks

With the order of the model thus determined, the next step in the process is to estimate the model. In spite of its apparent complexities, VAR is not difficult

Table 6.2 VAR Selection Process at Different Lags

	AIC	HQC	SIC	FPE
Maximum Lag Length: 8				
Optimal Lag: 8-8-8, 6				
Lag Coefficient	AIC(8) 3.191527e+01	HQC(8) 3.226515e+01	SIC(8) 3.370759e+01	FPE(6) 2.841255e+14
Maximum Lag Length: 7				
Optimal Lag: 7-7, 6-6				
Lag Coefficient	AIC(7) 3.364633e+01	HQC(7) 3.399176e+01	SIC(6) 3.522142e+01	FPE(6) 8.539863e+14
Maximum Lag Length: 6				
Optimal Lag: 6				
Lag Coefficient	AIC(6) 3.364750e+01	HQC(6) 3.397462e+01	SIC(6) 3.503610e+01	FPE(6) 6.514386e+14
Maximum Lag Length: 5				
Optimal Lag: 2				
Lag Coefficient	AIC(2) 3.454558e+01	HQC(2) 3.469457e+01	SIC(2) 3.513801e+01	FPE(2) 1.031986e+15
Maximum Lag Length: 4				
Optimal Lag: 2				
Lag Coefficient	AIC(2) 3.443653e+01	HQC(2) 3.459280e+01	SIC(2) 3.502556e+01	FPE(2) 9.225703e+14
Maximum Lag Length: 3				
Optimal Lag: 2				
Lag Coefficient	AIC(2) 3.441270e+01	HQC(2) 3.457497e+01	SIC(2) 3.499776e+01	FPE(2) 8.985431e+14
Maximum Lag Length: 2				
Optimal Lag: 2				
Lag Coefficient	AIC(2) 3.432564e+01	HQC(2) 3.449285e+01	SIC(2) 3.490630e+01	FPE(2) 8.218397e+14

Table 6.3 VAR Accuracy at Different Lags: Revenues

Training and Test Set	ME	RMSE	MAE	MAPE
VAR(1): Training Set	-240.7822	24575.60	13650.98	10.169719
VAR(1): Test Set	246.0198	11632.59	10527.44	6.902625
VAR(2): Training Set	2.425171e-12	7401.351	5932.053	7.191612
VAR(2): Test Set	3.945173e+03	9500.039	8299.338	5.221894
VAR(3): Training Set	-5456.477	10389.22	8175.721	10.128862
VAR(3): Test Set	3729.736	9984.47	8520.477	5.430906
VAR(4): Training Set	-10454.527	17353.46	13565.10	17.51972
VAR(4): Test Set	-2287.126	22875.43	20993.59	13.82124
VAR(5): Training Set	-9623.719	27703.12	20625.44	24.612220
VAR(5): Test Set	3661.703	15041.36	12378.96	7.923609
VAR(6): Training Set	-9160.858	35254.05	26936.25	30.49095
VAR(6): Test Set	-9702.604	57756.96	47898.34	30.37253

to estimate. The convention is to use OLS to estimate the system of equations, one equation at a time, followed by various tests to ensure that the estimated coefficients, as well as the model as a whole, are statistically sound. Since the model is estimated using OLS, it is important that the assumptions of OLS (discussed in Chapter 3) are also addressed. As long as the assumptions are satisfied, the estimated model will be consistent, and the results can be evaluated using traditional t and *F* tests.

Since our VAR is a two-equation, two-variable unrestricted model, it involves the estimation of two sets of parameters—one for revenue (Revenue Equation, Y_t) and the other for expenditure (Expenditure equation, X_t), similar to Equations 6.1 and 6.2. Also, since the model is estimated using

Table 6.4 VAR Accuracy at Different Lags: Expenditures

Training and Test Set	ME	RMSE	MAE	MAPE
VAR(1): Training Set	-235.750	21196.38	9069.146	5.791032
VAR(1): Test Set	3984.886	4739.12	3984.886	2.580858
VAR(2): Training Set	1.385812e-12	2765.540	2166.254	2.550564
VAR(2): Test Set	1.691690e+03	2687.617	1767.476	1.212944
VAR(3): Training Set	-4469.539	5066.254	4469.539	6.017757
VAR(3): Test Set	-3119.639	4736.160	3993.884	2.622186
VAR(4): Training Set	-8862.844	10222.77	8862.844	12.318054
VAR(4): Test Set	-6311.810	10993.02	9619.344	6.242754
VAR(5): Training Set	-8670.99	24195.92	17420.282	21.918285
VAR(5): Test Set	-4528.754	7208.84	6363.314	4.145041
VAR(6): Training Set	-9228.502	31100.86	24980.46	31.09661
VAR(6): Test Set	-33553.893	38962.09	33553.89	21.81378

OLS regression, the results of the estimated model can be interpreted the
same way as one would interpret a typical regression model. Additionally,
given the optimal order of the model, which turned out to be VAR(2), each
equation will now contain two sets of lags for model estimation:

$$Y_t = \alpha_1 + \beta_1 Y_{t-1} + \beta_2 Y_{t-2} + \gamma_1 X_{t-1} + \gamma_2 X_{t-2} + v_{1t} \tag{6.8}$$

$$X_t = \alpha_2 + \lambda_1 Y_{t-1} + \lambda_2 Y_{t-2} + \delta_1 X_{t-1} + \delta_1 X_{t-2} + v_{2t} \tag{6.9}$$

Interestingly, if our optimal model had an order four, VAR(4), each equation would have contained four lags, and if it had an order of 6, VAR(6), each
equation would have included six lags, and so forth. But, as noted earlier, the
addition of more lags to the same variables does not necessarily guarantee
that the estimated coefficients will be statistically significant because of the
possibility of statistical problems, such as multicollinearity. On the other
hand, collectively, for the model as a whole, they can be significant based on
the observed F statistics.

Table 6.5 presents the estimated equations for both variables, along with
the corresponding statistics such as standard errors, t ratios, F statistics, and
their p-values. Starting with the revenue variable, Y_t, it appears that individually Y at lag 2 and X at lag 2 are statistically significant (at the 10 and 5
percent levels of α, respectively). Next, looking at the expenditure variable,
X_t, we see that only X came out to be significant at lag 1 (at the 0.001 percent
level of significance), while the rest did not. This is to be expected when we
are dealing with lagged variables, as we noted earlier. On the other hand,
collectively, both models came out to be statistically significant (at the 0.001
percent level), as given by their respective F statistics and the p-values.

Although the estimated parameters of the model, as well as the estimated
equations, came out to be significant, based on the conventional t and F tests,
it is important to conduct a number of other tests, as we did for the ARIMA
models, to ensure the overall soundness of the model. Most of these tests are
based on residuals. Chapter 3 provided a good summary of a number of these
tests, especially those related to regression assumptions, but for the purpose
of keeping the discussion simple, we will focus here on tests pertaining to
two of the assumptions important in all time series analysis—normality and
autocorrelation.

As noted previously, the primary objective of residual tests is to determine
that the residuals are uncorrelated and that their distribution is normal. There
is a range of measures that we can use for this purpose, some of which were
discussed at length in Chapter 4, which range from simple visual plots such
as residual histogram, standard residual plots, ACF and PACF plots, and Q-Q

Table 6.5 VAR Estimates of Model Parameters

| | Revenue (Y) | | | | Expenditure (X) | | | |
| | $\hat{Y}_t = \hat{\alpha}_1 + \hat{\beta}_1 Y_{t-1} + \hat{\beta}_2 Y_{t-2} + \hat{\gamma}_1 X_{t-1} + \hat{\gamma}_2 X_{t-2}$ | | | | $\hat{X}_t = \hat{\alpha}_2 + \hat{\lambda}_1 X_{t-1} + \hat{\lambda}_2 X_{t-2} + \hat{\delta}_1 Y_{t-1} + \hat{\delta}_2 Y_{t-2}$ | | | |
Lag	Coefficient	Std. Error	t-Value	Pr(>|t|)	Coefficient	Std. Error	t-Value	Pr(>|t|)
Y(-1)	0.2390	0.1774	1.3472	0.1923	0.0300	0.0698	0.4298	0.6720
Y(-2)	-0.3272	0.1709	-1.9146	0.0692	0.0656	0.0672	0.9762	0.3400
X(-1)	-0.5410	0.5283	-1.0240	0.3175	1.1700	0.2079	5.6277***	0.0001
X(-2)	1.6953	0.5752	2.9473**	0.0077	-0.2454	0.2263	-1.0844	0.2900
Const.	12987.0231	4718.1061	2.7526*	0.0119	1456.1652	1856.5405	0.7840	0.4420

$R^2 = 0.9644$; Adjusted $R^2 = 0.9576$

Residual Standard Error: 8241; df = 21

F-Statistic = 142.3; df = 4, 21; $p = 6.843e{-}15$

$R^2 = 0.9941$; Adjusted $R^2 = 0.9930$

Residual Standard Error: 3243; df = 21

F-Statistic = 885.4; df=4, 21; $p = 2.2e{-}16$

Note: $p < 0.001$(***); $p < 0.01$(**); $p < 0.05$(*); $p < 0.1$(•)

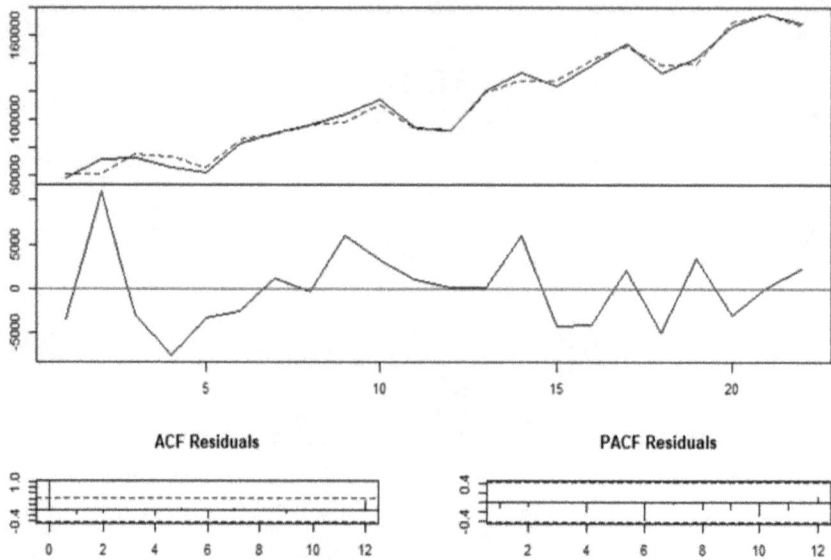

Figure 6.2   The Residual Plots for Revenue.

plots, to formal tests, such as Jarque-Bera (J-B) test, Ljung-Box test, among others. We will look at two sets of plots, the conventional residual plots and the Q-Q plots, followed by a couple of formal tests. Figures 6.2 and 6.3

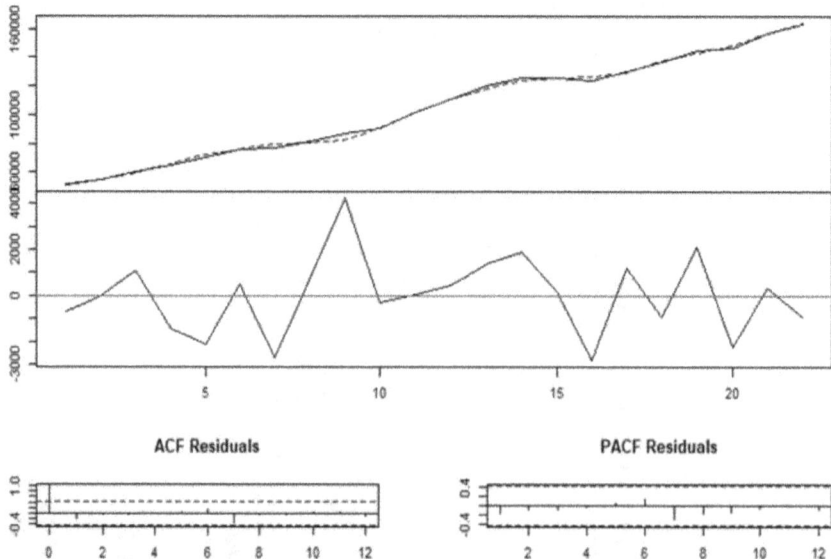

Figure 6.3   The Residual Plots for Expenditure.

show the residual plots for government revenues and expenditures (actual values in solid line and estimated values in broken line). As can be seen from the plots, residuals tend to fluctuate around the constant 0, indicating that they are normally distributed. This was also evident in the Q-Q plots for both variables (not shown here). As noted earlier, the Q-Q plots serve as suitable alternatives to residual histograms and other plots since they are much easier to interpret.

To further establish that the residuals are normally distributed, we use the J-B test of goodness-of-fit to determine if the residuals of the two variables approximate a normal distribution. J-B is essentially a χ^2 test and follows the same test procedures as conventional hypothesis testing with null and alternative hypotheses, H_0: The residuals are normally distributed if $\chi^2 = 0$; H_A: They are not normally distributed if $\chi^2 > 0$ (since χ^2 cannot be negative). In other words, the further the statistic is from zero, the more it fails to reject the null hypothesis. The test produces a χ^2 of 0.1977 with four degrees of freedom and a p-value of 0.9954. Since the observed test statistic is 0.1997, which is not too far from 0, and the p-value of the test is 0.9954, which is higher than the conventional significance level (α level) we use at 0.01 and 0.05, we fail to reject the null hypothesis that the residuals are normally distributed. In other words, the residuals are normally distributed. The Kolmogorov-Smirnov and Shapiro-Wilk tests also produced results (not shown here) that confirm this.

Finally, the model is tested for autocorrelation using a test commonly used for VAR, called the Portmanteau test, which is also a χ^2 test, and follows the same hypothesis testing procedure with a null hypothesis of no autocorrelation and alternative hypothesis of autocorrelation, H_0: There is no autocorrelation; H_A: There is autocorrelation. The test produces a χ^2 of 25.934 with 16 degrees of freedom and a p-value of 0547, significant up to lag 6, indicating the presence of no autocorrelation. In other words, since the observed p of 0.0546 is higher than the α level of 0.01 and 0.05, we cannot reject the null hypothesis of no autocorrelation, and the result is significant up to lag 6.[10] What is significant up to a specified lag means is that the past values of the variables do not affect the future values of the variables until the specified lag.

The presence of no autocorrelation is further supported by the Ljung-Box test discussed earlier. However, unlike the Portmanteau test, we conducted it individually for each equation rather than the model as a whole. The result produces a χ^2 of 1.8677, with six degrees of freedom and a p-value of 0.9315 for revenue, and a χ^2 of 2.5163, with the same degrees of freedom and a p-value of 0.8666 for expenditure.[11] Since both p-values are higher than the α level of 0.01 and 0.05, we cannot reject the null hypothesis of no autocorrelation. In other words, the residuals of the two variables are uncorrelated. Overall, the model appears to be statistically sound.

Forecasts

To complete the process, we now do the forecast of revenues and expenditures. Table 6.6 presents the forecasts for the next five years, along with 95% confidence intervals. According to the table, it appears that both revenues and expenditures will continue to increase at a fairly consistent pace for the forecast years, although the rate of growth will slow down a little toward the end of the forecast period. Since the revenue is expected to increase at a higher pace than the expenditure, there will be a budget surplus for each of the forecast periods.

Figure 6.4 shows the five-year revenue and expenditure forecasts for the government. Overall, the forecasts appear reasonable in light of the patterns observed in the original series that show a consistent increase in both revenue and expenditure over time, with revenues increasing at a greater pace than expenditures for the most part. However, as highlighted in Appendix A.3, government revenues experienced occasional ups and downs in the past reflecting how the state economy behaved, which may also be the case in the coming years, although the forecasts indicate consistent growth for the next several years. On the other hand, expenditure forecasts appear fairly consistent with the growth pattern observed in the recent past.

Finally, as we noted previously, the forecasts are estimates of actual values, not the actual values one would observe. That is why all forecasts, regardless of how good they appear, require constant monitoring. In other words, one needs to update the data on a regular basis and reestimate the models as new data become available to minimize the forecast errors and ensure the accuracy of the forecasts.

Returning to Cointegration

As noted earlier, cointegration is a common concern in all time series analysis that deals with two or more variables. In its bare essence, cointegration means correlation. In most economic studies, including those related to budgeting, there is a common understanding that there should be a long-term relationship among certain variables. Government revenue and expenditure would definitely fall into that category. The theory underlying this relationship is that these variables do not wander or drift away too far apart from one another in the long run. Formally, it means that one or more linear combinations[12] of these variables are stationary, although individually, they are not. If these variables are cointegrated, they cannot move too far away from one another. In contrast, a lack of cointegration would suggest that such variables do not have any long-run relationship; in principle, they can wander arbitrarily away from one another (Dickey et al., 1991). In other words, they are not correlated.

Table 6.6 Revenue and Expenditure Forecasts

Time	Revenue ($Million)	95% CI LB*	95% CI UB**	Expenditure ($Million)	95% CI LB*	95% CI UB**
t+1 (Yr.29)	173,567.3	157,415.8	189,718.8	170,714.5	164,359.0	177,070.0
t+2 (Yr.30)	183,954.1	167,093.9	200,814.3	177,359.5	167,519.5	187,199.4
t+3 (Yr.31)	193,626.7	175,352.5	211,901.0	183,971.8	171,624.6	196,319.0
t+4 (Yr.32)	200,228.0	178,740.8	221,715.3	191,048.8	176,896.3	205,201.4
t+5 (Yr.33)	206,022.5	182,325.7	229,719.3	198,538.5	182,827.2	214,249.8

*LB (Lower Bound); **UB (Upper Bound)

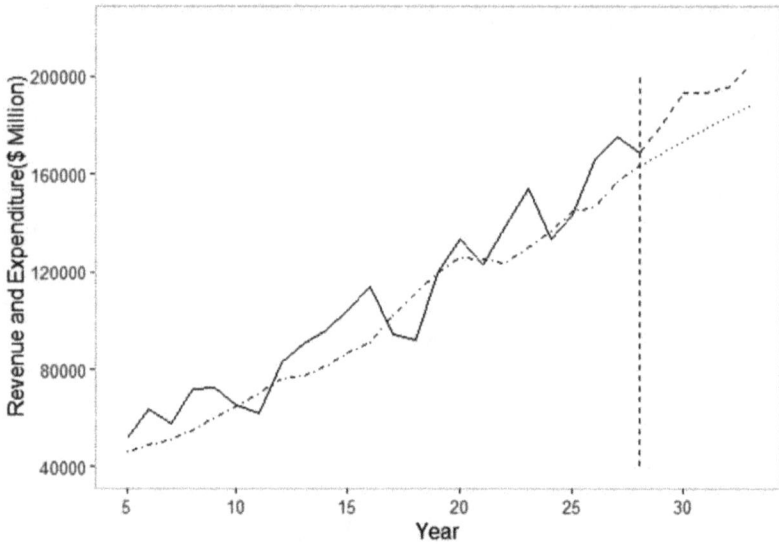

Figure 6.4   Five-Year Revenue (Solid Line) and Expenditure (broken line) Forecasts.

Cointegration Test

Although treated synonymously with correlation, cointegration is not quite the same as correlation. Correlation indicates how well two or more variables move together in the same or opposite direction. Cointegration does not test how well two or more series move together, rather that they differences between their means are constant (stationary). The test helps us to establish the presence of a statistically significant relationship between two or more time series that is much more robust than the relationship established by conventional correlation.

There is a range of tests that can be used for cointegration, such as the traditional Durbin-Watson test, KPSS test, Engle-Granger test, Phillips-Oulieris test, Johansen test, and so forth. Of these, Engle-Granger (1987) and Johansen (1991) tests are the two most frequently used cointegration tests.[13] Both tests follow the same conventional test procedures with a null and alternative hypothesis, H_0: There is no cointegration, and H_A: There is cointegration. Figure 6.5 shows the direction of growth in government revenues and expenditures over a 28-year period (top figure) and their difference (bottom figure). Looking at the difference, known as the spread, it appears that the two variables are moderately cointegrated in that they have the same long-run behavior, fluctuating around the constant, 0. In other words, they share a common stochastic trend suggesting that the series are jointly stationary.

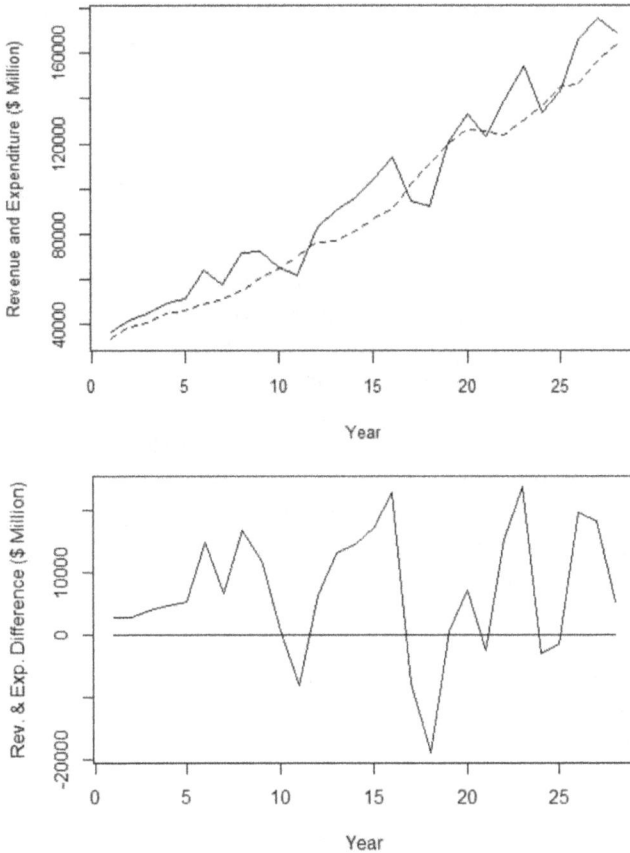

Figure 6.5 Revenue (solid line), expenditure (broken line)—(Top figure) and their spread (Bottom figure).

This long-term trend in the behavior of the two series is also supported by the Engle-Granger test conducted on the original series for a no-trend model with revenue as the response variable and expenditure as the input variable. The result produced a coefficient of -2.7592 with a p-value of 0.0807, indicating that we cannot quite reject the null hypothesis that the series are not cointegrated. In other words, they are cointegrated, albeit moderately.

A Note on Impulse Response Function

Interestingly, unlike the conventional regression analysis, the individual coefficients of VAR models are not always easy to interpret; as such, practitioners often use estimates based on what is known as impulse response function (IRF). The IRF is interpreted as how much a dependent variable will respond to one standard deviation shock to an independent variable for *m* periods, determined by the length period for which the standard error bands are above 0, for increase (or below 0, for decrease) after which the effect dissipates. More specifically, the IRF traces out the response of the dependent variable in a VAR model to shocks in the error terms, which, in our case, will be v_1 and v_2 in Equations 6.1 and 6.2.

To illustrate, suppose that v_1 in our revenue equation, Y_t, increases by the value corresponding to one standard deviation, then this change (shock) will change Y_t in the current, as well as future periods (years). However, since Y_t also appears in the expenditure equation, X_t, this change in v_1 will have an effect on X_t. Similarly, a change in one standard deviation in v_2 in equation, X_t, will have an effect on Y_t. The IRF traces the impact of such shocks for several periods into the future. Tables 6.7 and 6.8 show the changes in the two variables for the next six years.

As the tables show, the responses appear to reflect a pattern of change for the next several years in both revenues and expenditures that is much more reflective of the fluctuations we observed in the original series, especially for the revenue variable. This is where IRF plays an important role in providing additional information that does not seem obvious from VAR results. Although, on occasion, question has been raised about the importance of IRF, it remains a centerpiece of VAR analysis (Gujarati and Porter, 2009; McNees, 1987).

VECTOR ERROR CORRECTION

The greatest advantage of using VAR is that it provides a clear framework for describing the dynamic relationship among a number of variables that are stationary that conventional structural models do not provide. If the series is not stationary, one can always difference it to obtain stationarity, although, as we noted earlier, there are some disagreements if differencing is necessary when the goal is forecasting, assuming the series are cointegrated. In other words, the series may be individually nonstationary, but cointegrated in that the variables may have common underlying stochastic trends along which they move together on a nonstationary path.

However, when the series is not stationary, the VAR framework can be modified to produce consistent estimates of the relationship between the series. One way to achieve that is to use VEC, which is a special case of VAR for variables that are stationary in their differences, I(1), but are also cointegrated.

Table 6.7 Impulse Response: Revenue Function, Y$_t$

Time	Revenue ($Million)	95% CI LB*	95% CI UB**	Expenditure ($Million)	95% CI LB*	95% CI UB**
t+1	8240.711	5035.088	9116.806	405.953	-897.295	1466.195
t+2	1749.555	-929.108	3854.156	721.971	-1378.720	2220.920
t+3	-1980.383	-3808.245	588.091	1338.040	-1072.475	3084.335
t+4	-545.501	-3799.258	2075.182	1443.752	-865.789	2873.090
t+5	2004.939	-1575.634	4897.461	1214.599	-975.540	2368.682
t+6	2448.116	-402.668	4906.988	1091.095	-1067.748	2339.408

*LB (Lower Bound); **UB (Upper Bound)

Table 6.8 Impulse Response: Expenditure Function, X_t

Time	Revenue ($Million)	95% CI LB*	95% CI UB**	Expenditure ($Million)	95% CI LB*	95% CI UB**
t+1	0.000	0.000	0.000	3217.149	2049.560	3616.663
t+2	-1740.409	-4416.452	1774.176	3764.162	1581.663	4334.236
t+3	3001.894	691.964	4858.555	3562.442	1321.792	4882.966
t+4	5740.992	2639.802	7271.073	3220.157	909.092	4784.373
t+5	4687.174	909.762	6052.158	3262.325	1247.456	4775.867
t+6	2936.116	-15.152	5326.189	3543.739	1518.382	4976.707

*LB (Lower Bound); **UB (Upper Bound)

Basic Structure

To understand the relationship between the two models, let us look at two equations, similar to the equations we used for the VAR model, with the order reversed, as

$$X_t = \mu_1 + \gamma_1 d_{t1} + \alpha_{11} X_{t-1} + \alpha_{12} X_{t-2} + \ldots\ldots + \alpha_{1m} X_{t-m}$$

$$+ \beta_{11} Y_{t-1} + \beta_{12} Y_{t-2} + \ldots\ldots + \beta_{1m} Y_{t-m} + \epsilon_{t1} \qquad (6.10)$$

$$Y_t = \mu_2 + \gamma_2 d_{t2} + \alpha_{21} X_{t-1} + \alpha_{22} X_{t-2} + \ldots\ldots + \alpha_{2m} X_{t-m}$$

$$+ \beta_{21} Y_{t-1} + \beta_{22} Y_{t-2} + \ldots\ldots + \beta_{25} Y_{t-m} + \epsilon_{t2} \qquad (6.11)$$

The equations describe a system in which each variable is a function of its own lag, plus the lag of the other variable in the system. The maximum lag in the two equations is of order m, and structurally we have a VAR(m). Thus, if the two variables in the system are not stationary but stationary in differences I(m), then all one needs to do is take the differences and estimate the equations, using OLS. On the other hand, if the two variables are stationary, with I(m) and cointegrated, then the system of equations needs to ensure the cointegrating relations between the I(m) variables. This notion of cointegrated relationship in the model is the essence of VEC. Put simply, when the variables in a VAR are cointegrated, one should use VEC instead.

Operationally, since VEC is a special case of VAR, it follows the same basic steps as those used for VAR: (1) Difference the series, if they are non-stationary, (2) conduct tests for cointegration, (3) determine the optimal lag, (4) estimate the model, (5) check for accuracy of the estimated model, and (6) do the forecasts.

Stationarity

To illustrate, let us look at the federal budget with annual receipts and outlays (Appendix 5). Figure 6.6 shows the government receipts and outlays over a 70-year period.[14] As the figure shows, there has been a consistent increase in both receipts and outlays during this period, increasing more or less at the same pace for the first 30 years, after which outlays increasing at a faster pace than receipts. The result produced a deficit for the most part, with the exception of a couple of years around the year 50, which in real terms would be the years between 1998 and 2001. A careful look at the figure would further indicate that the two series are not stationary and that differencing is necessary to detrend the data.

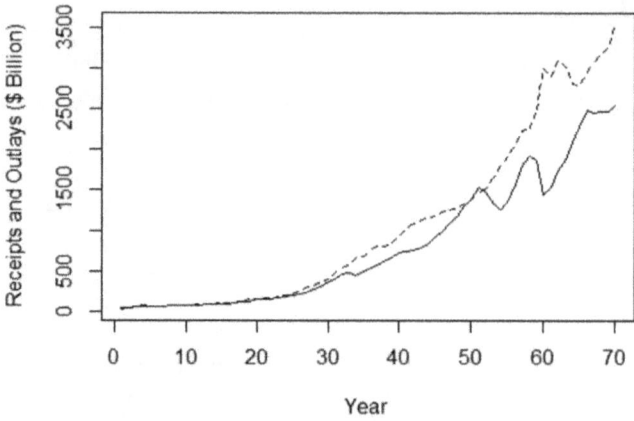

Figure 6.6   The Original series: Receipts (solid line), Outlays (broken line).

Figure 6.7 shows the series after first differencing, which appears to have detrended the data.

To further ensure that the two series are stationary, we conduct the hypothesis tests, as we did previously, using ADF and PP and look at the test results to draw the appropriate conclusion. The initial test results of the data without differencing indicate that they were not significant for both ADF and PP, but came out to be significant for the differenced series. The following provides a brief summary of the test results for ADF and PP:

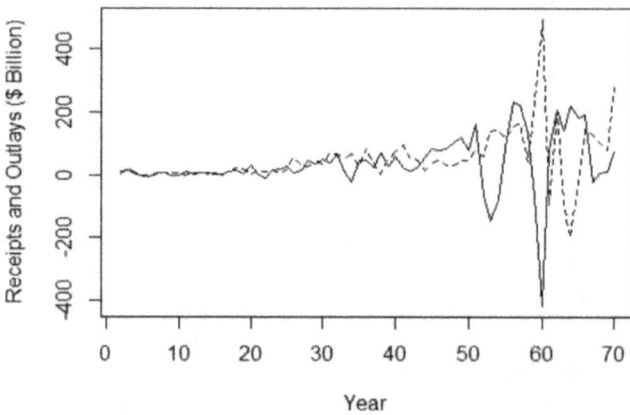

Figure 6.7   The Series after First Differencing.

Government Receipts: After first differencing
   Test Statistic (ADF): -6.2066, Lag order = 4, $p < 0.01$
   Test Statistic (PP): -37.832, Lag parameter = 3, $p < 0.01$
Government Outlays: After first differencing
   Test Statistic (ADF): -4.4552, Lag order = 4, $p < 0.01$
   Test Statistic (PP): -65.392, Lag parameter = 3, $p < 0.01$

As can be seen from the test results, both ADF and PP test statistics are quite low with low *p*-values, both significant at $p < 0.01$, indicating that the two series are stationary.

Cointegration Tests

As noted earlier, there are multiple different tests one can conduct for cointegration, two of which most frequently used are the Johansen test and the Engle-Granger test. Johansen test is particularly suitable where the system contains three or more variables, although it can be used for two variables. More importantly, it assesses the validity of a cointegrating relationship using the maximum likelihood estimates, as opposed to the Engle-Granger test, which uses ordinary least squares. On the other hand, it has an important weakness in that it is subject to asymptotic properties (large sample size) since small samples can produce unreliable results, which is not a problem with the Engle-Granger test. However, this should not be a problem in our case because our sample size is fairly large (n = 70). We will therefore use the Johansen test, since it is also more frequently used in VEC than the other tests.

Johansen Test

Two types of Johansen tests are commonly used in VEC: Trace test and maximum eigenvalue test.[15] Both tests check for the presence of no cointegration. To achieve this, the tests try to determine if the rank of a matrix, given by r, is equal to 0, 1, 2, and so forth.[16] Thus, the null hypothesis, H_0: r = 0 indicates no cointegration, while the alternative hypothesis, H_1: r > 0 indicates cointegrating relationship between two or more series. We will use the Trace test for our purpose since it is simple and relatively easy to interpret. The following provides a brief summary of the test results for the Trace test:

$r = 0$; *Trace Statistic* : 50.10; *5 Percent Critical Value* : 19.96;

1 Percent Critical Value : 24.60

$r \leq 1$; *Trace Statistic* : 13.01; *5 Percent Critical Value* : 9.24;

1 Percent Critical Value : 12.97

The results show the trace statistics for the two hypotheses, $r = 0$ and $r \leq 1$, along with their critical values at 5 and 1 percent, respectively. Thus, for the first test, $r = 0$, the trace statistic far exceeds the critical values at both 5 and 1 percent levels of significance, providing strong evidence to reject the null hypothesis of no integration. The second test, $r \leq 1$, also provides clear evidence to reject the null hypothesis of no cointegration, as the test statistic comfortably exceeds the critical value at both 5 and 1 percent levels of significance.

Lag Order, Model Specification, and Estimation

As with VAR, the next set of steps is to determine the order of the model for VEC, specify the model, estimate the model, check for the accuracy of the estimates, and do the forecasts. The order determines the maximum number of lags we can use to specify the model for estimation that will be optimal in that it will produce the least amount of information loss. As before, we use the same four criteria we used for VAR: AIC, HQ, SIC, and FPE. We used five lags for our purpose, although we could have used more. The general approach that is used to select the optimal lag is the one that would produce the least error for the criteria set used.

The following shows the five lags and their corresponding coefficients for each of the four criteria:

	Lag 1	Lag 2	Lag 3	Lag 4	Lag 5
AIC(n):	1.747794e+01	1.719610e+01	1.695432e+01	1.681215e+01	1.668387e+01
HQ(n):	1.758353e+01	1.735449e+01	1.716551e+01	1.707613e+01	1.700064e+01
SC(n) :	1.774556e+01	1.759752e+01	1.748956e+01	1.748120e+01	1.748672e+01
FPE(n):	3.896806e+07	2.941903e+07	2.313437e+07	2.011708e+07	1.775955e+07

Looking at the coefficients, it appears that lag 5 has the lowest error on all four criteria. Not only that, but it also has the lowest error for all five lag lengths—lag 1, lag 2, lag 3, lag 4, as well as lag 5, which makes it the preferred lag for the model. With the lag order thus determined, we can now specify the model that we will use for estimation, as shown below:

$$X_t = \mu_1 + \gamma_1 d_{t1} + \alpha_{11} X_{t-1} + \alpha_{12} X_{t-2} + \alpha_{13} X_{t-3} + \alpha_{14} X_{t-4} + \alpha_{15} X_{t-5}$$

$$+\beta_{11} Y_{t-1} + \beta_{12} Y_{t-2} + \beta_{13} Y_{t-3} + \beta_{14} Y_{t-4} + \beta_{15} Y_{t-5} + \epsilon_{t1} \tag{6.12}$$

$$Y_t = \mu_2 + \gamma_2 d_{t2} + \alpha_{21} X_{t-1} + \alpha_{22} X_{t-2} + \alpha_{23} X_{t-3} + \alpha_{24} X_{t-4} + \alpha_{25} X_{t-5}$$

$$+\beta_{21} Y_{t-1} + \beta_{22} Y_{t-2} + \beta_{23} Y_{t-3} + \beta_{24} Y_{t-4} + \beta_{25} Y_{t-5} + \epsilon_{t2} \tag{6.13}$$

where X_t and Y_t are receipts and outlays, respectively, μ_1 and μ_2 are the intercepts, γ_1 and γ_2 are the coefficients of error correction terms, and the rest of the terms are the same, as before.

The following presents the estimated equations for the two variables, along with their corresponding standard errors (in parentheses) and significance:

$$X_t = 33.7474 - 0.2012 d_{t1} + 0.6973 X_{t-1} - 0.0754 X_{t-2} - 0.3140 X_{t-3} + 0.2127 X_{t-4}$$

$$(15.7832)* \quad (0.0920)* \quad (0.1792)*** \quad (0.2107) \quad (0.2149) \quad (0.1975)$$

$$- 0.2164 X_{t-5} + 0.0635 Y_{t-1} + 0.02756 Y_{t-2} - 0.4165 Y_{t-3} + 0.1055 Y_{t-4} - 0.0549 Y_{t-5}$$

$$(0.1997) \quad (0.1819) \quad (0.1673) \quad (0.1701)* \quad (0.1586) \quad (0.1678)$$

$$Y_t = -14.7510 + 0.2886 d_{t2} + 0.1203 X_{t-1} - 0.2621 X_{t-2} + 0.0050 X_{t-3} + 0.5435 X_{t-4}$$

$$(13.7978) \quad (0.0804)*** \quad (0.1567) \quad (0.1842) \quad (0.1878) \quad (0.1727)**$$

$$-0.0008 X_{t-5} + 0.1113 Y_{t-1} + 0.1989 Y_{t-2} + 0.1960 Y_{t-3} + 0.3618 Y_{t-4} + 0.0820 Y_{t-5}$$

$$(0.1745) \quad (0.1590) \quad (0.1463) \quad (0.1487) \quad (0.1386)* \quad (0.1467)$$

Overall, the model appears to be good, with some coefficients that are significant, ranging between very high (***) and low (*), and some that are not significant.[17] To see if the results would further improve, the models were also estimated at lags 2 through 4, but none showed any major improvement. Obviously, we could have used much higher lags, but, as we noted earlier under VAR, which also applies to VEC, higher lags would take up too many degrees of freedom, resulting in statistical problems such as multicollinearity.

Forecasts

The process is complete once we do the forecasts of receipts and outlays. Table 6.9 shows the forecasts for the next five years, along with 95% confidence intervals. As the table shows, both receipts and outlays will continue to increase consistently for the forecast years, although outlays will increase at a much higher pace than the receipts, as it has been in recent years, producing a deficit for all five years.

Figure 6.8 presents the forecast plots for both receipts and outlays. Overall, the forecasts appear as one would expect in light of the pattern observed in the original series that show a consistent increase in government receipts and

Table 6.9 Forecasts of Receipts and Outlays

Time	Receipts ($Billion)	95% CI LB*	95% CI UB**	Outlays ($Billion)	95% CI LB*	95% CI UB**
t+1 (Yr.71)	2680.454	2556.199	2804.709	3573.281	3456.402	3690.159
t+2 (Yr.72)	2862.221	2659.720	3064.721	3660.840	3501.476	3820.204
t+3 (Yr.73)	2924.035	2682.858	3165.212	3753.203	3545.585	3960.821
t+4 (Yr.74)	2984.993	2731.737	3238.250	3892.807	3627.795	4157.818
t+5 (Yr.75)	3046.230	2792.455	3300.005	4006.202	3654.778	4357.626

*LB (Lower Bound); **UB (Upper Bound)

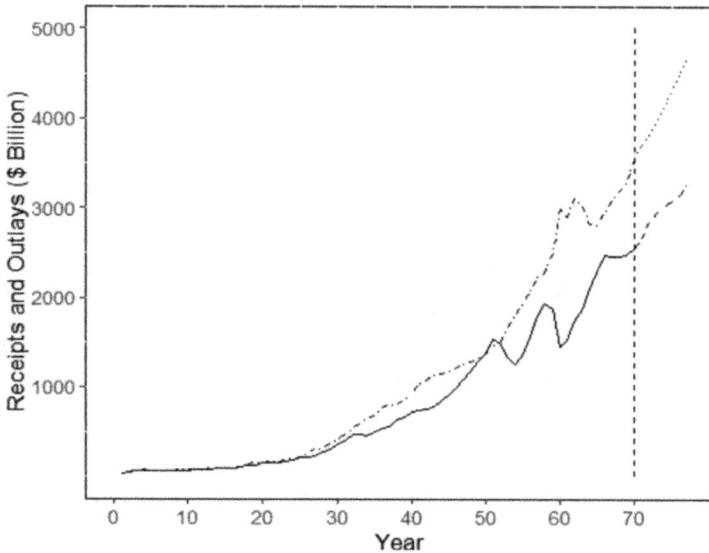

Figure 6.8   Five-Year Forecasts of Receipts and Outlays.

outlays. Additionally, as noted earlier, outlays appear to outpace the growth in receipts for all five years, producing a budget deficit consistent with the pattern observed during the second half of the study period. In fact, a seven-year forecast (not shown here) did not appear to improve the budgetary situation. Outlays will continue to outpace receipts at a much higher rate, producing over half a trillion dollars in deficit by the end of the seventh year.

SUMMARY

Causal models, in particular econometric models, have an important requirement, which could also be a weakness, in that they need to be correctly identified before estimating the model parameters to produce reliable forecasts. If not identified correctly, this can lead to difficulties in determining the exact structural relationship among the variables under consideration. VARs, and their cohort VEC, which belong to the family of multivariate autoregressive moving average (MARMA) models, but without the moving average, do not have any such requirement. This makes it relatively easy to use since it follows some of the same procedures as ARIMA models yet can produce good and reliable forecasts. This chapter has provided a broad overview of both VAR and VEC, including examples of model application with budgetary data from the real world. The chapter, in particular, looked at two issues that are integral to VAR modeling—that of causality and cointegration. It also provided a summary of impulse response function (IRF), which looks at how the variables in a model would respond to external shocks, especially when using VAR.

NOTES

1. A distributed-lag model is simply a time series model in which the effect of an independent variable occurs over time, instead of all at once. Thus, if a typical regression equation is used to predict the values of a dependent variable, Y, it will be based both on the current and the lagged (past) values of the independent variable, X, as can be seen from the following expression:

$$Y_t = \alpha + \sum_{i=0}^{T} \beta_t X_{t-i} + v_t \qquad [6.1]$$

where α and β are the regression parameters, and vt is the error term. For an ARMA process, vt will be a stationary error term.

2. When one is dealing with a system of equations, it is possible to use a method known as Seemingly Unrelated Regression (SURE), instead of VAR, to estimate the equations together. SURE applies to a situation where the equations have a contemporaneous cross-equation correlation in that the error terms of the regression equations are correlated. However, since each regression equation contains the same number of lagged endogenous variables, the OLS estimation of each equation separately produces identical and efficient estimates (Gujarati and Porter, 2009); hence, no need for SURE.

3. The data used in the example were the actual revenue and expenditure data for the State of Texas, obtained from the US Bureau of Census.

4. The *F* test used for Granger-Causality is the well-known Wald test. Developed by Abraham Wald, it is used to test the estimated parameters in a model, with the null hypothesis being that a set of parameters is equal to some values. The formula for the test statistic of a single parameter is as follows:

$$W = \frac{\left(\hat{\beta} - \beta_0\right)}{\left(Var\hat{\beta}\right)} \qquad [6.2]$$

The test is similar to hypothesis tests typically used in regression analysis, but it can be used to test multiple hypotheses about multiple parameters simultaneously (A. Lishinski, *Methods and Overview of Using EdSurvey for Running Wald Test*, https://www.air.org/sites/default/files/EdSurvey-WaldTest.pdf. Retrieved: March 17, 2021).

5. Interestingly, the Granger-Causality test run on differenced series also rejected the null hypothesis that X (Expenditure) does not Granger-cause Y (Revenue), although somewhat less strongly than when it was run on the original series, with an F

value of 3.2442 significant at $p = 0.0602$ with 22 degrees of freedom. However, when the test was run to see if Y Granger-causes X, it failed to reject the null hypothesis, indicating that government revenue does not Granger-cause government expenditure.

6. Cointegration is a statistical method for determining if there is a correlation between two or more time series in the long-term. The tests identify the scenarios where two or more non-stationary time series are integrated together in a way that that they do not drift away from one another in the long run. In other words, they help to identify the long-run parameters (or equilibrium) in a system of equations with variables with unit roots.

7. To explain, let us say that we have two variables, Y, the dependent or forecast variable, and X, the independent or predictor variable. Thus, given X, which is a predictor of Y, we can define it as a function F(X). The question that is appropriate for us, since we are using the Least Squares Method. i.e., the Least Square (LS) prediction of Y, given the observation X, is to find the function of F(X) that is close to Y such that the mean-squared error of prediction, $E[\{Y-F(X)\}]^2$, is minimized. The solution obviously will be the conditional expectation $F(X) = E(Y|X)$.

8. This is due to the fact that when we have a sample size of, say, n, and we are exploring the VAR models with, say, P lags, the models being compared VAR(1), VAR(2), ..., VAR(P) are fitted on the last n-P data points in the sample. Consequently, when we change P, our estimation sample also changes, which produces different results for the same lag length p. The effect of the changing estimation sample tends to be more pronounced for small samples (small n). Unfortunately, there is no precise answer to the problem; hence, we use a trial and error process. However, to make sure that the order of the model is the best (optimal), we use multiple decision criteria such as AIC, HQ, etc., followed by various accuracy measures for VAR at different lags such as ME, RMSE, MAPE, etc., to cross validate the decision.

9. The training set in this case consisted of 23 observations, from 1 to 23, and the test set the remaining five observations, from 24 to 28, for a total of 28 observations in our data set. The rule for selecting the holdout sample is straightforward: the sample length for holdout should be at least equal to the length of the forecast horizon. Thus, if the goal is to have three years of forecast, then withhold three observations, and if the goal is to have five years of forecast, then withhold five observations, and so forth. We ran the VAR model on both the training and the test set for VAR(1) to VAR(6), did forecasts for both, and finally compared the results to produce the accuracy level under four different measures – ME, RMSE, MAE and MAPE.

10. We could have used a different or much higher lag, but the software we used for data runs used lag 6 as the default lag. In fact, to test if the results would be significantly different we specified a lag of 10 which produced a $\chi 2$ of 35.365 with a p value of 0.3123, confirming further the presence of no autocorrelation in the model.

11. As before, the software produced the degree of freedom by default suggesting that with additional degrees of freedom it would produce a p value much higher than the current value; thereby, reinforcing the presence of no autocorrelation.

12. A linear combination is a mathematical expression constructed by multiplying a set of terms by a constant and adding them up, for instance, $Y = \beta_1 X + \beta_2 X$, where β_1 and β_2 are the constants, and Y is the linear combination of β_1 and β_2.

13. The Engle-Granger test, which is essentially an Augmented Dickey-Fuller (ADF) test, is based on the residuals of a static regression where they are tested for the presence of unit roots, discussed in chapter 4. In general, if the series are cointegrated, the residuals of cointegrated regression will be stationary. A couple of points that are worth noting here: ADF test is particularly suitable when one is dealing with two time series in a model, whereas Johansen test can be applied to any number of series. Also, ADF test requires that to apply it one needs to know or choose a priori the dependent variable; if not, it can produce spurious results (statistically significant coefficients with high R2, but meaningless relationship). Johansen test does not have any such requirement, which makes it considerably more flexible than ADF.

14. Economic Research, Federal Reserve Economic Data (FRED), St Louis, Federal Receipts and Outlays: 1950-2019. https://fred.stlouisfed.org/categories/5?t =annual [Retrieved June 15, 2021]

15. Trace test is based on trace, from linear algebra, where a trace is the sum of the diagonal elements in a square matrix. The maximum eigenvalue test, on the other hand, is based on the eigenvalue, λ, a scalar, which is obtained when a matrix is multiplied by a vector producing a vector and a single value, called scalar.

16. The rank of a matrix is given by the maximum number of linearly independent row or column vectors, and cannot not exceed the maximum number of rows and columns. Thus, for an m x n matrix, where m is the number of rows and n is the number of columns, if m<n, then rank of the matrix is m. Similarly, if m>n, then the rank of the matrix is n.

17. As a general rule, if the observed coefficients are twice the size of standard errors, they are considered statistically significant.

Part III

RECENT ADVANCES IN FORECASTING MODELS

Chapter 7

Some Recent Advances in Forecasting Models

Our focus in the previous chapters has been primarily on the principles of forecasting; in that context, we introduced several widely used forecasting models. Most of the works on these forecasting models have a long history; the literature on them is well established, and they are in common practice. In this chapter, we consider three recently developed forecasting models used in specific circumstances: Ensemble forecasting, state-space forecasting model, and neural network. Ensemble forecasting models are commonly used when the results of traditional models prove problematic. For example, an exponential weighted moving average model may prove to under forecast significantly in out-of-sample results. And on similar data, an ARIMA model may over forecast. In this case, we may have a need for an "average" of the forecasts. A state space forecast model combines information from many different variables that each reflects a certain portion of a concept underlying a variable. The concept here is that if we want to forecast a variable such as economic growth, we cannot perfectly observe economic growth. We observe only variables that capture certain elements of the economy. Combining information from many different variables increases the precision at which we are capturing the concept of economic growth.

Finally, using models of human thought processes, neural network models try to capture and process information in ways that traditional models cannot hope to achieve. The information handling and precision of these models are tremendous. If one has the computing capacity to implement these models and does so well, impressive gains in forecast accuracy can be achieved.

ENSEMBLE FORECASTING

The word ensemble is most often used in music and fashion. The dictionary definition of the word is "a group producing a single effect, such as: (a) Concerted music of two or more parts; (b) a complete costume of harmonizing or complementary clothing and accessories..." (Merriam-Webster, 2020). In the forecasting sense, ensembles impart the same meaning. It is a single forecast combined from a set (group) of other forecasts. Ensemble models combine the information from many individual forecasts to form point estimates or probability estimates of variables of interest (Kriz, 2019).

Ensemble forecasts were first used in weather forecasting. An example of this is the "spaghetti plots" that often accompany hurricane forecasts, as shown in Figure 7.1. In this graphic, the lighter shaded lines represent individual forecasts, and the thick bold line toward the center of the mass of individual forecasts is the ensemble forecast. That forecast has combined all information from the individual forecasts into one.

When would it make sense to use an ensemble forecast? Let us consider an analogy: Consider a person trying to make at 12:00 noon a forecast of rain for that afternoon. She might open an app or website to check the weather or simply look at the sky. But if she were making that forecast to prepare for some important event or during a period when the weather was particularly volatile, she might consult multiple sources of forecasts and compare them, updating her forecast with information from each successive information source (Kriz, 2019).

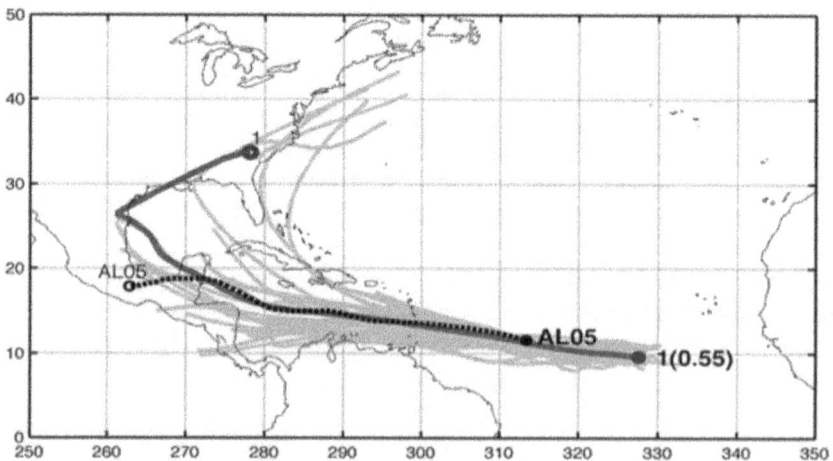

Figure 7.1   Ensemble Weather Forecast.

Morris (1974) established the theory of when a decision maker should get more information from professional experts when faced with a decision and how they should weigh that information against the existing body of knowledge and understanding (he also gave an example of weather forecasting). The answer is presented in Bayesian terms, with prior probabilities of an event or outcome updated as a function of the perceived accuracy of each expert, the strength of the prior probabilities, and the fundamental uncertainty of the variable of interest.

Model Framework

At the core of ensemble, forecasting is how to combine information from multiple forecasts to produce the forecasts that would be optimal. In a classic work, Bates and Granger (1969) established an empirical logic for how to combine information from different forecasts. They asked what an optimal weight (k) would be to combine two unbiased forecasts of a variable (forecast 1, we label this f_1 and forecast 2 - f_2) to produce a combined forecast C at time T:

$$C_T = k_T f_{1,T} + (1 - k_T) f_{2,T} \qquad (7.1)$$

such that the combined forecast variance σ_C^2 would be smaller than the individual variances σ_1^2 and σ_2^2. They find that in situations where the forecasts are uncorrelated, forecast errors should be minimized when the weight is inversely proportional to the relative forecast error variance of f_1:

$$k_T^{BG} = \frac{\sigma_2^{-2}}{\left(\sigma_1^{-2} + \sigma_2^{-2}\right)} \qquad (7.2)$$

There have been numerous methods developed for calculating weights for forecasts. Clemen (1989) found that simple averages produced gains in forecast accuracy in situations where forecasts were not highly correlated and not unbiased. This implies a weight for N forecasts, $f_1, f_2, \dots fN$, of:

$$k_T^{SA} = \frac{1}{N} \qquad (7.3)$$

Granger and Ramanathan (1984) studied ensemble forecasting in an early application of the method. They noted that individual forecasts were a form of information that could be used to determine weights. They proposed that the coefficients from a constrained or unconstrained linear regression of the actual values on the forecasts would yield a combined forecast with lower forecast errors. They proposed three regression variants to produce the optimal weights:

$$y_T = k_i^{GRA} f_{i,T} + u_t \qquad\qquad (7.4)$$

$$y_T = k_i^{GRB} f_{i,T} + u_t, \; st \sum_{i=1}^{N} k_i = 1 \qquad\qquad (7.5)$$

$$y_T = \alpha + k_i^{GRC} f_{i,T} + u_t \qquad\qquad (7.6)$$

Granger-Ramanathan variant A (Equation 7.4) is an unconstrained linear regression of the actual values (y_T) on the forecasts ($f_{i,T}$), dropping the constant term that is usually present in linear regressions. Variant B (Equation 7.5) adds the constraint that the weights should sum to one. Variant C (Equation 7.6) adds a constant term but removes the constraint that the weights add up to one. Granger and Ramanathan prove that in the presence of biased forecasts, variants A and B could produce biased estimates, but variant C will produce unbiased estimates in that the constant term would capture the average bias in the combined forecast.

Steps in Creating Ensemble Forecasts

To illustrate how to develop ensemble forecasts, let us use an example with data on sales tax receipts for a state government. We obtained data from the state's Department of Revenue on sales tax receipts by a quarter over a period of 71 quarters (Appendix 6).[1] The following provides the steps used in producing the forecasts, based on the framework discussed above: (1) Calculate individual forecasts, (2) calculate Bates-Granger and simple average ensemble models, (3) use Bates-Granger and simple average weights to calculate forecasts, (4) calculate Granger-Ramanathan weights using regression analysis, and (5) use Granger-Ramanathan weights to calculate forecasts.

Calculating Individual Forecasts

The first step in creating an ensemble forecast is to calculate the individual forecasts. For the data used in the study, we created three forecasts—a Holt-Winters Triple Exponential Smoothing forecast, a simple 4-quarter moving average forecast, and an ARIMA(1,0,0)(2,0,0) model. Figure 7.2 shows the results of each forecast and the actual data.

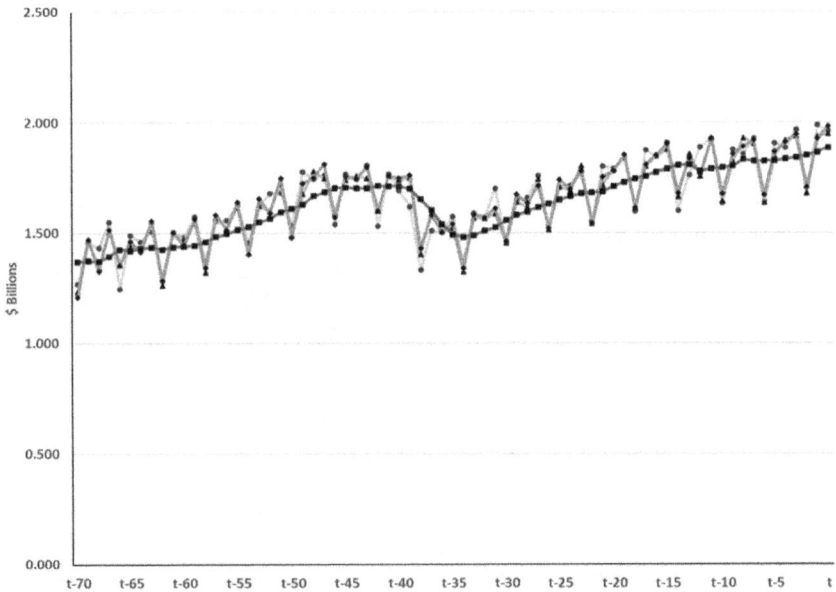

Figure 7.2   Individual Forecasts of Sales Tax Receipt Data.

The line with the circle-shaped marker is Actual Receipts. The line with the box-shaped marker is the 4-period moving average forecast, the line with the diamond-shaped marker is the forecast from a Holt-Winters smoother, and the line with the triangle-shaped marker is from an ARIMA forecast.

Calculations for the Bates-Granger and Simple Average ensemble models can be done entirely by hand or on a spreadsheet. From the R results of each of the analyses, we note the RMSE of each model. This is the error standard deviation (σ). For our data, the RMSEs are Holt-Winters: 48,086,579.26, ARIMA: 50,104,516.16, and MA(4): 108,174,229.63.

Following Equation 7.2, we square and invert each RMSE, producing the following measures: Holt-Winters: $1/(48,086,579.26)^2 = 4.32466E\text{-}16$, ARIMA: $1/(50,104,516.16)^2 = 3.98333E\text{-}16$, MA(4): $1/(108,174,229.63)^2 = 8.54579E\text{-}17$. Then, add these measures to find a total: $4.32466E\text{-}16 + 3.98333E\text{-}16 + 8.54579E\text{-}17 = 9.16257E\text{-}16$. Finally, divide each individual measure by the total to find the weight: Holt-Winters: $4.32466E\text{-}16/9.16257E\text{-}16 = 0.472$, ARIMA: $3.98333E\text{-}16/9.16257E\text{-}16 = 0.435$, MA(4): $8.54579E\text{-}17/9.16257E\text{-}16 = 0.093$. For the simple average, the weights will simply be $1/3 = 0.3333$.

Using Bates-Granger and Simple Average Weights to Calculate Forecasts

Once the weights have been determined, they are multiplied by the individual forecast values to create the ensemble forecast. For the first quarter in the forecast (t+1), the individual forecasts are: Holt-Winters: 2,021,144,963.39, ARIMA: 2,017,040,000.00, and MA(4): 1,903,812,393.40. Applying the Bates-Granger weights, the ensemble forecast would be: 2,021,144,963.39*0.472 + 2,017,040,000.00*0.435 + 1,903,812,393.40*0.093 = 2,008,416,941.74. The simple average ensemble forecast would be 2,021,144,963.39*0.3333 + 2,017,040,000.00*0.3333 + 1,903,812,393.40*0.3333 = 1,980,665,785.60.

Calculating Granger-Ramanathan Weights Using Regression Analysis

The Granger-Ramanathan weights are slightly more complicated to calculate. The first step in calculating the weights is to save the forecasts for the entire sample period. Then we regress the actual values on each of the forecast values. For our data, the regression for variant C would be:

$$SalesTax_T = \alpha + k_{HW}^{GRC} f_{HW,T} + k_{ARIMA}^{GRC} f_{ARIMA,T} + k_{MA4}^{GRC} f_{MA4,T} + u_t \quad (7.7)$$

Running the regression for the first time produces the following weights: $k_{HW}^{GRC} = 0.822908, k_{ARIMA}^{GRC} = 0.204236, k_{MA4}^{GRC} = -0.0795214$. The negative result for the 4-quarter moving average forecast presents a problem. The weights for the model must be positive, including a negative weight is problematic for calculations (if the values of the forecast are positive, applying a negative weight will tend to reduce the value of the ensemble forecast value versus increasing it). Therefore, we drop the moving average forecast term from the model and reestimate. The results indicate the following weights will be optimal: $k_{HW}^{GRC} = 0.779426, k_{ARIMA}^{GRC} = 0.192065$.

Using Granger-Ramanathan Weights to Calculate Forecasts

Applying these weights to the forecasts, we would arrive at an ensemble forecast of 2,021,144,963.39*0.779426 + 2,017,040,000.00*0.192065 = 1,962,735,721.84. This process would be repeated over the desired number of forecast observations to produce the ensemble forecast.

Ensemble forecasts tend to be the most accurate forecasts when the correlations among forecasts are relatively low and unbiased (except for Granger-Ramanathan variant C, which can produce unbiased ensemble forecasts even from biased individual forecasts). For example, a study by Kriz (2019) found that most ensemble methods outperformed individual forecasts of local sales tax revenues at the one-year and five-year time horizons.

STATE-SPACE FORECASTING

Developed in the late 1980s as a method of doing macroeconomic forecasting, state-space models relate the values of observed variables to an unobserved latent variable. A latent variable is another name for a variable that is not directly observable, like a characteristic or trait. For example, let us say that we are interested in people's satisfaction with some service. We cannot perfectly observe satisfaction. At best, we can ask how satisfied people feel about certain qualities of the service. Then we can look for commonalities in responses and interpret how satisfied people are. In other words, the observed variables provide some information about the commonality (these are traits or characteristics in behavioral research, we call them the "state" in forecasting terms). Reversing this logic, changes in the state variable create changes in observed variables.

This logic of the model is shown in Figure 7.3. As shown in the figure, the observed variables (squares) are partially predicted by the unobserved common state variable (oval). While the prediction contains an error, represented by the circles, the multiple measures of the state variable reflect the underlying value, which, in turn, drives the values of the observed variables.[2] In the example, the state variable is an economic index for the Omaha Metropolitan Statistical Area (OEI), while the observed variables are Employment in Transportation Services (transsvcs), the Chicago Federal Reserve Bank

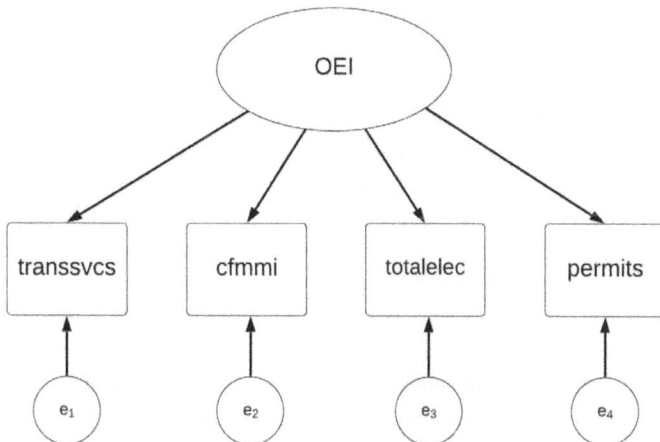

Figure 7.3   State-Space Concept.

Midwest Manufacturing Index (cfmmi), Total Electricity Sales in the Omaha MSA (totalelec), and Building Permits for Single-Family Residential Homes (permits).

Forms of State-Spaced Models

There are many forms of state-space models (see, for example, Commandeur and Koopman, 2007) for a review of and introduction to different types of models). One of the most important for forecasting of government finances is the dynamic factor model. In this type of model, a set of indicator variables evolve over time, and the model examines the relationships over time to deduce the single commonality (factor or state). The formulation of this model is shown in Equations 7.8 and 7.9:

$$X_t = \lambda(L)f_t + e_t \tag{7.8}$$

$$f_t = \Psi(L)f_{t-1} + \eta_t \tag{7.9}$$

The formulation relates the observed variables X to common factors f. The X and f are bolded, indicating that they are vectors of observed variables and factors, respectively. There may be only one or many factors as long as f < X. The factor(s) follow an autoregressive process. The observed variables can follow any stochastic process but most often also follow autoregressive processes.

Dynamic factor models can be used by forecasters to summarize the information contained in many different indicators. One example of this is in developing economic indicators to put into revenue and expenditure forecasts. These economic indicators can be embedded in multivariate forecasting models to capture the role of business cycles on fiscal variables. One could use a single indicator of economic activity, like personal income or output. But these indicators often only capture one aspect of economic activity and are sometimes estimates themselves, suffering from sampling error and subject to spurious changes or exogenous shocks. They also often lag, meaning that forecast models are not capturing the most recent information. Producing an estimate and forecast of dynamic factors and then using them in forecast models captures multiple dimensions of economic activity without inserting numerous indicators and reducing the tractability of the model.

There are numerous estimation procedures for these types of models. In the situation where the factors are not related over time ($\Psi = 0$), one can use simple factor analytic methods such as principal components analysis (PCA) on the data to extract components that reveal information about the latent factor. PCA is a statistical technique that transforms a set of variables into a much smaller set through using the correlations between variables (see Dunteman, 1989 for the general concept of PCA and Stock and Watson, 1989 for a discussion of using it in the dynamic factor model estimation). What results is a smaller set of variables that captures most of the information in the larger data. This estimates the common factors at each point in time.

When the factors are related over time, we must use statistical inference to estimate the time evolution of the factors. The most common methodology for this uses the Kalman filter. The Kalman filter is a means of extracting information from multiple time series that have a combination of a signal (movements that indicate the true direction of a series) and noise (random movements that mask or confound the signal). The filtering process combines the information from the time series and eliminates as much noise as possible. Essentially the weights in Equation 7.8—the factor loadings—are combined with an initial guess about the value of the unknown factor at time t, then the factor loadings and value of the unknown factor are "passed forward" in time to $t+1$, combined with the autoregressive coefficient ψ in Equation 7.9 and updated to estimate the value of the observed variables at $t+1$. The process repeats over all observations T, producing estimates of the observed variables. This process is done iteratively, with each iterative "pass" updating estimates of factor loadings and the unobserved factor. Once the error between the predicted observed variables and actual observed variables over time is minimized, the factors have been identified as closely as possible.

A second method is to use maximum likelihood estimation, where the combination of loadings from the latent factor to the observed variable is determined by the maximization of the likelihood that the weights match the true weights in the population. If there are missing observations, which will occur in many instances, but particularly if the periodicity of all the variables in the data is not the same, this methodology has been amended to include the Expectation Maximization procedure for imputing data (DFM-EM, see Doz, Giannone, and Reichlin, 2012). This involves estimating the values of observation for a given variable based on past values of the variable or past relationships with other variables.

An example of an application using state-space techniques is the Chicago Fed National Activity Index (CFNAI—Brave and Lu, 2010). It combines 85 indicators of national economic activity into a single dynamic factor representing the underlying condition of the economy. The index is based on the academic research of Stock and Watson (1999) into using multiple measures to forecast inflation and business cycles. There are subcomponents of the index for various sectors of the economy which give insights into the dynamics of the following economic aggregates: Production and income;

employment, unemployment and hours worked; personal consumption and housing; and sales, orders, and inventories.

Once we have obtained the factor or factors representing the underlying condition of the economy, we can use it in a time series regression analysis, ARIMA, vector autoregression, or other models to forecast revenues and expenditures. In this way, we reduce the dimensionality of the data (from multiple indicator variables to one or a few factors that capture the information in the variables), which may improve forecast accuracy.

Steps in Dynamic Factor Modeling

Let us look at an example based on a study conducted for a large metropolitan government. The data used in the study focus on the condition of the regional economy over a period of 157 quarters (Appendix 7).[3] We will use a dynamic factor model to extract the factor common to four different time series: Average Hourly Earnings of all private sector employees (we will refer to this as AHE, the data source is the U.S. Bureau of Labor Statistics, State and Metro Area Employment, Hours, and Earnings report), Total Nonfarm Private Employment (NPE, from the U.S. Bureau of Labor Statistics, State Employment, and Unemployment report), New Private Housing Units Authorized by Building Permits (BP, source is the U.S. Census Bureau, Housing Units Authorized by Building Permits report), and Commercial and Industrial Electric Utility Sales (CIE, source is the U.S. Energy Information Administration, Form EIA-861M (formerly EIA-826) detailed data). All data are seasonally adjusted with monthly periodicity.

We proceed in three steps: (1) Test for stationarity and differencing, if necessary, (2) estimate unobserved factors using DFM-MLE, and (3) extract the latent factor and check for consistency with prevailing facts.

Testing for Stationarity and Differencing, if Necessary

We first tested for stationarity using the Kwiatkowski-Phillips-Schmidt-Shin test (KPSS).[4] The test revealed that all variables required differencing to induce stationarity.

Estimating Unobserved Factors Using DFM-MLE

The factors were then determined using the DFM-MLE approach. The Log-Likelihood statistic indicated that the best fit model was one with an AR(1) process for the factor (Equation 7.8) and an AR(2) process for the observed variables (Equation 7.9). The loadings of each variable on the first factor—which we take to represent the underlying state of the economy—are: AHE: -0.414, NPE: 0.567, BP: 2.309, CIE: 0.132. This indicates that building permits loaded the heaviest on the resulting factor, with electrical sales having the lowest loading.

Extract the Latent Factor and Check for Consistency with Prevailing Facts

Figure 7.4 shows the resulting dynamic factor we assume as the economic indicator. The way that the indicator was constructed from the first differenced data implies that a zero value will indicate no change in economic condition, with progressively positive (negative) values indicating improvement (deterioration) of economic activity.

One of the limitations of the DFM method is that there are no standards for assessing goodness of fit. Most times, it is incumbent on the analyst to check the credibility of the model. In this case, the economic indicator seems to fit the perceived facts from news and other sources about the condition of the metropolitan economy. The economic downturn in observations 8-25 is clear, followed by a strong recovery, then a leveling off until around observation 115, when a short burst of economic growth was realized, followed by moderation, and then a definite improvement at the end of the period. Once the values of this factor variable are saved, they can be used in a revenue or

Figure 7.4 Economic Indicator for the Metropolitan Study Area.

expenditure analysis to reflect summarized information on the state of the Pittsburgh economy over time.

Forecasts of the factor can be made in a way similar to that of Time Series Regressions in Chapter 4. The component loadings are like regression coefficients. If we know or have estimates of the variables going forward, we can apply the loadings to forecast the factor in future periods.

NEURAL NETWORK

Neural network models are another advanced methodology for forecasting revenues and expenditures. Although the roots of these models go back to the 1940s, only with the advent of "Big Data" in the late 1990s and early 2000s, these models began to receive renewed interest. In these models, the thought processes of humans are modeled to capture and process information in ways that traditional models can never hope to achieve. The term neural network may cause consternation as it seems complex for most students, even those with considerable background in statistics. However, as we will see, these models are nothing more than applied statistical models. They do differ from the models we have seen before in significant ways. They are potentially non-linear and based on numerical maximization algorithms custom-built to the purpose, as opposed to primarily linear models in generic statistical applications appropriate for many types of problems.

Model Structure

The word neural in the title is meant to invoke the workings of the human brain. These models seek to replicate the process of cognition in human minds, allowing for the identification of "fuzzy" patterns and shapes in applications ranging from facial recognition to text analysis. In general, a neural network model consists of at least three "layers"—an input layer that recognizes information, a "hidden" layer or layers that process the input information, and an output layer that creates a prediction (Figure 7.5). These layers are connected through weights (the lines in the figure) that create a value in the next layer.

To see how these layers work, let us examine a stylized example. Suppose that we are trying to predict the value of a house. We have data on several variables, including the square footage of the house, the number of bedrooms, distance from the city center, and the age of the house (McCullum, 2021). In the simplest form of a neural network, we apply weights to each input variable to produce a predicted price (Figure 7.6). The formula in the Figure

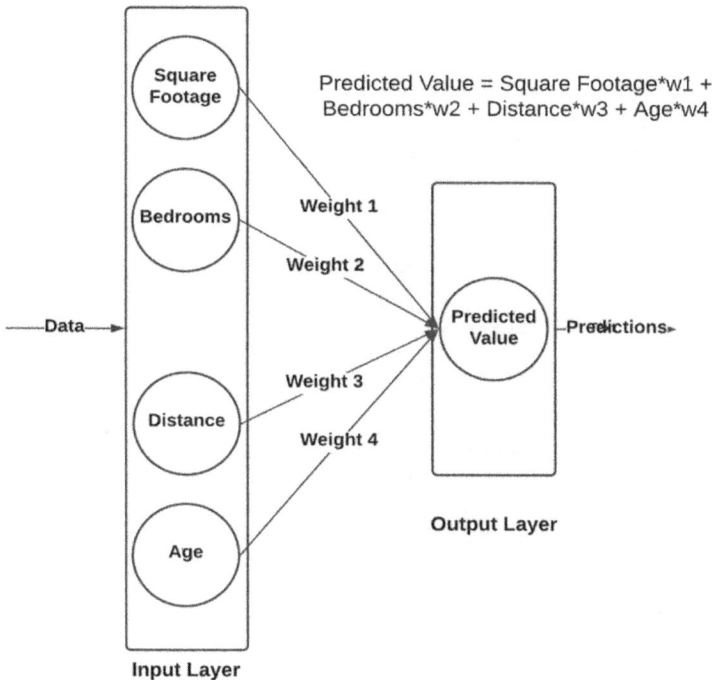

Predicted Value = Square Footage*w1 + Bedrooms*w2 + Distance*w3 + Age*w4

Figure 7.5   Two-Layer Neural Network Model of House Prices.

should seem familiar—a simple two-layer input-output neural network is simply a linear regression model, as discussed in an earlier chapter.

As long as this simple model applies to the prediction of house prices, then we need to go no further than the simple two-layer input-output neural network. However, if things get complicated—for example, where the actual model of housing prices differs based on the distance to the city center, we need a way to capture this. Enter the hidden layers. The hidden layers take inputs from the input layer (or other hidden layers) and apply new weights to "feed-forward" a new prediction to other hidden layers or the output layer. Let us assume that the actual model for housing prices has one set of weights for houses less than 5 miles from the city center and another set of weights for houses more than 5 miles. We add a hidden layer to the model for that condition. If the hidden layer is "activated" by an observation more than 5 miles from the city center, the new set of weights applies. However, if the layer is not activated, then the original weights apply. This type of hidden layer is sometimes called a "conditional" or "Boolean" hidden layer—its value is either zero or one depending on whether it is activated (Figure 7.7).

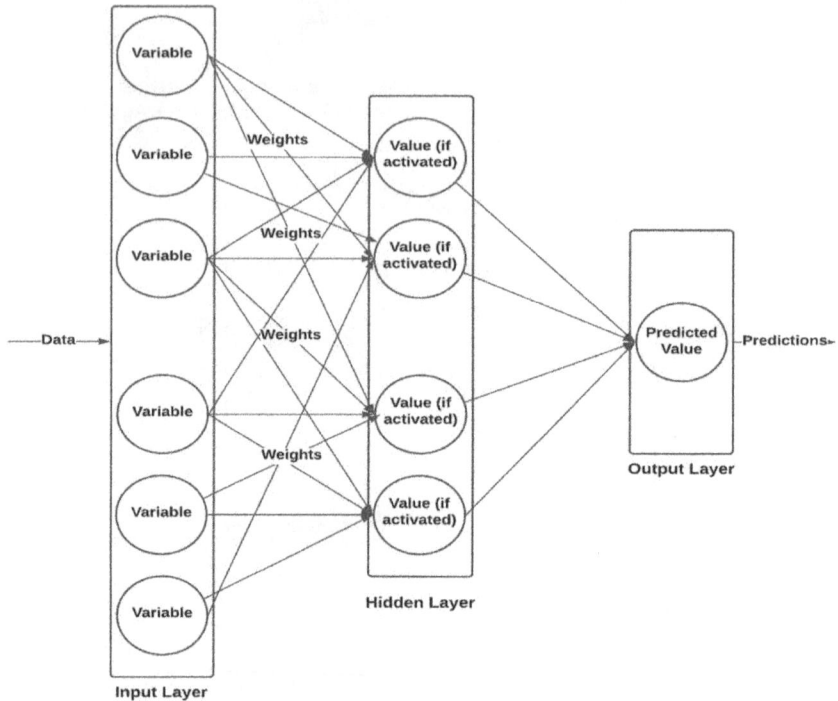

Figure 7.6   Basic Neural Network Structure.

The conditional hidden layer is only one type. Hidden layer activation may be based on specific calculations, certain threshold values, or certain relationships among different calculations or values. The flexibility of this type of model is a definite strength. Many types of linear and nonlinear forms can be applied to the data. The trade-off for this flexibility is a level of complexity that can be daunting to explain, which can require a large amount of computing power to estimate.

We have discussed how neural networks feed input information forward through weights and hidden layers to create a predicted output value. This process is also called forward propagation. Readers might be thinking of two questions at this point: (1) How are the weights determined, and (2) how is the number of hidden layers determined? To answer those questions, we must introduce a new term called backpropagation (or "backprop"). Backprop is how neural network models "learn" through adjusting weights and the number of layers. To understand this, consider our model from Figure 7.6. This model has one hidden layer and a series of weights leading from the input layer to the hidden layer and from the hidden layer to the output layer. The output layer value (the prediction) is compared to an actual value. The result

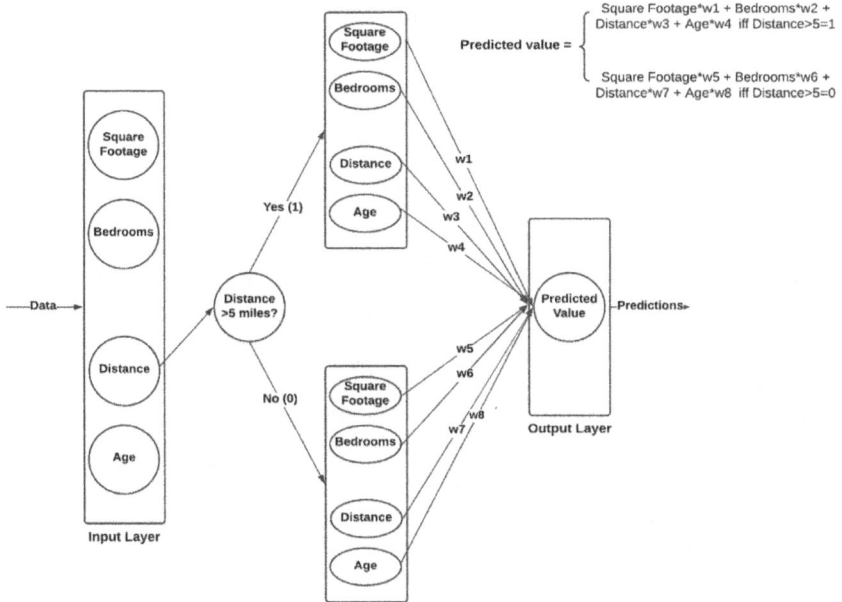

Figure 7.7   Neural Network Model with Boolean Hidden Layer.

is an error value, as discussed in chapter 2. Suppose there is enough data on actual relationships between input and output values. In that case, the model with weights and one layer is compared to the data, producing a summary error measure such as mean-squared error (MSE). The model then adjusts weights considering the MSE and then recalculates the errors. It can also add or subtract layers as necessary to reach a minimum on the MSE.[5]

Learning can be "supervised" or "unsupervised." Supervised learning (described above) is used when there is sufficient data on both inputs and outputs to adjust weights and layers based on output predictions. In cases where there is not sufficient data on inputs and outputs, we rely on unsupervised learning. This type of learning is often used in applications where outputs are not well defined, such as text predictions. In this situation, outputs are determined through a sort of "clustering" analysis, where patterns of outputs are identified and classified into different clusters. The weight and layer structure are then determined to provide the most significant distinction between different clusters.

This process of modeling using neural networking is typically done through two stages. The model is "trained" using supervised or unsupervised learning on "training data" in the first stage. This data is a sampled subset from the total amount of data available. The remaining data is used to "test" the model developed during the training phase. There are many ways to sample data for training and testing, which are beyond the scope of this text.[6]

Neural Networks and Time Series Data

Applying neural networks in a time series data structure presents some specific problems. Three of the problems involve the time series structure itself, the recency of data points, and the noisiness of the data. To see this, assume that the data has been following a positive linear trend with an AR(1) error term. The neural network needs to be trained such that the relationship between sequential observations reflects the trend-AR(1) structure of the data. Each sequential observation can be evaluated against the predicted value, and the model can be adjusted accordingly. Such a model that adjusts sequentially is called a "recurrent neural network" (RNN). RNNs can be very powerful in predicting time-series data.

Now assume that a new observation comes in far from the predicted value generated by the previous iteration of the RNN. The question is whether this observation represents:

1. A mismeasured value
2. A deviation due to noisiness of the data
3. A change in the trend, AR term, or the entire structure of the model (this is called a structural break)

If the situation is mismeasurement (1), we do not want to estimate the model again, introducing more noise. If the problem is due to a noisy observation (2), we may estimate again but will put a lower weight on this observation to estimate the model's parameters. However, if a structural break has occurred, we need to reformulate the model moving forward.

A relatively new type of model has been developed to deal with this type of situation, a long short-term memory model (LSTM). LSTM is a form of RNN, but with "gates" introduced to filter data from new observations. The gates assess new observations against the model's predictions formed up to the prior observation. If the value of the new observation is substantially different from that prediction, it pauses the model from updating through backprop as it usually would. Then the model assesses the following observation. Suppose the next observation is within the limit predicted by the model. In that case, the model uses that observation to backprop, adjust the weights and layers, and forget the prior observation. Thus, the model concludes that either (1) or (2) happened, and there is no need to reinitialize the model estimation. However, suppose the second observation is also far from the prediction of the existing model. In that case, the model begins to think that a structural break (3) has taken place, continuing to pause updating. Depending on how sensitive the model has been set to be, the model would reset at the structural breakpoint after a few observations.

Extended Example

NNs, RNNs, and LSTMs can be used to forecast many variables. In this example, we examine forecasts for sales tax receipts in the state of Illinois. We obtain quarterly data on sales tax receipts in different industries and counties throughout the state over a then aggregate the county-level data to produce statewide sales tax receipts for an apparel industry (Appendix 8).[7] Figure 7.8 shows a graph over time.

At first, the data were modeled as a single-hidden-layer RNN for each industry (as shown in Figure 7.8 above). The single hidden layer structure proved adequate in the training data. However, during modeling, it was determined that common factors drove each industry. Therefore, we modeled all data together and added a hidden layer that activates depending on the industry. We also modeled the data using an LSTM module with forget and updating gates, as shown in Figure 7.9.

Running the model produces forecasts at different horizons. The methodology for producing the forecasts mirrors that of ARIMA models in chapter 4. The models produce weights for each of the historical observations in the

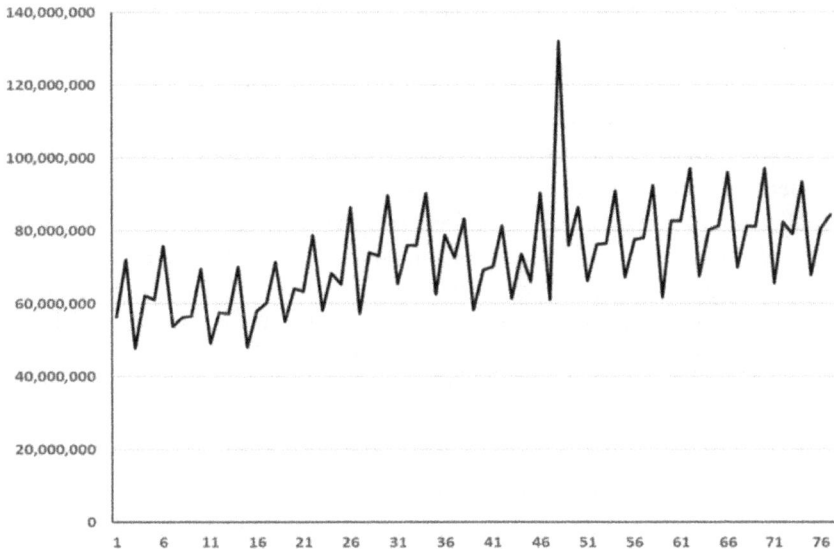

Figure 7.8　Quarterly Sales Tax Receipts, Apparel.

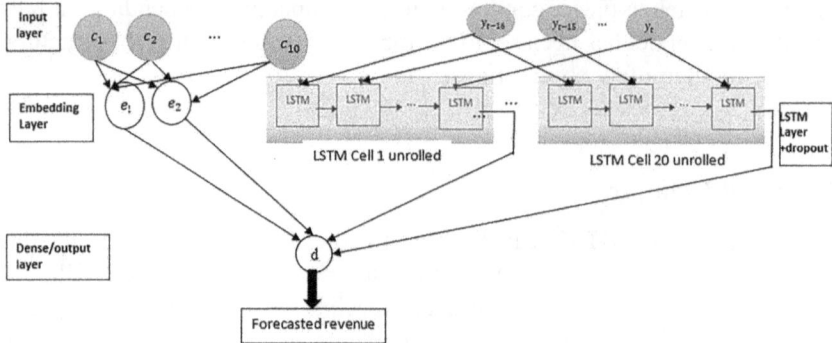

Figure 7.9   LSTM Model, Sales Tax Receipts.

model; those weights are then rolled forward recursively. We evaluated the RNN and LSTM models against the best-fitting ARIMA model at the one-quarter ahead time horizon, using the MAPE to measure forecast accuracy.[8] The results of the model for various industries are shown in Table 7.1. The RNN model performs best in most industries, except for Drugs & Retail. This industry had remarkable stability, where a pattern-following model like ARIMA can perform very well.

SUMMARY

This chapter has provided an overview and analysis of three recently developed models used for more specific forecasting purposes than conventional forecasting models. Ensemble forecasting models capture information from numerous forecasts and combine them into a single forecast that may have smaller errors than the individual forecasts that go into them. They are used in situations where more traditional models produce biased estimates and significant out-of-sample errors. State-space models combine information on variables that measure some component of a variable that cannot be observed directly, such as economic growth. The combined information produces a "factor" that can be said to be an estimate of the unobserved variable. Neural networks are models that use the same information processing approach that is used in the human mind to create complex but very accurate models of phenomena. They have become more widely used over the past decade or so and have been shown to have good qualities when applied appropriately to time-series data.

Table 7.1 MAPE, Different Models and Industries, Sales Tax Receipt Data

Model/Industry	Agriculture and All Others	Apparel	Automotive and Filling Stations	Drinking and Eating Places	Drugs and Retail	Food
RNN	3.07	2.79	2.54	0.50	11.48	3.36
LSTM	4.16	4.16	4.44	1.47	10.69	3.91
ARIMA	5.51	7.39	3.34	3.87	9.87	8.03
Model/Industry	Furniture and Household, Radio	General Merchandise	Lumber Building and Hardware	Manufacturing	Mean Across Industries	
RNN	2.72	2.89	3.07	3.77	3.63	
LSTM	3.04	5.34	4.00	6.80	4.80	
ARIMA	5.06	9.50	6.85	3.91	6.30	

NOTES

1. The data for the study came from State of Illinois: The data begins in the third quarter of 1999 and ends in the third quarter of 2018. Source: Sales Tax Receipts: Illinois Department of Revenue, Sales Tax Statistics https://www2.illinois.gov/rev/research/taxstats/SalesTaxStatistics/Pages/default.aspx

2. We've defined "state" in the term state-space, but not "space." The space refers to the Euclidean space the state variables exist within. In other words, the range of the observations.

3. Based on an actual study conducted for the City of Pittsburgh. The data used in the study came from the following sources:

    a. Average Hourly Earnings: U.S. Bureau of Labor Statistics, State and Metro Area Employment, Hours, and Earnings report https://www.bls.gov/sae/

    b. Total Nonfarm Private Employment: U.S. Bureau of Labor Statistics, State Employment and Unemployment report https://www.bls.gov/lau/

    c. New Private Housing Units Authorized by Building Permits: U.S. Census Bureau, Housing Units Authorized by Building Permits report https://www.census.gov/construction/bps/

    d. Commercial and Industrial Electric Utility Sales: U.S. Energy Information Administration, Form EIA-861M (formerly EIA-826) detailed data) https://www.eia.gov/electricity/data.php

4. This is a test for stationarity similar to the Augmented Dickey-Fuller (ADF) test introduced in chapter 4. The difference is that whereas the ADF test is a test of the null hypothesis that the data is not stationary, the null for the KPSS test is that the data is stationary.

5. This is very similar to the Kalman filter and maximum likelihood estimation methods introduced in the section on state-space forecasting models.

6. Interested readers can consult Hancock (2012) on the specifics of training and testing of models.

7. The data came from the State of Illinois: Quarterly Sales Tax Receipts: Illinois Department of Revenue, Standard Industrial Classification (SIC) Code Reporting https://www.revenue.state.il.us/app/kob/index.jsp

8. We used a form of testing data called rolling cross-validation where the model is trained on successively longer training period, always with a one-step-ahead test period.

Conclusion

The forecasting methods discussed in the text are among the most widely used methods in time series forecasting. Most of these methods, with some exceptions, especially those discussed in the previous chapter, are conceptually simple yet versatile enough that they can be applied to almost any forecasting situation. As such, they are often called "mechanical methods" of forecasting, drawing an analogy with forecasting methods used in engineering, in part because they are based on the assumption that future is a derivative of the past. But there are methods that do not necessarily assume that the future is an extension of the past, rather that it can be predicted based on the present. Methods of this type are commonly known as "barometric methods," which are primarily used for dealing with specific forecasting problems.

This concluding chapter provides a brief overview of three commonly used barometric methods in forecasting—statistical indicators, diffusion index, and a composite index. The last two are considered variations of the first, and, together, they are often called qualitative indicators. The chapter also highlights several topics that are integral to most discussions on forecasting, in particular, challenges to time series forecasting, the need to evaluate forecasts and forecasting methods, forecast monitoring, and, finally, producing a multi-year forecast to determine if there will be a budget surplus or deficit. It concludes with some commonsense rules of do's and don'ts of forecasting.

STATISTICAL INDICATORS

Statistical indicators are mostly used to forecast changes in the direction of an economy as it goes through the peaks and troughs in a business cycle. Three types of statistical indicators are commonly used for this purpose: Leading indicators, coincident indicators, and lagging indicators. Leading indicators are primarily used to identify and forecast the changes in an economy, in particular the business cycle. As an economy goes through periodic ups and downs, it is necessary to have a sense of when the economy will go through a trough or reach its peak. The movements in leading indicators can predict the movements in the business cycle before the economy does; hence, the term leading indicators.

The government uses multiple such indicators to track these changes. Important among these indicators are returns on short-term Treasury Bills (yield curve), average work week (production workers, manufacturing hours), average weekly claims (unemployment insurance), new orders for consumer goods and materials, new business formations, contracts for plants and equipment, new building permits (private housing), changes in inventories on hand and order, changes in total liquid assets, stock prices (500 common stocks), and money supply, especially M2. In addition, the government also uses traditional indicators such GDP, Consumer Price Index (CPI), and Producer Price Index (PPI), among others.

Unlike the leading indicators, which are used to predict changes in the cycle, the coincident indicators indicate the movement in the economy the same way as the business cycle, at approximately the same time. As such, they do not predict the future, rather they tell us what is happening at the present time. For instance, suppose we want to know if the economy has entered a recession. It takes several months to gather GDP data, so if we rely on GDP data to time a recession, we cannot determine if a recession has started until we can analyze the GDP data, which might be months after a recession has already begun. But if we look at coincident indicators, we can get current information that tells us what is currently happening in the economy. Thus, coincident indicators are used to determine what is currently happening when the more comprehensive, i.e., detailed GDP data are unavailable. These indicators typically include employees on nonagricultural payrolls, industrial production, personal income, and manufacturing and business sales.

Finally, the lagging indicators are used for those activities that are slow to respond to changing business and economic conditions. This is because these indicators measure what has already occurred. Examples of lagged indicators would include labor cost per unit of output, manufacturing inventory, commercial and industrial loans outstanding, the average duration of unemployment, the ratio of consumer installment debt to personal income, and the average prime rate charged by banks. Lagged indicators are most effective when used in combination with leading indicators to determine trends.

The last point suggests that as good as these indicators are, by themselves, they may not produce sufficient information about the direction of the economy. Therefore, they are often used in combinations, such as by taking an average of the individual components to produce an aggregate index. A good example is an index currently used by the US Conference Board, which uses an average of all three indicators to provide a good predictor of the direction of change in the economy.

Diffusion Index

Next, the diffusion indexes are used to see if a change in a particular indicator or a group of indicators reflects a shift in the general trend in the economy or it is just an isolated incident. For instance, suppose that four of 12 leading indicators have been increasing in recent months, the diffusion index would thus be 4/12 or 33.33 percent. Using a diffusion index, economists define a critical percentage, usually set at 50 percent. If the diffusion index is above this critical percentage, it is an indication that economic activities are increasing, and the converse is true if it is less than 50 percent. The intensity of the trend in either direction reflects how far the activity is from this critical percentage.

Unfortunately, the direction of the indexes may not always be precise. For instance, it is possible that some indexes may peak during the early stages of a business expansion and then settle down at a slow to moderate pace until the recession sets in. This may not have any forecasting value if they fail to capture the underlying trend. However, despite their occasional irregularities, the diffusion indexes are considered a useful measure for examining the direction of the economy, especially the business cycle.

Composite Index

Finally, the composite indexes, including those used by the Conference Board, are mostly used for predicting the movement in the aggregate economy, including turning points. Turning points occur when a series takes a sudden turn from a trend toward the peak or trough in a cycle. A convenient way to forecast the movement in an aggregate economy is to use a weighted average or a composite index of a group of indicators or data series, also known as component series. The weight of each indicator or series is based on how well it performs on a set of criteria related to forecasting, such as economic significance, statistical reliability, conformity to business expansions and contractions, and so forth. In general, if the component series is chosen carefully, the composite index based on those series can contain a lot of information about the aggregate economy that may prove to be more reliable than any of its individual components (Ratti, 1985).

While all three measures discussed above provide sufficient information about when changes in the cycle will take place, they do not provide an iron-clad guarantee that the predictions will be accurate every time. There were many instances in the past when these indicators failed to accurately predict when the turning points in the cycle will occur, but that does not diminish their overall effectiveness. To avoid this problem, the government has been using a combination of indexes, including the diffusion index, to gauge the direction of business activity, the rate of change to measure both the direction and degree of business activity, and the NBER's (National Bureau of Economic Research) reference cycle to trace the peaks and troughs of the business cycle, among others.

CHALLENGES TO TIME SERIES FORECASTING

Forecasting is a challenging exercise. From the first step of defining the forecasting objective, selecting the appropriate method, collecting relevant data, applying the method, testing the results and, finally, producing the forecast is a complex undertaking. Of these, selecting the appropriate forecasting method is particularly important because of the range of methods that are available to a forecaster, which has increased both in number and complexity over the years. This simple recognition of the challenges to forecasting, in particular the availability of a wide range of methods, is what drives the forecasters to constantly search for better forecasting methods. Unfortunately, there is no guarantee that the most sophisticated methods will produce better and more accurate forecasts. Simple extrapolation methods such as naïve forecasting or percentage average, if applied properly, can produce forecasts that are as good as those produced by sophisticated methods (Makridakis et al., 1982).

Given that methods abound, the real challenge for a forecaster is to select the method or methods that would be most appropriate for a forecasting problem; in other words, one that would produce the most accurate forecasts (least forecast errors). Unfortunately, it is easier said than done because of the presence of intervening factors that can render perfectly accurate forecasts, especially time series forecasts, difficult. The factors can range from estimation uncertainty (due to systematic and random errors, which we addressed to some extent in Chapter 3), to overfitting and difficulties in modeling trends (due to the limited number of observations in a time series, which we addressed to some extent in Chapters 4 and 5), to modeling shocks and instability (due to sudden changes in a policy or structural breaks to which forecasting models fail to adapt, which we touched a little when we discussed the impulse response function in Chapter 6). From a forecasting perspective, what is important, first and foremost, is to determine what contributes to these issues and, second, what measures can be taken to address them.

The question eventually boils down to which method or methods would produce the best forecast. As noted earlier, it is not quite as simple to suggest a prescription that would provide a good forecasting method. Nevertheless, studies abound that attempt to address this issue. Two general lessons emerge from the vast array of time series studies (Stock, 2001): Simple linear models perform as well, if not better than complex nonlinear models, and gains from univariate to multivariate time series models are marginal, although not always. So, where does the future hold for forecasting methods? Unfortunately, there is no precise answer to the question. According to Stock (2002), the future of forecasting, in particular economic forecasting, hinges on the development of computer-intensive methods and the real-time availability of large data sets with complex patterns of historical dependence. Some of the methods discussed in the previous chapter, plus the whole range of new methods that are emerging lend support to Stock's reflection on new directions in forecasting.

EVALUATING FORECASTS AND FORECASTING METHODS

As it should be obvious, forecasts are not perfect. They seldom are. Forecasters, as well as those who use forecasts, are aware of it. One way to address the problem is to examine the forecasting methodology in its entirety to determine what contributes to the problem. There are different approaches one can use for this purpose. Armstrong (2001), for instance, suggests an interesting approach based on the systems concept with inputs and outputs. Inputs, in this context, would include model assumptions, as well as the data used in the study. Outputs, on other hand, would include the actual forecasts and their level of accuracy. It is difficult to say which one is more important: Inputs or Outputs? One may argue that testing inputs are more important in evaluating forecasting methods than testing outputs. In reality, both are necessary (Armstrong, 2001): Testing inputs can help determine the superiority of one method over another for a given forecasting problem, while testing outputs can produce information that can tell how to improve the model.

Interestingly, the search for better forecasting methods is an unending process, given the wide range of methods one can choose from. In each case, the question will be the same: How best to select a method that, in the final analysis, would produce good and reliable forecasts.

Evaluating Forecast Errors

All forecasting studies have a common objective, which is to produce forecasts that would be good and reliable with the least forecast error. The conventional approaches to measure forecast errors, such as MAD, MSE,

MAPE, and so forth, while serving as the first important step in determining the accuracy of a forecast, it may be necessary to use other measures to further ensure that the results are good and reliable. The simplest way to achieve this is to compare the forecasts obtained with a particular method against those obtained with other methods to see how well they compare. This is a common practice at the national level where multiple organizations (e.g., Data Resources Incorporated, Chase Econometrics, Wharton Econometric Associates, academic institutions, and others) develop forecasts on the same set of variables. Most of these variables are macroeconomic variables such as unemployment, inflation, gross domestic product, budget deficit, and so on. The forecasts can easily serve as a benchmark against which individual forecasts can be compared to measure their accuracy.

Another, perhaps, more effective way to produce reliable forecasts is to take an average of the forecasts produced by different methods into a single forecast. This is known as a composite forecast, similar to the composite index discussed earlier. Composite forecasts are useful in situations where the forecaster is not sure what specific forecasting method to use. By taking an average or some combination of the forecasts, the forecaster can avoid large errors. The rule of thumb is to use at least five different forecasts on the same set of variables. A common assumption in selecting multiple methods is that there are qualitative differences among the methods so that the forecaster can assign a different weight to the forecasts produced by each method and take a weighted average.

Dealing with Forecasting Bias

Alice Rivlin, the first Director of Congressional Budget Office (CBO), once made an interesting observation that during her tenure as the Director of CBO she came across three types of forecasts: Optimistic (forecasts that consistently overestimate), pessimistic (forecasts that consistently underestimate), and pragmatic (forecasts that are neither). Obviously, each forecast will have a direct effect on the budgetary decision of a government. For instance, an optimistic forecast can easily lead to overspending that cannot be supported by the amount of revenue the economy will generate for the government, resulting in a budget deficit. Conversely, a pessimistic forecast can easily lead to underspending, given the amount of revenue the economy will generate for the government, resulting in a budget surplus. The latter may come at the cost of reduced government expenditures that can lead to reduced collective consumption, which, in turn, can lead to a reduction in the collective welfare of society.

The scenario described above is possible, in particular, when one is using a causal model, where the forecaster has to make some assumptions about how the explanatory (predictor) variables will behave in the future that will have a direct effect on the forecast variable. If the assumptions are optimistic, the forecast will be optimistic. Conversely, if they are pessimistic, the forecast will be pessimistic. To give an example, suppose that the economic growth (forecast variable) of a government depends on consumption spending (C), private investment (I), government spending (G), and trade balance (M), the explanatory variables in this case. The government wants to forecast the growth rate for the next several years. If we assume that each of the explanatory variables in the coming years will be high and positive (an unlikely scenario, given the recent trend in the state of the economy), the economic growth will also be high, and vice versa.

The point is, whether the overestimation and underestimation of future economic growth, called bias in estimation, are deliberate or unintended, the government must make every effort to minimize the bias by adjusting the projected growth against the actual growth. This is where forecast monitoring becomes critically important, which allows a government to trace the direction of bias and make the necessary adjustment in the budgetary decisions (overspend or underspend) to conform to actual data.

FORECAST MONITORING

All forecasts need to be monitored on a regular basis to determine how well they are performing against the actual values in order to establish their reliability. The ultimate test of a forecasting model is its ability to sustain the production of acceptabe, reliable, forecasts. Over time, the forces driving the data in a series may change, causing the forecast accuracy to decline and the models less reliable. Additionally, the series may develop a trend, the functional form of a trend may change, the seasonal patterns may become unpredictable, and the like. What this means is that when changes occur in a series, it may be necessary to change the model or update the model structure to reflect the changing conditions.

While updating can help improve the situation, it may not always be able to keep up with the changes affecting the forecasts, in which case it may be necessary to build into the forecasting scheme an accuracy monitor to indicate any loss of accuracy. One such measure of accuracy monitoring is tracking signal (TS). This method allows for comparison of forecasts with actual observations as they become available. There are different ways of developing tracking signals; the simplest is to divide the forecast errors, called the running sum of forecast errors (RSFE), by their mean absolute deviation (MAD). It is given by the expression

$$TS = \frac{RSFE}{MAD} = \frac{\sum_{i=1}^{n}\left(Y_{t+i} - \hat{Y}_{t+i}\right)}{MAD} \qquad (C.1)$$

where Y_t is the observed value of the variable Y at time t, which is usually the current period and $\hat{Y}_{t+i}$ is the forecast value for i^{th} period beyond the current period (for i = 1, 2,......,n). In general, a positive signal indicates the actual observation is higher than the forecast value, while a negative signal indicates the opposite. While TS does not have a precise upper limit, it can be close to 0. In general, the closer it is to 0, the better the forecast.

To give an example, let us suppose that we have six years of forecasts for LOST revenue of a local government. Table C.1 shows the computations of the tracking signal for LOST revenue for the government. Assume that we have the actual (observed) values of LOST revenue corresponding to six years of the forecasts. Since the signals are cumulative, the TS for Year 6 explains the overall error for all six forecast years, *t*+1 through *t*+6, as shown below:

$$TS = \frac{0.2752}{0.4728} = 0.58$$

which is 0.58 (expressed in terms of MAD)

As can be seen from the table, most of the signals are close to 0, indicating that the forecasts were quite good (which may not be the case in reality since the values were arbitrarily selected) but to ensure that they are statistically sound it may be necessary to compare the tracking signals against some predetermined control limits with upper and lower bounds. If the signals fall within these limits, they should be considered good, meaning that the forecasts are good, and if they lie outside the limits, the signals are considered tripped, indicating poor forecasts.

Unfortunately, there is no cut-and-dried formula for determining the control limits for tracking signals. As such, forecasters frequently use a convention to determine the limits that are based on the area under the normal curve. Since the maximum length the curve can extend from the center of gravity is $\pm 4\sigma$, one can argue that ± 1 MAD is equivalent to approximately 0.8 standard deviation, ± 2 MADs to 1.6 standard deviations, ± 3 MADs to 2.4 standard deviations, and ± 4 MADs to 3.2 standard deviations.[1] This means that for a forecast to be in control, 89 percent of the errors must fall within ± 2 MADs, 98 percent within ± 3 MADs, and 99.9 percent within ± 4 MADs. Going back to the LOST revenue example, we can see that our hypothetical tracking signal falls within the acceptable limits, drifting between -0.87 MAD and $+0.58$ MAD, thus indicating that the forecasts were reasonably good.

Table C.1 Computation of Tracking Signal for LOST Revenue (in $Million)

Time	Forecast Value	Actual Value	Error	RSFE*	Forecast Error	Cumulative Error	MAD	TS
t+1	24.4278	25.1368	0.7090	0.7090	0.7090	0.7090	0.7090	1.00
t+2	25.8943	26.2799	0.3856	1.0946	1.0946	1.8036	0.9018	1.21
t+3	26.7373	25.3732	-1.3641	-0.2695	0.2695	2.0731	0.6910	-0.39
t+4	27.5990	27.3649	-0.2341	-0.5036	0.5036	2.7736	0.5768	-0.87
t+5	27.8466	28.4083	0.5617	0.0581	0.0581	2.5617	0.4730	0.12
t+6	28.4016	28.1845	0.2171	0.2752	0.2752	2.8369	0.4728	0.58

*RSFE (Cumulative total); MAD=Cumulative Error/n; TS=RSFE/MAD

THE END PRODUCT: CONSTRUCTING
A MULTIYEAR FORECAST

The old adage that the quality of a pudding lies in tasting also applies to forecasting. How good a forecast is, depends on how close it is to the actual value and what it can tell us about the future. One way to assess the merit of a forecast, especially for a government budget, is to construct a multiyear forecast for several years into the future to assess the long-term outlook of the government's revenue and expenditure; in other words, to determine if there will be a major budget gap in the future, as we did with some of our forecasting methods. In fact, the 1974 Budget and Impoundment Control Act requires the federal budget to include a multiyear forecast when preparing the annual budget, which subsequently became a standard for most state and local governments.

However, questions have been raised as to how many years of forecasts are necessary, since errors tend to increase faster as the forecast period is lengthened. In most cases, a five-year forecast should suffice. Beyond that, forecasts could become only marginally better than random noise (Penner, 2001). Nevertheless, long-term forecasts are necessary to allow the decision makers plenty of time to decide what measures to take in the event the normal budget shortfalls resulting in budget deficits become serious and persistent. In the same vein, since most government budgets are prepared on an annual basis, it is important that forecasts are continuously updated as new information becomes available to minimize forecast errors.

To give an example, let us look at a study involving a large US city that was experiencing persistent budget shortfalls (Khan, 2003). It was conducted at a time when long-term forecasts started receiving a lot of attention, especially at the local level, in part because most state and large metropolitan governments were already using long-term forecasts, and in part because of the potential for a budget crisis resulting from persistent deficits. The study consisted of both simple trend line and single-equation regression models. A total of 15 equations were used to produce a six-year revenue and expenditure forecast for the General Fund (GF) of the government.

The following provides a brief summary of the equations used in the study:

GF Revenues: (By Source)

Property Tax Revenue $(PTR_t) = [\{(NVTP_t \times PC_t)/1,000\} \times MR_t$

Net Value of Taxable Property $(NVTX_t) = \alpha + \beta Time$

Business and Excise Txaes $(BEXT_t) = \alpha + \beta_1 CPOP_t + \beta_2 RCPI_t + e_t$

Intergovernmental Revenue $(IGR_t) = [(FAST_t + CSSTC_t) - LOGT_t]$

Federal and State Transfer $(FAST_t) = \alpha + \beta Time$

City Share of Sales Tax Collections $(CSSTC_t) = [(GSSTC_t)(0.1)] \times k(constant)$

County Sales tax Collection $(GSSTC_t) = \alpha + \beta SSTR_t + e_t$
Local Option Gasoline Tax $(LOGT_t) = \alpha + \beta CPOP_t + e_t$
Business Licenses and Permits $(BLP_t) = \alpha + \beta_1 RCPI_t + \beta_2 CPI_t + e_t$
Fines and Forfeiture $(FAF_t) = \alpha + \beta Time_{t-1}$
Miscellaneous Charges and Revenue Sources $(MCRS_t) = \alpha + \beta Time$

GF Expenditures: (By Category)
  City Personnel Services $(CPS_t) = \alpha + \beta CPS_{t-1} + e_t$
  City Operating Expenses $(COE_t) = \alpha + \beta_1 COE_{t-1} + \beta_2 CPOP_t + e_t$
  City Capital Expenses $(CCE_t) = \alpha + \beta_1 INFR_{t-1} + e_t$
  Special Programs and Accounts $(SPAC_t) = \alpha + \beta Time_{t-1}$

where MR is the millage rate, CPOP is city population, RCPI is real county personal income, SSTR is state sales tax revenue, CPI is a consumer price index, and INFR is the inflation rate.

Table C.2 shows the six-year revenue and expenditure forecasts, along with the projected deficits and surpluses. As the table shows, the expenditures were projected to exceed the projected revenues for five of the six years, indicating a rather gloomy budget prospect for the government. Fortunately for the government, the deficits were expected to be large in the early years of forecasts and then decline gradually. What the deficit figures essentially mean is that the projected revenues would not be sufficient to sustain the projected growth in running the operations of the government, especially during the early years of the forecast period.[2]

It should be worth noting that although the operating budget deficits, in particular those related to the General Fund of a government (since it is by far the largest of all governmental funds), by law, are not permitted for state and local governments, especially during the preparation stage of the budget, they are not uncommon during the implementation phase of the budget. The deficits can be a real problem if the trend continues, thus raising serious questions about the long-term fiscal health of a government. This is where methods such as trend monitoring become useful.

There are other methods, besides trend monitoring, that one can use for this purpose, in particular, to determine what contributes to the budget gap. A good example is gap analysis[3] that can help the decision makers determine what contributes to the gap and the course of action that would be necessary to deal with the problem before it gets out of control. At the same time, the decision makers, as well as those who will use the forecasts, must understand that there is no methodological solution to a budgetary problem, in particular, the deficit problem, although it can be minimized if it is the result of poor forecasts.

Table C.2   GF Budget Forecasts ($Million)

Revenues	t+1	t+2	t+3	t+4	t+5	t+6
PTR	91.6758	94.6333	99.0289	103.4245	107.7563	112.1519
PEXT	39.3505	40.6399	41.9293	43.5884	45.3812	47.1481
IGR	29.9658	30.6794	31.7899	33.5295	35.4268	37.1332
BLP	6.5395	6.7264	6.9166	7.1003	7.2872	7.4291
FAF	2.0222	2.0879	2.1536	2.2192	2.2849	2.3506
MCRS	27.1610	28.9622	30.7634	32.5646	34.3659	36.1671
Total	196.7148	203.7279	212.5817	222.4265	232.4893	242.3800
Expenditures	t+1	t+2	t+3	t+4	t+5	t+6
CPS	154.4425	160.9593	167.1165	172.9338	172.4301	183.6230
COE	33.3362	32.5133	31.8198	31.1995	30.9265	30.9510
CCE	0.5547	0.6381	0.6751	0.6581	0.6085	0.6913
SP&E	17.6722	19.0938	20.5154	21.9370	23.3586	24.7802
Total	206.0056	213.2045	220.1268	226.7244	233.3237	240.0455
Surplus (Deficit)	(9.2908)	(9.4754)	(7.5451)	(4.2979)	(0.8344)	2.3345

DO'S AND DON'TS OF FORECASTING

Before concluding our discussion, it is important to highlight a few do's and don'ts of forecasting. While most forecasters carefully follow the basic guidelines of forecasting, several rules are worth keeping in mind. Most of these rules are based on common sense. Paul Saffo (2007) nicely summarizes six rules useful for effective forecasting: (1) Define a cone of uncertainty, (2) look for the S-curve, (3) embrace the things that don't fit, (4) hold strong opinions weakly, (5) look back twice as far as look forward, and (6) know when not to make a forecast. Let us go over the rules briefly.

Cone of uncertainty, the first rule, broadens one's understanding by revealing overlooked possibilities and unexamined assumptions that can improve forecasting performance. The job of a forecaster is to map out the cone in a manner that would help the decision makers exercise strategic judgment. The rule for mapping is simple in that it should not be too wide to include every single possibility under the sun that is unrealistic and too narrow that would leave out the most likely possibilities. A well-designed brainstorming session, preferably before the forecasting process, can help develop a balanced set of possibilities.

In forecasting, as in most data-driven studies, the data do not follow a straight-line pattern; if they did, forecasting would be simple, predictable, and less complicated. In most instances, the patterns follow an S-shaped curve, starting slowly and increasing incrementally, then exploding suddenly, and finally tapering off, or even disappearing.[4] The art of forecasting is to identify the pattern as it begins to emerge, well ahead of the inflection point. But finding the inflection point is extremely difficult because no one can predict when and how fast an event will occur that will change the behavior of the data, especially in the short run.

The third rule is not to ignore things that may not fit conventional wisdom. Since the goal of forecasting is to predict the future based on the past and the present, it is possible that traces of the future can be found in the present. According to Saffo, the entire left of the S-curve is paved with small traces, which, when aggregated, could produce a hint of what is to come. This is where the barometric methods such as those discussed earlier can be useful.

The next three rules are very much self-explanatory. First, it is important not to over-rely on information that seems to reinforce the conclusion because no information is permanent and can instantly change for a variety of reasons over which the forecaster may not have much control, thereby, affecting the forecasting outcome. The point is—unthinkable can happen. The sinking of the Titanic, the unsinkable ship, is probably one of the best and most tragic examples in history. Next, which is somewhat related to Rule 2, one must look for turns, not the straight ways—a common mistake most forecasters

make because of the difficulty in determining the inflection points with precision. As such, the forecaster must peer far enough into the past to identify
patterns. This may partly explain why methods such as Box-Jenkins and
ARIMA models often require lengthy time series.

Finally, a common mistake most forecasters make is not knowing when
not to forecast. The point is there are moments when forecasting is relatively easy, and there are moments when it is impossible, even for the most
seasoned forecaster. When that happens, especially the latter, it is wise not
to do a forecast; the best an organization can do is develop a consensus
forecast based on rigorous brainstorming, even if the agreement is not
one hundred percent. As the author puts it, "the cone of uncertainty is not
static, it expands and contracts as the present rolls into the future, and as
certain possibilities come to pass while others are closed off" (Saffo 2007,
Page 11).

SUMMARY

There has been significant growth in forecasting methods over the years
both in number and complexity, as well as in analytical rigor, along with
an increase in the choice of methods available to a forecaster. This final
chapter has briefly discussed several additional methods used in forecasting,
especially those related to the business cycle. While we have covered a good
number of methods, it is impossible to cover the vast array of methods that
are available to a forecaster in a few chapters or even in a single book. In the
same vein, there is no hard-and-fast rule for selecting the best method; much
depends on the objective of the forecast, the quality of data, the knowledge
and skill of the forecaster, and the forecasting environment, in particular, the
forecast user's willingness to understand that forecasts are not actual values
but estimates of actual values one would observe in the future. As long as the
methods used are sound, data are reliable, the forecasting objective is clear,
and the environment in which forecasting takes place is conducive, the forecasts should be reliable and good.

NOTES

1. To see how it works, we can look at a standard normal curve, say, for ±1.6 standard deviations (i.e., the Z value from a standard normal table). The area under the
curve corresponding to this value will be approximately 0.89 or 89.0 percent, which
will represent ±2 MADs. Likewise, for ±2.4 standard deviations, the area under the
curve will be approximately 0.98 or 98 percent, which will represent ±3MADS. For

±3.2 standard deviations, the area under the curve will be approximately 0.99 or 99 percent, representing ±4 MADs.

2. To follow up on the forecast results, the government continued to experience the budget deficits, as indicated in the study, which became a concern for the government to the point that the county government had to intervene and eventually bail out the government. The government was forced to undertake a number of expenditure control and other measures to eventually come out of the budget doldrums, including some recommended in the study.

3. Gap analysis is a process that compares actual performance or result with what was expected or desired and then uses that information to plan ways for improvement. More specifically, the method provides a way to identify suboptimal or missing strategies, structures, capabilities, processes, practices, technology or skills, and then recommends steps to meet the goals or targets (Weller, 2018). Although developed for firms and businesses, the method can be applied to government, in particular for analyzing budget gaps.

4. One of the most well-known S-shaped power curves is the Gordon Moore's Law, initially developed to predict the time it takes to double the number of transistors in an integrated circuit, which was roughly 18 months (Saffo, 2007). Interestingly, Moore's prediction held for 10 years; he then revised the prediction to two years, becoming later the Moore's Law. He later developed a second law that deals with rates at which costs of technology tend to go down, but it is difficult to say how long his predictions will hold, especially the second law, since these are not the natural laws of physics.

Appendix

SELECTED DATA TABLES

Table A.1 Taxable Retail Sales and Predictor Variables, FY 1982–2016

Year	Taxable Retail Sales	MSA Population	MSA Personal Income
t-34	8,669,602,500	8,047,477	109,395,378
t-33	8,887,387,300	8,044,580	115,119,544
t-32	9,949,189,700	8,067,923	126,059,797
t-31	10,792,777,900	8,072,070	133,134,084
t-30	11,745,900,700	8,078,098	140,925,456
t-29	11,876,943,800	8,099,059	150,341,810
t-28	12,616,565,900	8,116,756	163,860,875
t-27	13,476,034,700	8,153,134	173,455,150
t-26	14,700,651,200	8,203,210	185,603,988
t-25	13,475,040,300	8,304,560	190,254,106
t-24	13,242,800,000	8,412,788	205,709,815
t-23	13,951,300,000	8,512,911	213,635,012
t-22	13,760,000,000	8,605,735	225,126,232
t-21	14,660,000,000	8,693,383	240,970,377
t-20	15,509,000,000	8,782,253	255,962,866
t-19	15,470,000,000	8,862,719	271,380,395
t-18	16,190,000,000	8,949,190	289,952,881
t-17	15,470,000,000	9,035,654	303,979,339
t-16	16,910,000,000	9,113,234	328,950,610
t-15	16,837,500,000	9,169,580	338,244,810
t-14	16,810,600,000	9,206,032	342,226,257
t-13	15,861,800,000	9,233,303	346,839,229
t-12	17,030,000,000	9,260,676	359,247,215
t-11	17,651,840,000	9,276,302	376,684,966
t-10	21,306,960,000	9,297,749	403,783,779
t-9	21,231,120,000	9,337,140	427,291,505
t-8	19,480,880,000	9,384,555	436,265,773
t-7	17,990,960,000	9,429,498	407,956,816
t-6	18,677,840,000	9,471,637	414,871,122
t-5	18,677,840,000	9,493,862	434,962,900
t-4	20,059,840,000	9,516,555	459,669,792
t-3	20,816,000,000	9,535,961	468,263,079
t-2	21,960,400,000	9,543,893	496,338,979
t-1	24,664,000,000	9,532,569	519,692,602
t	25,270,640,000	9,512,999	529,121,652

Source: From the City of Chicago (retail sales) and the Chicago-Naperville-Elgin MSA (population and per capita income).

Table A.2   General Sales Tax Revenue: Quarterly Data

N of Qtrs. (Quarter)	Sales Tax Revenue ($Million)	N of Qtrs. (Quarter)	Sales Tax Revenue Sales Tax Rev. ($Million)	N of Qtrs. (Quarter)	Sales Tax Revenue ($Million)
1-Q1	3676.314	23-Q3	5547.248	45-Q1	7151.766
2-Q2	3835.809	24-Q4	5007.777	46-Q2	7248.544
3-Q3	3964.583	25-Q1	4974.838	47-Q3	7367.274
4-Q4	3883.405	26-Q2	4686.458	48-Q4	6998.104
5-Q1	3904.886	27-Q3	4903.542	49-Q1	7173.469
6-Q2	3913.394	28-Q4	4909.866	50-Q2	7071.422
7-Q3	4094.585	29-Q1	5060.191	51-Q3	7075.589
8-Q4	4011.545	30-Q2	5033.583	52-Q4	6931.030
9-Q1	4236.440	31-Q3	5385.575	53-Q1	7058.524
10-Q2	4283.424	32-Q4	5422.183	54-Q2	6918.111
11-Q3	4681.717	33-Q1	5559.179	55-Q3	7274.981
12-Q4	4486.350	34-Q2	5699.471	56-Q4	7151.123
13-Q1	4749.354	35-Q3	5988.986	57-Q1	7452.506
14-Q2	4851.322	36-Q4	6038.661	58-Q2	7576.926
15-Q3	5095.817	37-Q1	6373.034	69-Q3	8001.233
16-Q4	5053.431	38-Q2	6327.128	60-Q4	7893.054
17-Q1	5182.774	39-Q3	6371.577	61-Q1	8360.016
18-Q2	5171.403	40-Q4	6389.221	62-Q2	8341.699
19-Q3	5485.482	41-Q1	6754.232	63-Q3	8501.957
20-Q4	5220.188	42-Q2	6554.858	64-Q4	8471.729
21-Q1	5639.003	43-Q3	6754.461	65-Q1	8708.532
22-Q2	5405.531	44-Q4	6813.039	---	---

Source: Generated from the monthly data (See Appendix A.3).

Table A.3   General Sales Tax Revenue: Monthly Data

N of Months (Month)	Sales Tax Rev. ($Million)	N of Months (Month)	Sales Tax Rev. Sales Tax Rev. ($Million)	N of Months (Month)	Sales Tax Rev. Sales Tax Rev. ($Million)
1-Sept	1124.239	31-Mar	1369.080	61-Sept	1682.625
2-Oct	1195.259	32-Apr	1573.775	62-Oct	1739.839
3-Nov	1356.816	33-May	1543.495	63-Nov	1983.067
4-Dec	1253.354	34-Jun	1493.727	64-Dec	1869.447
5-Jan	1316.143	35-Jul	1605.669	65-Jan	1928.333
6-Feb	1266.312	36-Aug	1649.958	66-Feb	1749.468
7-Mar	1186.019	37-Sept	1516.966	67-Mar	1582.020
8-Apr	1461.063	38-Oct	1604.078	68-Apr	1652.715
9-May	1317.501	39-Nov	1730.278	69-May	1773.042
10-Jun	1185.906	40-Dec	1679.232	70-Jun	1571.720
11-Jul	1272.013	41-Jan	1765.299	71-Jul	1650.951
12-Aug	1425.486	42-Feb	1651.286	72-Aug	1752.167
13-Sept	1168.178	43-Mar	1531.544	73-Sept	1471.728
14-Oct	1290.716	44-Apr	1735.717	74-Oct	1517.871
15-Nov	1445.992	45-May	1786.170	75-Nov	1696.859
16-Dec	1357.715	46-Jun	1632.718	76-Dec	1653.055
17-Jan	1396.261	47-Jul	1690.890	77-Jan	1655.305
18-Feb	1340.609	48-Aug	1859.166	78-Feb	1595.182
19-Mar	1209.879	49-Sept	1622.758	79-Mar	1458.929
20-Apr	1342.905	50-Oct	1653.819	80-Apr	1675.495
21-May	1458.761	51-Nov	1894.826	81-May	1775.442
22-Jun	1291.678	52-Dec	1832.811	82-Jun	1606.973
23-Jul	1456.703	53-Jan	1856.237	83-Jul	1686.543
24-Aug	1488.059	54-Feb	1796.434	84-Aug	1766.675
25-Sept	1334.327	55-Mar	1644.761	85-Sept	1571.260
26-Oct	1367.421	56-Apr	1704.914	86-Oct	1617.701
27-Nov	1581.676	57-May	1870.513	87-Nov	1844.622
28-Dec	1581.676	58-Jun	1769.704	88-Dec	1807.885
29-Jan	1573.726	59-Jul	1867.029	89-Jan	1828.141
30-Feb	1543.962	60-Aug	2002.270	90-Feb	1749.549

(*continued*)

Table A.3 **(Continued)**

N of Months (Month)	Sales Tax Rev. ($Million)	N of Months (Month)	Sales Tax Rev. Sales Tax Rev. ($Million)	N of Months (Month)	Sales Tax Rev. Sales Tax Rev. ($Million)
91-Mar	1603.786	121-Sept	2012.490	151-Mar	2164.355
92-Apr	1866.404	122-Oct	2137.197	152-Apr	2368.946
93-May	1951.993	123-Nov	2405.171	153-May	2397.729
94-Jun	1722.585	124-Dec	2250.554	154-Jun	2197.874
95-Jul	1859.803	125-Jan	2299.316	155-Jul	2365.147
96-Aug	1976.791	126-Feb	2204.591	156-Aug	2495.503
97-Sept	1756.136	127-Mar	2088.683	157-Sept	2128.221
98-Oct	1874.567	128-Apr	2272.151	158-Oct	2290.300
99-Nov	2068.768	129-May	2452.205	159-Nov	2499.590
100-Dec	1980.195	130-Jun	2244.730	160-Dec	2437.750
101-Jan	2000.944	131-Jul	2335.869	161-Jan	2439.299
102-Feb	2007.847	132-Aug	2571.167	162-Feb	2397.932
103-Mar	1874.114	133-Sept	2172.037	163-Mar	2229.512
104-Apr	2069.596	134-Oct	2413.647	164-Apr	2427.420
105-May	2094.951	135-Nov	2662.860	165-May	2494.191
106-Jun	1984.037	136-Dec	2347.292	166-Jun	2426.348
107-Jul	2047.323	137-Jan	2557.121	167-Jul	2553.076
108-Aug	2341.674	138-Feb	2462.861	168-Aug	2473.082
109-Sep	1959.860	139-Mar	2120.521	169-Sep	2350.987
110-Oct	2028.036	140-Apr	2297.667	170-Oct	2448.338
111-Nov	2339.232	141-May	2579.916	171-Nov	2777.601
112-Dec	2165.947	142-Jun	2213.508	172-Dec	2737.942
113-Jan	2122.783	143-Jul	2399.053	173-Jan	2659.479
114-Feb	2082.847	144-Aug	2560.908	174-Feb	2603.812
115-Mar	1977.862	145-Sep	2212.936	175-Mar	2390.434
116-Apr	2150.903	146-Oct	2283.474	176-Apr	2753.627
117-May	2260.456	147-Nov	2575.012	177-May	2748.993
118-Jun	2165.543	148-Dec	2323.088	178-Jun	2758.659
119-Jul	2196.961	149-Jan	2456.940	179-Jul	2729.561
120-Aug	2391.728	150-Feb	2295.561	180-Aug	2929.349*

Source: Office of Comptroller, Texas, Monthly State Revenue Watch, Transparency: State Revenue and Spending, Associated Data Files; https://comptroller.texas.gov/transparency/revenue/watch/
*Estimate.

Table A.4   State Revenue and Expenditure

Period (Time)	Revenue ($Million)	Expenditure ($Million)	Period (Time)	Revenue ($Million)	Expenditure ($Million)
t-27	168,759.292	163,424.749	t-13	95,820.765	81,277.051
t-26	175,350.481	156,921.554	t-12	90,489.755	77,163.705
t-25	166,225.637	146,454.872	t-11	82,621.328	76,386.043
t-24	143,412.914	144,881.577	t-10	61,979.817	70,036.258
t-23	133,653.200	136,514.037	t-9	65,525.245	64,685.858
t-22	154,164.430	130,357.427	t-8	72,322.692	60,425.369
t-21	138,928.002	123,646.575	t-7	71,648.633	54,761.328
t-20	123,217.215	125,554.913	t-6	57,807.137	51,064.773
t-19	133,266.128	126,005.369	t-5	63,864.034	48,887.370
t-18	120,506.772	119,871.583	t-4	51,459.160	46,081.839
t-17	92,274.744	110,998.477	t-3	49,421.533	44,643.310
t-16	94,310.376	101,920.390	t-2	45,034.889	40,966.651
t-15	113,832.250	90,852.662	t-1	42,019.015	39,080.298
t-14	103,964.436	86,660.158	t	36,721.807	33,893.797

Source: State & Local Government Finances, Historical Datasets and Tables. US. Bureau of Census; https://www.census.gov/programs-surveys/gov-finances/data/datasets.html

Table A.5 Federal Receipts and Outlays (In $Billion): 1950–2019

Year	Receipts	Outlays	Year	Receipts	Outlays
1950	37.336	42.038	1985	547.866	769.396
1951	48.496	44.237	1986	568.927	806.842
1952	62.573	65.956	1987	640.886	809.243
1953	65.511	73.771	1988	667.747	860.012
1954	65.112	67.943	1989	727.439	932.832
1955	60.370	64.461	1990	750.302	1027.928
1956	68.162	65.668	1991	761.103	1082.539
1957	73.201	70.562	1992	788.783	1129.191
1958	71.587	74.902	1993	842.401	1142.799
1959	70.953	83.102	1994	923.541	1182.380
1960	81.851	81.341	1995	1000.711	1227.078
1961	82.279	86.046	1996	1085.561	1259.580
1962	87.405	93.286	1997	1187.242	1290.490
1963	92.385	96.352	1998	1305.929	1335.854
1964	96.248	102.794	1999	1382.984	1381.064
1965	100.094	101.699	2000	1544.607	1458.185
1966	111.749	114.817	2001	1483.563	1516.008
1967	124.420	137.040	2002	1337.815	1655.232
1968	128.056	155.798	2003	1258.472	1796.890
1969	157.928	158.436	2004	1345.369	1913.330
1970	159.348	168.042	2005	1576.135	2069.746
1971	151.294	177.346	2006	1798.487	2232.981
1972	167.402	193.470	2007	1932.896	2275.049
1973	184.715	199.961	2008	1865.945	2507.793
1974	209.299	216.496	2009	1450.98	3000.661
1975	216.633	270.780	2010	1531.019	2902.397
1976	231.671	301.098	2011	1737.678	3104.459
1977	278.741	328.675	2012	1880.489	3018.975
1978	314.169	369.585	2013	2101.832	2821.07
1979	365.309	404.941	2014	2285.926	2800.231
1980	403.903	477.044	2015	2479.518	2948.773
1981	469.097	542.956	2016	2457.785	3077.943
1982	474.299	594.892	2017	2465.566	3180.429
1983	453.242	660.934	2018	2475.16	3260.472
1984	500.363	685.632	2019	2549.061	3540.339

Source: Economic Research, Federal Reserve Economic Data (FRED), St Louis, Federal Receipts and Outlays: 1950-2019. https://fred.stlouisfed.org/categories/5?t=annual

Table A.6   Sales Tax Receipts and Forecast: Quarter 3, 1999–Quarter 3, 2018

Observation (Quarter)	Actual Receipts	ARIMA Forecast	Holt-Winters Forecast	MA4 Forecast
t-70	1,268,437,280	1,231,389,310	1,208,000,472	1,370,605,623
t-69	1,452,124,699	1,470,924,323	1,470,096,156	1,374,505,428
t-68	1,432,927,025	1,343,698,904	1,328,530,629	1,371,263,170
t-67	1,549,725,114	1,507,658,825	1,515,115,346	1,394,587,773
t-66	1,245,848,941	1,356,237,046	1,354,697,891	1,425,803,530
t-65	1,489,035,309	1,439,201,916	1,463,098,666	1,420,156,445
t-64	1,460,569,299	1,429,117,467	1,414,380,681	1,429,384,097
t-63	1,507,876,344	1,551,941,477	1,555,700,282	1,436,294,666
t-62	1,285,367,179	1,265,431,272	1,286,058,708	1,425,832,473
t-61	1,501,820,557	1,496,224,485	1,501,164,691	1,435,712,032
t-60	1,481,491,917	1,473,496,379	1,445,589,419	1,438,908,345
t-59	1,574,095,819	1,545,981,417	1,562,085,617	1,444,138,999
t-58	1,371,304,250	1,322,026,387	1,343,098,977	1,460,693,868
t-57	1,553,767,645	1,571,539,034	1,581,863,898	1,482,178,136
t-56	1,557,248,692	1,520,914,436	1,512,320,484	1,495,164,908
t-55	1,625,565,761	1,615,418,796	1,638,333,238	1,514,104,101
t-54	1,455,718,202	1,408,506,745	1,403,891,985	1,526,971,587
t-53	1,619,241,141	1,622,065,395	1,654,220,577	1,548,075,075
t-52	1,678,848,294	1,598,135,202	1,589,653,396	1,564,443,449
t-51	1,681,737,045	1,723,456,689	1,748,324,048	1,594,843,350
t-50	1,532,910,238	1,491,667,337	1,478,666,912	1,608,886,171
t-49	1,775,807,526	1,676,840,397	1,723,800,782	1,628,184,180
t-48	1,743,964,947	1,777,716,821	1,748,784,173	1,667,325,776
t-47	1,761,076,696	1,746,967,841	1,810,587,866	1,683,604,939
t-46	1,537,690,181	1,589,857,089	1,569,825,261	1,703,439,852
t-45	1,766,250,314	1,739,601,480	1,755,306,382	1,704,634,837
t-44	1,740,884,597	1,756,806,476	1,744,768,742	1,702,245,534
t-43	1,805,842,864	1,748,011,669	1,797,341,141	1,701,475,447
t-42	1,529,805,812	1,600,123,048	1,600,089,633	1,712,666,989
t-41	1,765,607,161	1,757,424,799	1,758,139,715	1,710,695,896
t-40	1,692,432,745	1,738,942,574	1,747,252,858	1,710,535,108
t-39	1,616,636,393	1,748,420,134	1,759,964,185	1,698,422,145
t-38	1,334,037,060	1,402,864,396	1,429,288,214	1,651,120,527
t-37	1,510,303,021	1,600,884,510	1,580,113,973	1,602,178,340
t-36	1,505,600,056	1,507,735,424	1,501,073,945	1,538,352,305
t-35	1,572,928,026	1,521,935,047	1,542,010,118	1,491,644,133
t-34	1,369,452,367	1,324,946,533	1,341,486,353	1,480,717,041
t-33	1,589,192,053	1,568,585,556	1,582,089,423	1,489,570,868
t-32	1,568,441,672	1,564,048,952	1,568,058,081	1,509,293,126
t-31	1,700,730,312	1,585,942,396	1,610,734,042	1,525,003,529
t-30	1,459,681,623	1,454,792,392	1,461,388,709	1,556,954,101
t-29	1,647,499,991	1,637,987,785	1,672,574,532	1,579,511,415
t-28	1,657,499,757	1,615,910,033	1,632,617,813	1,594,088,399
t-27	1,756,810,457	1,740,982,067	1,712,723,856	1,616,352,921
t-26	1,535,355,940	1,516,164,386	1,519,991,849	1,630,372,957
t-25	1,707,100,253	1,707,030,390	1,737,898,099	1,649,291,536

(continued)

Table A.6 (Continued)

Observation (Quarter)	Actual Receipts	ARIMA Forecast	Holt-Winters Forecast	MA4 Forecast
t-24	1,712,365,977	1,690,013,348	1,698,242,519	1,664,191,602
t-23	1,769,953,768	1,801,921,390	1,778,221,623	1,677,908,157
t-22	1,553,656,536	1,542,207,057	1,543,008,064	1,681,193,985
t-21	1,800,435,087	1,716,698,885	1,751,527,340	1,685,769,134
t-20	1,790,524,477	1,783,403,660	1,779,467,634	1,709,102,842
t-19	1,837,302,630	1,839,998,972	1,851,712,374	1,728,642,467
t-18	1,596,428,099	1,611,212,092	1,613,219,024	1,745,479,682
t-17	1,874,509,158	1,799,723,997	1,808,712,551	1,756,172,573
t-16	1,844,660,318	1,847,315,601	1,850,731,961	1,774,691,091
t-15	1,908,627,213	1,875,927,007	1,901,915,584	1,788,225,051
t-14	1,600,476,806	1,663,843,208	1,678,650,833	1,806,056,197
t-13	1,761,081,581	1,854,816,466	1,836,895,732	1,807,068,374
t-12	1,887,489,533	1,755,647,669	1,766,079,304	1,778,711,479
t-11	1,925,875,300	1,929,433,029	1,926,289,856	1,789,418,783
t-10	1,633,821,779	1,641,029,914	1,675,566,459	1,793,730,805
t-9	1,877,040,710	1,822,089,591	1,854,137,584	1,802,067,048
t-8	1,856,538,848	1,929,194,020	1,890,374,407	1,831,056,830
t-7	1,927,766,225	1,904,013,242	1,918,153,871	1,823,319,159
t-6	1,642,236,755	1,636,893,607	1,670,692,355	1,823,791,890
t-5	1,904,936,811	1,844,954,518	1,865,671,041	1,825,895,634
t-4	1,885,036,409	1,919,734,100	1,909,981,735	1,832,869,660
t-3	1,966,722,496	1,937,478,584	1,945,880,053	1,839,994,050
t-2	1,700,727,418	1,678,843,988	1,703,730,810	1,849,733,118
t-1	1,986,780,433	1,935,126,896	1,926,085,092	1,864,355,783
t	1,961,019,227	1,946,808,609	1,981,335,720	1,884,816,689
t+1 (Qtr.72)*		2,017,040,000	2,021,144,963	1,903,812,393

Source: Produced from data runs.
*Forecast.

Table A.7   Regional Economic Data, Multiple Variables (by Quarter)

Qtr.	AHE	NPE	BP	CIE	Obs	AHE	NPE	BP	CIE
0	20.059	1016.233	426.641	7803.803	79	24.331	1038.428	302.615	7975.83
1	19.999	1014.885	416.135	7624.17	80	24.600	1038.003	258.972	7651.727
2	19.955	1017.565	559.561	8062.995	81	24.644	1037.902	330.325	7517.148
3	20.104	1016.000	384.553	7506.85	82	24.532	1037.357	354.664	7230.561
4	20.039	1019.976	422.162	7825.021	83	24.821	1037.640	268.619	7642.732
5	20.107	1023.311	317.101	8258.919	84	24.443	1037.378	313.518	8113.702
6	20.133	1020.877	355.725	8304.766	85	24.856	1037.131	267.558	7603.063
7	20.008	1021.560	394.330	8747.179	86	24.784	1038.015	323.950	7712.387
8	20.129	1020.605	399.677	8156.595	87	24.689	1040.402	359.135	7185.334
9	19.999	1021.260	396.904	8098.341	88	24.406	1041.975	419.162	7378.629
10	19.930	1022.071	326.156	7742.625	89	24.388	1043.225	385.562	7620.452
11	20.267	1021.805	308.129	7979.269	90	24.211	1041.801	443.065	8071.775
12	20.257	1023.040	333.942	8118.35	91	24.113	1043.072	269.465	8015.769
13	20.315	1023.452	341.485	7718.947	92	24.095	1043.804	448.693	7711.605
14	20.399	1022.433	311.432	7968.696	93	23.877	1043.852	377.201	7519.52
15	20.263	1025.062	313.422	7599.108	94	24.055	1042.773	314.631	7158.249
16	20.316	1025.814	320.662	7772.795	95	23.727	1044.435	313.491	7575.125
17	20.500	1024.879	300.278	8361.936	96	23.574	1044.362	90.056	7693.934
18	20.322	1024.202	298.774	8562.37	97	23.908	1042.292	301.116	7638.657
19	20.307	1023.584	281.304	8163.316	98	24.062	1040.655	79.376	7937.385
20	20.318	1022.539	245.397	8266.385	99	23.982	1042.698	468.307	7138.274
21	20.431	1021.626	259.618	7717.566	100	24.201	1044.182	340.272	7305.255
22	20.496	1018.399	203.576	7526.562	101	24.085	1044.036	199.949	7661.253
23	20.362	1014.650	154.050	7701.741	102	24.121	1045.547	123.295	8247.384
24	20.353	1009.581	136.792	8005.294	103	24.240	1046.935	115.326	7991.906
25	20.428	1006.647	174.103	7041.145	104	24.045	1045.704	108.386	7900.68
26	20.471	1001.793	214.382	7604.132	105	23.972	1046.082	106.142	7416.999
27	20.479	996.725	241.917	7111.027	106	24.027	1047.105	103.764	6961.854
28	20.534	994.505	213.092	7310.057	107	23.752	1046.467	138.389	7255.865
29	20.522	990.963	239.598	7436.282	108	23.927	1045.659	126.284	7742.884
30	20.561	988.521	219.709	7855.373	109	23.912	1045.296	123.030	7503.001
31	20.718	987.513	227.056	8237.874	110	23.833	1045.866	172.391	7349.593
32	20.651	986.727	244.434	7460.127	111	23.622	1048.473	123.486	6905.534
33	20.668	986.100	229.889	7394.614	112	23.998	1044.814	114.425	7158.044
34	20.773	986.807	269.666	7039.9	113	23.814	1043.998	126.153	7604.405
35	20.684	988.310	374.066	7467.08	114	23.818	1046.008	111.272	8074.404
36	20.737	987.263	328.938	7802.022	115	23.940	1045.872	134.815	8316.722
37	20.854	982.323	253.580	7150.958	116	23.928	1046.410	218.344	8011.568
38	20.781	988.732	257.343	7691.103	117	24.194	1046.125	132.746	7449.462
39	20.840	993.780	262.845	7357.723	118	24.275	1048.360	168.091	6997.491
40	20.906	993.370	291.137	7601.377	119	24.374	1046.573	131.236	7550.257
41	20.913	996.966	283.099	8161.937	120	24.535	1049.617	85.358	7700.981
42	20.969	1002.153	251.914	8532.401	121	24.702	1051.651	179.516	7247.786
43	21.205	1004.246	246.194	8243.574	122	24.803	1051.780	479.083	7449.886
44	21.127	1002.835	259.540	7952.801	123	25.080	1054.750	128.345	7192.057
45	21.232	1004.481	236.871	7387.388	124	25.026	1055.571	181.844	7212.217
46	21.224	1005.842	327.182	7102.736	125	25.252	1056.949	110.006	7556.987
47	21.297	1008.463	585.662	7839.973	126	25.444	1056.880	106.339	8153.668

(continued)

Table A.7   (Continued)

Qtr.	AHE	NPE	BP	CIE	Obs	AHE	NPE	BP	CIE
48	21.344	1011.699	392.136	8472.444	127	25.423	1059.357	113.507	8134.548
49	21.366	1011.833	252.113	7659.905	128	25.440	1061.960	113.242	7617.664
50	21.541	1013.907	212.881	7616.928	129	25.603	1063.175	129.728	7482.466
51	21.573	1015.853	235.796	7201.248	130	25.360	1063.421	114.630	7255.596
52	21.993	1017.796	193.879	7476.535	131	25.718	1064.831	137.542	7507.827
53	22.120	1020.477	201.469	8062.354	132	25.987	1065.397	140.299	7916.975
54	22.369	1021.134	227.509	8219.209	133	25.858	1068.155	138.084	7452.148
55	22.371	1022.614	252.786	8256.631	134	25.859	1069.032	126.579	7520.969
56	22.417	1026.622	243.742	7795.841	135	26.011	1068.332	107.038	7304.97
57	22.578	1027.143	238.627	7603.496	136	26.160	1069.251	136.280	7481.006
58	22.685	1029.111	215.271	7237.74	137	26.295	1068.166	123.206	7532.465
59	22.770	1029.762	279.361	7518.951	138	26.729	1070.800	160.909	8298.511
60	22.907	1032.756	274.436	7629.238	139	26.605	1070.427	178.579	8459.73
61	22.938	1035.801	302.359	7340.308	140	27.267	1071.733	132.189	8265.952
62	23.060	1041.357	281.048	7632.475	141	26.811	1074.108	121.662	7414.76
63	23.225	1038.067	274.641	7012.739	142	27.156	1074.447	131.324	7058.602
64	23.167	1037.095	283.919	7728.59	143	27.667	1074.368	114.676	7670.932
65	23.164	1035.980	296.081	7479.339	144	27.388	1077.314	121.618	7876.174
66	23.483	1034.843	310.229	8294.727	145	27.290	1076.475	130.415	7323.863
67	23.448	1034.690	296.300	8183.886	146	27.320	1077.816	121.414	7577.002
68	23.870	1035.214	314.485	7712.315	147	27.477	1078.121	127.222	6998.914
69	23.640	1037.814	322.847	7439.127	148	27.529	1077.944	117.771	7408.983
70	23.665	1038.746	302.430	7083.982	149	27.812	1077.114	146.783	7376.589
71	23.941	1037.703	326.564	7421.9	150	27.403	1079.366	132.705	7939.069
72	23.995	1036.910	288.540	7540.755	151	27.364	1081.093	130.078	8218
73	23.910	1040.308	360.741	7496.777	152	27.330	1080.498	129.176	7786.795
74	24.024	1039.412	337.862	7544.516	153	27.177	1080.005	155.566	7474.042
75	24.046	1036.979	292.966	7168.022	154	27.162	1080.376	148.153	6967.379
76	24.111	1036.802	317.352	7378.311	155	27.204	1081.775	146.214	7139.188
77	24.295	1037.781	488.048	7649.549	156	27.009	1081.359	618.513	7559.506
78	24.158	1039.266	781.745	8392.201	157	27.090	1081.580	145.242	7217.224

Multiple Sources:
1. Average Hourly Earnings: U.S. Bureau of Labor Statistics, State and Metro Area Employment, Hours, and Earnings report, https://www.bls.gov/sae/
2. Total Nonfarm Private Employment: U.S. Bureau of Labor Statistics, State Employment and Unemployment report, https://www.bls.gov/lau/
3. New Private Housing Units Authorized by Building Permits: U.S. Census Bureau, Housing Units Authorized by Building Permits report, https://www.census.gov/construction/bps/
4. Commercial and Industrial Electric Utility Sales: U.S. Energy Information Administration, Form EIA-861M (formerly EIA-826) detailed data) https://www.eia.gov/electricity/data.php

Table A.8   Quarterly Sales Tax Receipts: Apparel Industry

Quarter	Apparel	Quarter	Apparel	Quarter	Apparel
1	56,388,179.68	27	57,221,109.98	53	76,488,451.61
2	72,003,787.55	28	73,924,790.15	54	90,777,308.94
3	47,668,945.22	29	73,000,427.65	55	67,238,516.42
4	62,148,863.56	30	89,687,794.91	56	77,544,347.19
5	61,172,001.86	31	65,397,616.77	57	77,978,024.48
6	75,768,297.67	32	75,871,717.35	58	92,309,762.23
7	53,632,184.24	33	75,909,121.58	59	61,727,063.62
8	56,257,057.88	34	90,236,286.49	60	82,662,380.51
9	56,436,864.22	35	62,583,300.91	61	82,618,372.00
10	69,504,108.18	36	78,697,586.25	62	97,112,946.09
11	48,972,189.81	37	72,683,136.69	63	67,478,559.65
12	57,502,218.45	38	83,208,593.82	64	80,168,185.42
13	57,226,487.97	39	58,302,621.64	65	81,241,692.68
14	70,039,006.27	40	69,142,376.86	66	96,075,287.49
15	47,995,631.06	41	70,134,310.44	67	69,917,846.63
16	57,971,995.84	42	81,300,186.95	68	81,070,080.11
17	60,260,608.61	43	61,454,987.03	69	81,111,920.79
18	71,486,796.70	44	73,550,077.28	70	97,153,585.02
19	55,011,738.78	45	66,108,488.29	71	65,549,914.01
20	64,116,022.55	46	90,246,899.03	72	82,279,935.45
21	63,334,546.85	47	61,112,209.86	73	79,083,664.29
22	78,809,063.97	48	131,890,753.60	74	93,350,197.58
23	58,159,082.75	49	75,874,972.09	75	67,827,093.62
24	68,252,691.91	50	86,418,643.85	76	80,518,509.17
25	65,333,319.29	51	66,160,986.84	77	84,313,064.98
26	86,327,484.48	52	76,140,590.26		

Source: State of Illinois: Quarterly Sales Tax Receipts: Illinois Department of Revenue, Standard Industrial Classification (SIC) Code Reporting, https://www.revenue.state.il.us/app/kob/index.jsp

Bibliography

Adelman, I., & Adelman, F. L. (1959). The Dynamic Properties of the Klein-Goldberger Model. *Econometrica, 27*(4), 596–625.

Armstrong, J. S. (2001). Evaluating Forecasting Methods. In J. S. Armstrong (Ed.), *Principles of Forecasting: A Handbook for Researchers and Practitioners*. New York: Klower Publishers, 443–472.

Batchelor, R. A., & Bowe, C. (1974). Forecasting UK International Trade: A General Equilibrium Approach. *Applied Economics, 6*(2), 109–141.

Bates, J. M., & Granger, C. W. J. (1969). The Combination of Forecasts. *Operations Research, 20*(4), 451–468.

Bernstein, P. L. (2019). *Against the Gods: The Remarkable Story of Risk*. New York: John Wiley & Sons.

Blackley, P. R., & DeBoer, L. (1993). Bias in OMB's Economic Forecasts and Budget Proposals. *Public Choice, 76*(3), 215–232.

Box, G. E. P., & Jenkins, G. M. (1976). *Time-Series Analysis: Forecasting and Control* (Revised Edition). San Francisco, CA: Holden Day.

Box, G. E. P., & Jenkins, G. M. (1970). *Time Series Analysis: Forecasting and Control*. Holden-Day.

Box, G. E. P., & Tiao, G. C. (1975). Intervention Analysis with Applications to Economic and Environmental Problems. *Journal of the American Statistical Association, 70*(349), 70–79.

Brave, S., & Lu, C. (2010). *A Snapshot of the Midwest Economy: Past and Present* (No. 280; Chicago Fed Letter), Federal Reserve Bank of Chicago.

Breiman, L. (1996). Bagging Predictors. *Machine Learning 24*, 123–140.

Bretschneider, S., & Gorr, W. (1992). Economic, Organizational, and Political Influences on Biases in Forecasting State Sales Tax Receipts. *International Journal of Forecasting, 7*(4), 457–466.

Bretschneider, S., & Schroeder, L. (1985). Revenue Forecasting, Budget Setting and Risk. *Socio-Economic Planning Sciences, 19*(6), 431–439.

Bretschneider, S., & Schroeder, L. (1988). Evaluation of Commercial Economic Forecasts for Use in Local Government Budgeting. *International Journal of Forecasting, 4*(1), 33–43.

Brooks, C. (2014). *Introductory Econometrics for Finance.* Cambridge: Cambridge University Press.

Brown, R. G. (1956). *Exponetial Smooting for Predicting Demand.* Cambrige, MA: Arthur D. Little, Inc.

Buxton, E., Kriz, K., Cremeens, M., & Jay, K. (2019). An Auto Regressive Deep Learning Model for Sales Tax Forecasting from Multiple Short Time Series. *2019 18th IEEE International Conference on Machine Learning and Applications (ICMLA)*, 1359–1364.

Cassidy, G., Kamlet, M. S., & Nagin, D. S. (1989). An Empirical Examination of Bias in Revenue Forecasts by State Governments. *International Journal of Forecasting, 5*(3), 321–331.

Cholette, P. A., & Lamy, R. (1986). Multivariate ARIMA Forecasting of Irregular Time Series. *International Journal of Forecasting, 2*(2), 201–216.

Cipra, T. (2006). Exponential Smoothing for Irregular Time Series. *Applications of Mathematics, 51*, 597–604.

Cipra, T., Trujillo, J., & Rubio, A. (1995). Holt-Winters Method with Missing Observations. *Management Science, 41*, 174–178.

Clemen, R. T. (1989). Combining Forecasts: A Review and Annotated Bibliography. *International Journal of Forecasting, 5*(4), 559–583.

Clower, E. (2021). A Guide to Conducting Cointegration Tests. *APTECH.* Retrieved June 15, 2021, from https://www.aptech.com/blog/a-guide-to-conducting-cointe-gration-tests.

Commandeur, J. J. F., & Koopman, S. J. (2007). *An Introduction to State Space Time Series Analysis.* Oxford: Oxford University Press.

Conway, R. S. (1979). Simulation Properties of a Regional Interindustry Econometric Model. *Papers of the Regional Science Association 43*, 45–57.

Cragg, J. G., & Malkiel, B. G. (1968). The Consensus and Accuracy of Some Predictions of the Growth of Corporate Earnings. *Journal of Finance, 23*(1), 67–84.

Dagum, E. B., & Bianconcini, S. (2016). *Seasonal Adjustment Methods and Real Time Trend-Cycle Estimation.* New York: Springer.

Dalkey, N., & Helmer, O. (1962). *An Experimental Application of the Delphi Method to the Use of Experts.* Memorandum RM-727/1-Abridged. Santa Monica, CA: The RAND Corporation.

Davidson, R., & McKinnon, J. G. (2004). *Econometric Theory and Methods.* New York: Oxford University Press.

Dickey, D. A., Jansen, D. W., & Thornton, D. L. (1991). A Primer on Cointegration with an Application to Money and Income. *Federal Reserve Bank of St. Louis Review, 73*(March–April), 58–78.

Diebold, F. X. (1998). *Elements of Forecasting.* Cincinnati, OH: South-Western College Publishing.

Doz, C., Giannone, D., & Reichlin, L. (2012). A Quasi-Maximum Likelihood Approach for Large, Approximate Dynamic Factor Models. *Review of Economics & Statistics*, *94*(4), 1014–1024.

Duan, X., & Zhang, X. (2020). ARIMA Modelling and Forecasting Irregularly Patterned COVID-19 Oubreaks using Japanese and South Korean Data. *Data in Brief*, *31*, August 2020. Retrieved February 5, 2021, from https://www.sciencedirect.com/science/article/pii/S2352340920306739.

Dunteman, G. H. (1989). *Principal Components Analysis*. Newbury Park, CA: Sage.

Elsberry, R. L., Tsai, H., & Jordan, M. S. (2014). Extended-Range Forecasts of Atlantic Tropical Cyclone Events during 2012 Using the ECMWF 32-Day Ensemble Predictions. *Weather and Forecasting*, *29*(2), 271–288.

Engle, R. F., & Granger, C. W. J. (1987). Co-Integration and Error Correction: Representation, Estimation, and Testing. *Econometrica*, *55*(2), 251–276.

Fanchon, P., & Wendel, J. (1992). Estimating VAR Models Under On-Stationarity and Cointegration: Alternative Approaches to Forecasting Cattle Prices. *Applied Econometrics*, *24*(2), 207–217.

Feenberg, D. R., Gentry, W., Gilroy, D., & Rosen, H. S. (1989). Testing the Rationality of State Revenue Forecasts. *The Review of Economics and Statistics*, *71*(2), 300–308.

Gardner, E. S. (1985). Exponential Smoothing: The State of the Art. *Journal of Forecasting*, *4*, 1–28.

Gardner, E. S. (2006). Exponential Smoothing: The State of the Art-Part II. *International Journal of Forecasting*, *22*, 637–666.

Gentry, W. M. (1989). Do State Revenue Forecasters Utilize Available Information? *National Tax Journal*, *42*(4), 429–439.

Geweke, J. (1978). Testing the Exogeneity Specification in the Complete Dynamic Simultaneous Equation Model. *Journal of Econometrics,* *7*(2), 163–185.

Geweke, J. (1982). Measurement of Linear Dependence and Feedback between Multiple Time Series. *Journal of the American Statistical Association,* *77*(378), 304–313.

Geweke, J. F., & Singleton, K. J. (1981). Latent Variable Models for Time Series: A Frequency Domain Approach with an Application to the Permanent Income Hypothesis. *Journal of Econometrics,* *17*(3), 287–304.

Gilchrist, W. (1976). *Statistical Forecasting*. New York: John-Wiley & Sons.

Granger, C. W. J. (1969). Investigating Causal Relations by Econometric Models and Cross-Spectral Methods. *Econometrica*, *37*(4), 424–438.

Granger, C. W. J., & Newbold, P. (1986). *Forecasting Economic Time Series* (2nd ed.). New York: Academic Press.

Granger, C. W. J., & Ramanathan, R. (1984). Improved Methods of Combining Forecasts. *Journal of Forecasting*, *3*(2), 197–204.

Gujarati, D. N., & Porter, D. C. (2009). *Basic Econometrics*. New York: McGraw-Hill.

Hamilton, J. D. (1994). *Time Series Analysis*. Princeton, NJ: Princeton University Press.

Hancock, M. (2012). *Practical Data Mining*. Boca Raton, FL: CRC Press.

Harvey, A., Koopman, S. J., & Penzer, J. (1998). Messy Time Series: A Unified Approach. *Advances in Econometrics*, *13*, 103–143.

Harvey, A. C. (1990). *The Econometric Analysis of Time Series* (1st MIT Press ed., 2nd ed.). MIT Press.

Holt, C. C. (1957a). *Forecasting Seasonals and Trends by Exponentially Weighted Averages* (O.N.R. Memorandum No. 52). Carnegie Institute of Technology, Pittsburgh USA. Reprinted in *International Journal of Forecasting*, *20*(1), 5–10.

Holt, C. C. (1957b). Forecasting Trends and Seasonal by Exponentially Weighted Averages. Office of Naval Research Memorandum 52, reprinted in Holt, C.C. Forecasting Trends and Seasonal by Exponentially Weighted Average. *International Journal of Forecasting*, *20*(1), January–March 2004, 5–10.

Hossain, Z., Rahman, A., Hossain, M., & Karami, J. H. (2019, January). Over-Differencing and Forecasting with Non-Stationary Time Series Data. *The Dhaka University Journal of Science*, *67*(1), 21–26.

Hyndman, R. J., & Athanasopoulos, G. (2018). *Forecasting: Principles and Practice* (2nd ed.). Melbourne: OTexts. Retrieved March 11, 2022, from http://OTexts.com /fpp2.

Hyndman, R. J., & Koehler, A. B. (2006). Another Look at Measure of Forecast Accuracy. *International Journal of Forecasting*, *22*(4), October–December, 679–688.

Jaisal, R. K., Lohani, A. K., & Tiwari, H. L. (2015). Statistical Analysis of Change Detection and Trend Assessment in Climatological Parameters. *Environmental Processes*, *2*(August), 729–749.

Johansen, S. (1988). Statistical Analysis of Cointegration Vectors, *Journal of Economic Dynamics and Control*, *12*(2–3), 231–254.

Johansen, S. (1991). Estimation and Hypothesis Testing of Cointegration Vectors in Gaussian Vector Autoregression Models. *Econometrica*, *59*(6), 1551–1580.

Johansen, S., & Juselius, K. (1990). Maximum Likelihood Estimation and Inference on Cointegration - with Applications to the Demand for Money. *Oxford Bulletin of Economics and Statistics*, *52*(2), 169–210.

Jöreskog, K. G., & Goldberger, A. S. (1975). Estimation of a Model with Multiple Indicators and Multiple Causes of a Single Latent Variable. *Journal of the American Statistical Association, 70*(351), 631.

Khan, A. (2003). Forecasting the General Fund Budget of a Local Government: The City of Pleasantville. In A. Khan & W. Bartley Hildreth (Eds.), *Case Studies in Public Budgeting and Financial Management* (pp. 195–208). New York: Marcel Dekker.

Koop, G. (2000). *Analysis of Economic Data*. John Wiley & Sons.

Krause, G. A., & Corder, J. K. (2007). Explaining Bureaucratic Optimism: Theory and Evidence from U.S. Executive Agency Macroeconomic Forecasts. *American Political Science Review*, *101*(1), 129–142.

Kriz, K. A. (2019). Ensemble Forecasting. In D. W. Williams & T. D. Calabrese (Eds.), *The Palgrave Handbook of Government Budget Forecasting* (pp. 413–426). Cham, CH: Palgrave Macmillan.

Kydland, F. E., & Prescott, E. C. (1982). Time to Build and Aggregate Fluctuations. *Econometrica*, *50*(6), 1345–1370.

Lee, K. L., & Billings, S. A. (2002). Time Series Prediction Using Support Vector Machines, the Orthogonal and the Regularized Orthogonal Least-Squares Algorithms. *International Journal of Systems Science, 33*(10), 811–821.

Lejung, G. M., & Box, G. E. P. (1978). On a Measure of Lack of Fit in Time-Series Models. *Biometrika, 65*, 67–72.

Linden, A. (2015). Conducting Interrupted Time-Series Analysis for Single and Multiple-Group Comparisons. *The Stata Journal, 15*(2), 480–500.

Litterman, R. (1979). *Techniques of Forecasting using Vector Autoregressions* (No. 115; Federal Reserve Bank of Minneapolis Working Papers).

Lucas, R. E. (1976). Econometric Policy Evaluation: A Critique. *Carnegie-Rochester Conference Series on Public Policy, 1*, 19–46.

Maddala, G. S., & Kim, I. M. (1998). *Unit Roots, Cointegration, and Structural Change.* Oxford: Oxford University Press.

Makridakis, S. (1986). The Art and Science of Forecasting: An Assessment and Future Directions. *International Journal of Forecasting, 2*(1), 15–39.

Makridakis, S., Anderson, A., Carbone, R., Fildes, R., Hibon, M., Lewandowski, R., & Winkler, R. (1982). The accuracy of extrapolation (time series) methods: Results of a forecasting competition. *Journal of Forecasting, 1*(2): 111–153.

Makridakis, S., & Wheelright, S. C. (1978). *Interactive Forecasting: Univariate and Multivariate Methods.* San Francisco, CA: Holden-Day, Inc.

Makridakis, S., Wheelright, S. C., & Hyndman, R. J. (1998). *Forecasting: Methods and Application.* New York: John Wiley & Sons.

Mccauley, F. R. (1931). *The Smoothing of Time Series.* New York: National Bureau of Economic Research, Inc.

McCullum, N. (n.d.). *How Do Neural Networks Really Work?* Retrieved July 19, 2021, from https://nickmccullum.com/python-deep-learning/how-do-neural-networks-really-work/.

McNees, S. (1987). Vector Autoregression and Reality. *Journal of Business and Economic Statistics, 5*, 437–454.

Merriam-Webster. (2020). *Ensemble | Definition of Ensemble.* Retrieved May 23, 2020, from https://www.merriam-webster.com/dictionary/ensemble.

Morris, P. A. (1974). Decision Analysis Expert Use. *Management Science, 20*(9), 1233–1241.

Nau, R. (2014). *The Mathematical Structure of ARIMA Models.* Fuqua School of Business, Duke University. Retrieved November 22, 2019, from https://faculty.fuqua.duke.edu/~rnau/Mathematical_structure_of_ARIMA_models--Robert_Nau.pdf.

Newey, W. K., & West, K. D. (1987). A Simple Positive Semi-definite Heteroskedasticity and Autocorrelation Consistent Cvariance Matrix. *Econometrica, 55*(3), 703–708.

Olson, R. S., & LaFaive, M. D. (2007). *A Michigan School Money Primer: For Policymakers, School Officials, Media, and Residents.* Midland, MI: Mackinac Center for Public Policy.

Pankratz, A. (1983). *Forecasting with Univariate Box–Jenkins Models: Concepts and Cases.* New York: John Wiley & Sons.

Penner, R. G. (2001). *Errors in Budget Forecasting.* Washington, DC: The Urban Institute.

Ramanathan, R. (2002). *Introductory Econometrics with Applications* (5th ed.). Harcourt College Publishers.

Saffo, P. (2007). Six Rules for Effective Forecasting. *Harvard Business Review*, July–August 2007. Retrieved January 15, 2022, from https://hbr.org/2007/07/six-rules-for-effective-forecasting.

Schuster, A. (1906). On the Periodicities of Sunspots. *Philosophical Transactions of the Royal Society of London: Series A, Containing Papers of a Mathematical or Physical Character*, *206*, 69–100.

Sims, C. A. (1972). Money, Income, and Causality. *American Economic Review*, *62*(4), 540–552.

Sims, C. A. (1980). Macroeconomics and Reality. *Econometrica*, *48*(1), 1–48.

Slutzky, E. (1937). The Summation of Random Causes as the Source of Cyclic Processes. *Econometrica*, *5*(2), 105–146.

Stock, J. H. (2002). Time Series: Economic Forecasting. In *International Encylopedia of Social and Behavioral Sciences* (pp. 15721–15724). Amsterdam: Elsevier Science Limited.

Stock, J. H., & Watson, M. W. (1999). Forecasting inflation. *Journal of Monetary Economics*, *44*(2), 293–335.

Strum, A. (2019). *Illinois Economic and Fiscal Policy Report*. https://www2.illinois.gov/sites/budget/Documents/Economic and Fiscal Policy Reports/FY 2019/Economic-and-Fiscal-Policy-Report-FY20-FINAL.pdf.

The Weather Channel. (2021). *Hurricane Spaghetti Models: Four Things You Need to Know to Track Storms Like the Pros | The Weather Channel - Articles from The Weather Channel | weather.com*. The Weather Channel. Retrieved August 16, 2021, from https://weather.com/science/weather-explainers/news/spaghetti-models-tropics-tropical-storm-hurricane.

US. Bureau of Census. (2017). X-13ARIMA-SEATS Reference Manual. Version 1.1, January 18, 2017, Center for Statistical Research and Methodology, US Bureau of Census, Washington DC. Retrieved March 23, 2021, from https://www.census.gov/ts/x13as/docX13AS.pdf.

Voorhees, W. R. (2006). Consistent Underestimation Bias, the Asymmetrical Loss Function, and Homogeneous Sources of Bias in State Revenue Forecasts. *Journal of Public Budgeting, Accounting & Financial Management*, *18*(1), 61–76.

Weller, J. (2018). The Complete Guide to Gap Analysis. *Smartsheet*. October 17, 2018. Retrieved July 7, 2019, from https://www.smartsheet.com/gap-analysis-method-examples.

White, H. (1980). A Heteroskedasticity-consistent Covariance Matrix Estimator and a Direct Test for Heteroskedasticity. *Econometrica*, *48*(4), 817–838.

Winters, P. R. (1960). Forecasting Sales by Exponentially Moving Averages. *Management Science*, *6*(3), 324–342.

Wooldridge, J. M. (2006). *Introductory Econometrics: A Modern Approach* (3rd ed.). Thomson Higher Education.

Wright, D. J. (1986). Forecasting Data Published at Irregular Time Series Intervals using Extensions of Holt's Method. *Management Science*, *32*, 499–510.

Yule, G. U. (1927). On a Method of Investigating Periodicities in Disturbed Series, with Special Reference to Wolfer's Sunspot Numbers. *Philosophical Transactions of the Royal Society of London: Series A, Containing Papers of a Mathematical or Physical Character, 226,* 267–298.

Zarnowitz, V. (1967). *An Appraisal of Short-Term Economic Forecasts.* New York: National Bureau of Economic Research.

Zhang, G., Patuwo, B. E., & Hu, M. Y. (1998). Forecasting with Artificial Neural Networks: The State of the Art. *International Journal of Forecasting, 14*(1), 35–62.

Index

Jarque-Bera Goodness-of-fit test, 115,
170
Johansen test, 174, 181; maximum
eigenvalue test, 181, 188; trace test.
See trace test
judgmental forecasts, 14

Kalman filter, 199
Kolmogorov-Smirnov test, 115, 171
Koop, G., 161
KPSS test, 174, 200

lagging indicators, 212
lag order, 118, 139, 148, 181–82
latent factor, 199–201
leading indicators, 212–13
least squares method, 37, 123, 141; least
squares criteria, 123, 141
linear combination, 187
linear regression model, 83
linear trend, 61
Ljung-Box Q test, 115–16, 124, 136,
143, 152; optimal lag, 164–66, 168,
179, 182; order of the series, 109
log-likelihood statistic, 200
long short-term memory (LSTM)
model, 206

Macauley, F.R., 11
machine learning process, 13
Makridakis, 14, 21
margin of error, 3
Maximum eigenvalue test, 181, 188
maximum likelihood estimation (MLE),
86, 122, 141, 199
mean absolute deviation (MAD), 48–49
mean absolute percentage error
(MAPE), 50
mean absolute scaled error (MASE),
141, 150, 155
mean percentage error (MPE), 49–50
mean-squared error (MSE), 47–48
mean square successive differencing
(MSSD), 53
model-building approach, 105

model identification, 121–22, 148–50,
160
modeling shocks, 215
Morris, P.A., 193
moving average parameter, 106, 132
moving average process, 11, 121, 135–
36, 148, 154
multicollinearity, 93, 165, 168, 183
multivariate autoregressive moving
average (MARMA), 158

naïve model, 21
National Bureau of Economic Research,
46
neural network (NN), 13, 17, 190,
202–8; Boolean (conditional) hidden
layer, 205; feed-forward, 203; hidden
layer, 203–5, 207; input layer, 203;
output layer, 203–4; recurrent neural
network (RNN), 206; single hidden
layer, 207
nonlinear trend, 61
no perfect collinearity, 89
normality, 52, 115, 124, 168

Office of Management and Budget, 4–5
optimal lag, 164–65, 179
Ordinary Least Squares (OLS) method.
See least squares method

parametric test, 39–40; nonparametric
test, 39–40
partial autocorrelation, 110, 114, 116,
121, 135, 150, 158
partial autocorrelation function (PACF),
111
Pearson's Product Moment Correlation
Coefficient, 40
percentage average method, 22–24, 38
periodogram, 11
Phillips-Perron test, 114, 129, 181
point estimates. *See* point forecasts
point forecasts, 3, 43; confidence
forecasts, 43
political acceptance, 5

About the Authors

Aman Khan, PhD is professor of political science and public administration at Texas Tech University in Lubbock, Texas, where he teaches public budgeting, financial management, policy analysis, and quantitative methods. He is the author, coauthor of several dozen publications in professional journals and edited volumes, including seven books. His most recent publications include *Cost and Optimization in Government (3rd Edition)*, *Fundamentals of Public Budgeting and Finance*, and *US Infrastructure: Challenges and Directions for the 21st Century* (coeditor, Klaus Becker). He previously served as director of the Graduate Program in Public Administration at Texas Tech University and also briefly taught graduate finance at a business school. In addition, he frequently provided consulting services to various local governments on budget forecasting. Dr. Khan is the founder and current director of the Institute of Governmental Finance, which provides, among others, professional training to middle and upper-level public managers and elected officials.

Kenneth A. Kriz, PhD is university distinguished professor at the University of Illinois at Springfield. Dr. Kriz conducts research focusing on subnational debt policy and administration, public pension fund management, government financial risk management, economic and revenue forecasting, and behavioral public finance. Dr. Kriz is a frequent presenter at public economics and public budgeting and financial management conferences and has published more than 40 journal articles and book chapters along with a textbook on quantitative research methods in public administration. Dr. Kriz has consulted with several public and nonprofit organizations on financial and economic matters. Dr. Kriz served as vice-chairperson of the City of Omaha, Nebraska Civilian Employees Retirement System from 2006 to 2011 and on the Board of Trustees of the Wichita, Kansas Police & Fire Retirement System and on the Joint Investment Committee for the city's pension funds from 2014 to 2018. Dr. Kriz was a fulbright scholar in the Republic of Estonia during academic year 2004–05 and a fulbright senior specialist in the Czech Republic in 2008.